# THE FAITH INSTINCT

ALSO BY NICHOLAS WADE

*The Nobel Duel: Two Scientists' 21-Year Race to Win the World's Most Coveted Research Prize*

*Betrayers of the Truth: Fraud and Deceit in the Halls of Science* (with William Broad)

*Before the Dawn: Recovering the Lost History of Our Ancestors*

# THE FAITH INSTINCT

*How Religion Evolved and Why It Endures*

NICHOLAS WADE

THE PENGUIN PRESS

*New York*

*2009*

THE PENGUIN PRESS
Published by the Penguin Group
Penguin Group (USA) Inc., 375 Hudson Street, New York, New York 10014, U.S.A. •
Penguin Group (Canada), 90 Eglinton Avenue East, Suite 700, Toronto, Ontario,
Canada M4P 2Y3 (a division of Pearson Penguin Canada Inc.) • Penguin
Books Ltd, 80 Strand, London WC2R 0RL, England • Penguin Ireland,
25 St. Stephen's Green, Dublin 2, Ireland (a division of Penguin Books Ltd) •
Penguin Books Australia Ltd, 250 Camberwell Road, Camberwell, Victoria 3124,
Australia (a division of Pearson Australia Group Pty Ltd) •
Penguin Books India Pvt Ltd, 11 Community Centre, Panchsheel Park,
New Delhi – 110 017, India • Penguin Group (NZ), 67 Apollo Drive, Rosedale,
North Shore 0632, New Zealand (a division of Pearson New Zealand Ltd) •
Penguin Books (South Africa) (Pty) Ltd, 24 Sturdee Avenue,
Rosebank, Johannesburg 2196, South Africa

Penguin Books Ltd, Registered Offices:
80 Strand, London WC2R 0RL, England

First published in 2009 by The Penguin Press,
a member of Penguin Group (USA) Inc.

LIBRARY OF CONGRESS CATALOGING IN PUBLICATION DATA
Wade, Nicholas.
The faith instinct : how religion evolved and why it endures / Nicholas Wade.
p.   cm.
Includes bibliographical references and index.
ISBN 978-1-59420-228-5
1. Religion—Philosophy.   I. Title.
BL51.W133 2009
201—dc22
                                                                2009028497

Printed in the United States of America
1   3   5   7   9   10   8   6   4   2
DESIGNED BY AMANDA DEWEY

# CONTENTS

# 1

# THE NATURE OF
# RELIGION

For the last 50,000 years, and probably for much longer, people have practiced religion. With dance and chants and sacred words, they have ritually marked the cycles of the seasons and the passages of life, from birth to adolescence, to marriage and to death.

Religion has brought meaning to millions in their personal lives. Its rituals have given believers assurance of control over unpredictable adversities. In the face of daunting fears, of famine, sickness, disaster or death, religion has always been a wellspring of hope. "Though thou art worshipped by the names divine / Of Jesus and Jehovah," wrote the poet William Blake, "Thou art still / The son of morn in weary night's decline, / The lost traveler's dream under the hill."

Religions point to the realm of the supernatural, assuring people that they are not alone in the world. Most religions teach that there is an afterlife and some promise a better existence there, often for lives lived correctly in this world or to compensate for its misfortunes. The Wana people of Sulawesi believe that as they are last on earth, so they will be first in paradise.

Faith brings personal rewards but it is as a social force that religion carves its place in history. In religion's name, people have fed the hungry, cared for the sick, founded charities and hospitals. Religion creates circles of trust whose members may support one another in calamity or find hosts and trading partners in distant cities. In societies throughout the world, religious rites are intimately associated with the communal activities of music and dance. Religion has fostered and inspired artists' expressions of shared devotion, from medieval cathedrals, to the painters of the Renaissance and the masses of Palestrina, Bach and Haydn.

Religion, above all, embodies the moral rules that members of a community observe toward one other. It thus sustains the quality of the social fabric, and did so alone in early societies that had not developed civil authorities. It binds people together for collective action, through public rituals that evoke emotional commitment to a common cause.

There is no church of oneself. A church is a community, a special group of people who share the same beliefs. And these are not ordinary, matter-of-fact views but deeply held emotional attachments. By expressing the common creed together, in symbolic rituals, in group activities involving song and movement in unison, people signal to each other their commitment to the shared beliefs that bind them together as a community. This emotional bonding is captured in the probable derivation of "religion" from *religare*, a Latin word meaning to bind.

Religion may tie together the members of a village church, or of an entire country. It can unite people who may share neither common kinship, nor ethnicity nor even language. When nations feel their existence is at stake, they often define their cause by religion, whether in Europe's long wars with Islam, or Elizabethan England's defiance of Catholic Spain, or the Puritans' emigration to New England, or the foundation of Israel.

So indelibly and distinctively does religion shape the fabric of societies that it has become the defining feature of the cultures around which great civilizations are built, such as those of Western Christianity or Islam or Hinduism.

Religion has a darker side too, drawn from excesses of the fierce loyalty it inspires. Acts of particular cruelty have been committed against internal foes, the perceived disrupters of orthodoxy. Under religion's banner, societies have conducted inquisitions, murdered people deemed to be heretics or witches, and tortured or exiled those who worshipped different gods.

Religion is almost always prominent in a society's response to external foes. It has routinely been invoked to justify and sustain wars, and has helped foment many, between Christian and Muslim, Protestant and Catholic, Shi'a and Sunni. Few religious wars have been more atrocious than the Aztec empire's ravenous search for victims who were sacrificed every day, sometimes by the thousands in a single ceremony, so that the streams of their blood could nourish the Aztec sun god.

What is religion, that it can evoke the noblest and most sublime of human behaviors, yet also the cruelest and most despicable? Is religion just a body of sacred knowledge bequeathed from one generation to the next? Or does religion, being much more than just a cultural heritage, spring from a deeply ingrained urge to worship?

"Like any other human activity," writes the historian of religion Karen Armstrong, "religion can be abused, but it seems to have been something that we have always done. It was not tacked on to a primordially secular nature by manipulative kings and priests but was natural to humanity."[2]

Religion is so natural to humanity that it seems to be part of human nature, as if a propensity for belief in the supernatural were genetically engraved in the human mind, and expressed as spontaneously as the ability to appreciate music or to learn one's native language. "No society known to anthropology or history is devoid of what reasonable observers would agree is religion, even those such as the former Soviet Union which have made deliberate attempts to extirpate it," wrote the anthropologist Roy Rappaport.[3]

Given the time, energy and treasure spent on building religious monuments, fighting holy wars and offering sacrifices to the gods, Rappaport wrote, he found it hard to imagine that religion had not contributed positively to human adaptation, the process of genetic change that occurs in response to natural selection. "Surely so expensive an enterprise would have been defeated by selective pressures if it were merely frivolous or illusory. . . . Religion has not merely been important but crucial to human adaptation," he wrote in 1971.[4]

But Rappaport's insight was not followed up for many years, in part because of a reluctance by anthropologists to believe that any part of human behavior might be genetically shaped.

## The Nature of Religion

The emergence of religious behavior has long been hard to reconstruct because of the severe lack of evidence. The people of 50,000 years ago, the period when modern humans dispersed from their African homeland, have vanished, leaving behind no material trace of their existence, let alone of their religious beliefs. People at that time lived as hunters and gatherers, and continued to do so until 15,000 years ago. Only then were the first permanent settlements built, by which time religion had long been an established feature of human societies.

But many new strands of evidence have been accumulating. These now make it possible at least to sketch out a possible origin for this most mysterious of human behaviors, as well as a rough time line for its development. Recent work by students of human evolution has provided the context in which a new form of social coordination would have been needed, a requirement that religion would have filled well. By analyzing the DNA of living people around the world, it is possible to identify societies that have long been isolated from others and whose religious behaviors may reflect those of the ancestral human population. New interpretations by archaeologists record how this early form of religious behavior, practiced by hunters and gatherers, was modified for the more sophisticated needs of settled societies.

Thus from a growing body of work by researchers in several different fields, it is now possible to piece together a reasonable account of how and why religious behavior evolved to be an ingrained part of human nature, and to trace some of the cultural innovations by which the early religion of hunter gatherers was shaped to the different needs of settled societies.

The purpose of this book is to try to understand religious behavior from an evolutionary perspective. Some of the implications that emerge from this approach may be unwelcome to believers, others to atheists. People of faith may not warm to the view that the mind's receptivity to religion has been shaped by evolution. Those who regard religion as an obscurantist obstacle to rational progress may not embrace the idea that religious behavior evolved because it conferred essential benefits on ancient societies and their successors.

Despite these understandable attitudes, the evolutionary approach to religion does not necessarily threaten the central positions of either believers or atheists. Believers would be right to take the view that Darwin's theory specifies no purpose for the biological process it explains and cannot trespass into whatever religions have to say about the meaning of life. Evolution describes how the human body and behavior have been shaped, but has nothing to say about any ultimate purpose behind this process. Biological drives for all functions essential to survival are embedded in the human brain; it need surely be no scandal to people of faith that an instinct for religious behavior is one of those necessities. That the mind has been prepared by evolution to believe in gods neither proves nor disproves their existence.

Atheists, for their part, may not at all welcome the idea that religious behavior strengthens the moral fabric, enhances social cohesion and was so central to the survival of early human societies that all that lacked it have perished. But even that perspective does not compel them to acknowledge the hand of a deity in shaping human values. Religious behavior can be studied for its own sake, regardless of whether or not a deity exists.

THE THEME OF THE pages ahead is that an instinct for religious behavior is indeed an evolved part of human nature. Because of the decided survival advantage conferred on people who practiced a religion, the behavior had become written into our neural circuitry by at least 50,000 years ago, and probably much earlier.

To see why religion is likely to be an evolved behavior, it helps to compare it with language. Like language, religion is a complex cultural behavior built on top of a genetically shaped learning machinery. People are born with innate instincts for learning the language and the religion of their community. But in both cases culture supplies the content of what is learned. That is why languages and religions differ so widely from one society to the next, while remaining so similar in their basic form.

Just as language operates on top of many other behaviors that had evolved earlier, such as neural systems for hearing and generating sounds, religious behavior too depends on several other sophisticated faculties, such as sensitivity to music, the moral instinct and of course language itself. Like language, religious behavior in all societies develops at a specific age, as if an innate learning program is being triggered on cue.

As with language, religion is most significant as a social behavior. One can speak or pray to oneself, but both are most meaningful when done in company. That is because both faculties are instruments of communication.

Many human behaviors are shared with other animals, especially our fellow mammals, leaving little room for doubt that traits like a mother's urge to protect her children have a strong genetic basis. And it is easy to envisage that mothers who watch closely over their young will leave more surviving offspring than will less vigilant mothers. So over the course of a few generations genes that promote protective instincts will displace genes allowing maternal indifference, and the upshot will be development of a strong instinct for maternal care.

The same argument applies to the development of language and religion, though is less demonstrably true because they are uniquely human behaviors and there are no other species in which these faculties can be directly studied. Still, it has long seemed likely on grounds of general plausibility that language has a genetic basis. The rules of sentence formation are so complex that babies must presumably possess an innate syntax-generating machinery, rather than having to figure out the rules for themselves. The existence of such a neural mechanism would explain why infants learn to speak so effortlessly, and at a specific age, as if some neural developmental program is being rolled out at that time. Evolution has not yet had time to engineer similar programs for reading and writing, which is why they must be taught so laboriously in school.

Arguments about the innateness or otherwise of language have been hard to resolve because so little is known about the genes that define the architecture of the human brain. But with recent advances in decoding the human genome, the first genes affecting language have started to come to light, beginning with the discovery in 2001 of the FOXP2 gene which affects several neural and muscular skills underlying the articulacy of speech.

People survive as social groups, not as individuals, and little is more critical to a social species than its members' ability to communicate with one another. Because of the primacy of language the effectiveness of the other modes of communication, such as religion or gesture, often goes unappreciated. Just as language is a system for communicating thought, religious behavior is a way of signaling shared values and emotions. Any genetic variation that made these systems more effective is likely to have been quickly favored by natural selection. This is particularly true if natural selection operates on groups of individuals as well as at the level of individuals alone, as is more usual. Group level selection is controversial among evolutionary biologists, but even its sternest opponents do not say that it cannot exist, only that it is likely to be insignificant in most cases. There are special circumstances in human evolution, discussed below, that would have allowed group selection to operate much more powerfully than usual.

It's easy enough to see why natural selection would have favored genes underlying the faculty of language, given the immense advantage to members of a social species of being able to share thoughts and information. But why should religious behavior have evolved? What benefit does religion confer, other than spiritual fulfillment? How can religious behavior make a difference on the only scale measured by natural selection, that of leaving more progeny?

To understand the influence exerted by religion in early societies, it helps to distinguish between its personal aspects, which are probably more familiar to people today, and its role as a social force.

## The Social and Personal Nature of Religious Belief

Asked to define religion, many people will describe the personal importance of their belief, whether as a feeling of communion with the sacred, a source of hope and solace, a compass of moral behavior, an explanation of misfortune, or a wellspring of meaning in life. In his book *The Varieties of Religious Experience,* the psychologist William James emphasized the personal above any other element of religion. Religion, as he defined it, "shall mean for us the feelings, acts, and experiences of individual men in their solitude, so far as they apprehend themselves to stand in relation to whatever they may consider the divine. Since the relation may be either moral, physical, or ritual, it is evident that out of religion in the sense in which we take it, theologies, philosophies, and ecclesiastical organizations may secondarily grow."[5]

But however strongly religion may seem to grow out of people's personal beliefs, the practice of religion is heavily social. It is because of their personal beliefs that people desire to worship together with others of the same faith. People may pray alone, but religious services and rituals are communal. A religion belongs to a community and shapes members' social behavior, both toward one another (the in-group) and toward non-believers (the out-group). The social aspect of religion is extraordinarily significant because the rules for behavior toward others are in effect a society's morality.

One need look no further for a reason why people are so attached to their religion. The quality of a society—its cohesiveness, its freedom from crime, its members' willingness to help others, the rarity of lying, cheating and freeloading—is shaped by the nature of its morality and by the strength of people's adherence to community standards. Both of these—standards of morality, and the extent of compliance with them—are set or heavily influenced by religion. People will defend their religion because it undergirds so much else of what gives life quality.

Those standards of morality underwritten by religion have a curious feature about them, one that is not generally acknowledged by moral philosophers who see morality as being based on universal principles. Practical morality is not universal. Compassion and forgiveness are the behaviors owed to one's in-group, but not necessarily to an out-group, and certainly not to an enemy.

Toward hostile societies human behavior is steely, implacable and often genocidal. Foes may be demonized or regarded as subhuman, and the moral restraints owed to members of one's own society need not be extended to them. And religion is often intimately involved in warfare because it is invoked by leaders to justify aggression, to sustain morale, and to spur soldiers to the ultimate sacrifice.

From this perspective, one can begin to see how crucial religion may have been over the centuries in ensuring a society's survival. It enhances the quality of a society and makes it worth fighting for, and it inspires people to lay down their lives in the society's defense. Other things being equal, groups with a stronger religious inclination would have been more united and at a considerable advantage compared with groups that were less cohesive. People in the more successful groups would have left more surviving children, and genes favoring an instinct for religious behavior would have become commoner each generation until they had swept through the entire human population.

The social function of religion, as opposed to the personal, is the one that seemed significant to Émile Durkheim, a founder of sociology. Durkheim saw religion as playing a mediating role between people and the society in which they live. "The faithful are not mistaken when they believe in the existence of a moral power to which they are subject and from which they receive what is best in themselves. That power exists, and it is society," Durkheim wrote in his book *The Elementary Forms of Religious Life*, first published in 1912. He went on to note that "religion is first and foremost a system of ideas by means of which individuals imagine the society of which they are members and the obscure yet intimate relations they have with it."[6]

People do not of course worship society directly. Durkheim's insight was that the relationship between religion and society could be seen to work in two directions, at least in terms of their functions. Religion imbues a society with moral standards and belief in a supernatural enforcer behind them; society embraces religion and follows its dictates, while shaping them toward solving current problems. Religion is far more than belief in supernatural powers, in Durkheim's view. Magicians and sorcerers, after all, summon unearthly forces to do their bidding, but they do not draw people to one another—there is no church of magic. Religious beliefs, on the other hand, are shared, and bind together all those who hold them.

This line of thought led Durkheim to his well-known definition: "*A religion is a unified system of beliefs and practices relative to sacred things, that is to say, things set apart and forbidden—beliefs and practices which unite into one single moral community called a Church all those who adhere to them.*"[7] In showing that religion and church are inseparable, Durkheim added, the definition underlines that religion "must be an eminently collective thing."

For those familiar with thinking of religion in personal terms, it may seem strange to conceive of religion as an agent of society's collective will, in addition to whatever else it may be. But consider how intimately religion is involved in important social functions, such as the rite of marriage. In the Anglican branch of Christianity, toward the conclusion of the service, the priest joins together the right hands of the man and woman, and issues the solemn warning, "Those whom God hath joined together, let no man put asunder."

These are powerful words because at that moment, in their own eyes and in those of society, the man and woman indeed become married, and their union is spiritually indissoluble. The arrangement is one that all in the community recognize, whether they were present or not. "There are hardly any words in the Prayer Book which more solemnly declare the faithful conviction of the Church that God ratifies the work of His priests," writes John Henry Blunt, author of *The Annotated Book of Common Prayer*.[8] And of course society too, through the priest's words and the communal service, ratifies the marriage.

There may be a civil procedure as well, but it does not carry the same weight. It is the religious ceremony that evokes the emotional conviction that two people have been truly married.

In the initiation rites observed by many peoples, which commonly occur as part of a religious ceremony, a boy becomes a man, not just metaphorically but because his community thereafter treats him like a man. In coronation rites, whether by anointment or the placement of a crown or diadem on his head, a man becomes a king. Religions are powerful creators of social fact. And it's not merely facts they create, but a binding emotional knowledge that these facts are sacred truths.

It's easy to underestimate the remarkable nature of the effect achieved by religious belief, just as it is easy to underestimate language, since we take both faculties for granted. Language lets people convey precise thoughts from the mind of one individual to that of another, an extraordinary feat of biological engineering achieved by no other living species. Equally unparalleled, religion binds a group of individuals together in beliefs and principles they consider so sacred and inviolable that they feel compelled to submit their usually lively sense of self-interest to that of the group. Just as language achieves almost perfect communication, religion brings about an emotional commitment so powerful that people will make almost any sacrifice that their religion requires, including that of their life.

Durkheim's work strongly influenced social anthropologists such as Bronislaw Malinowski and Alfred Radcliffe-Brown, both of whom reached much the same conclusions. "Religion needs the community as a whole so that its members may worship in common its sacred things and its divinities," Malinowski wrote, "and society needs religion for the maintenance of moral law and order."[9]

Durkheim's views on religion later fell out of favor with social scientists for several reasons, including reinterpretation of the early ethnographic data about Australian Aborigines, on which Durkheim's theory was largely based. But his ideas have recently become an inspiration to biologists seeking to understand the role of religion in early human evolution. The reason is that they point strongly to the survival value of religious behavior. A society that develops a strong moral fabric, whose members are emotionally committed through powerful rituals to their community's well-being, is likely to prevail in warfare over a society with weaker bonds. Groups that used religion to coordinate collective activities, such as planting fields at the right time or managing natural resources, would have been more effective and better able to survive.

Natural selection, a motive force of evolution, is about survival and who leaves more children. Many of the social aspects of religious behavior offer advantages—such as a group's strong internal cohesion and high morale in warfare—that would lead to a society's members having more surviving children, and religion for such reasons would be favored by natural selection. This is less true of the personal aspects of religion. Religion may help people overcome the fear of death, or find courage in facing disease and catastrophe, but these personal beliefs seem unlikely to enable them to have more surviving offspring, natural selection's only yardstick of success. Rather, the personal rewards of religion are significant because they draw people to practice it, without which the social benefits could not have been favored by natural selection.

## Defining Religion

What then is religion? The word itself has a range of meanings, referring sometimes to a set of beliefs in the supernatural, sometimes to an organized community of adherents to a faith. Religion has been notoriously hard to define, perhaps because each observer seeks to emphasize a different aspect. Even the great sociologist Max Weber ducked the task. He opened his essay on the sociology of religion by warning readers they must wait to hear exactly what it is—"Definition can be attempted, if at all, only at the conclusion of the study"—yet he provided none at the end either.

But if, as argued here, religious behavior emerged because of its evolutionary role, definition becomes less elusive. From the evolutionary perspective, as laid out in the chapters ahead, the essential elements of religious behavior may be summarized as follows. Starting around the age of adolescence, people learn and become emotionally committed to the rituals, religious practices and sacred symbols of their community. The rituals involve rhythmic activity, whether singing and vigorous dancing, as in hunter gatherer religions, or just singing, as in many modern religions. They may include painful initiation rites that induce lasting emotional memories and commitment. The rituals evoke a sense of awe as celebrants feel that they or their priests are in contact with agents of the supernatural realm.

Through moving or singing in unison, in a state of emotional elevation, individuals develop a fervent sense of togetherness, a desire to put the group's interests above their own and to do whatever is needed, up to the sacrifice of their own life, in the group's defense.

In practicing their religion, people come to know what is right for themselves and their community: it is what the supernatural powers have decreed.

In every religion, the supernatural powers live in a different realm and yet, strange as this may be, they are not unreachable. Their behavior can be influenced by appropriate rituals, prayers and sacrifice. A religious community thus implicitly negotiates with its supernatural lawgivers. The negotiators who interact with the gods are the whole community in the case of primitive societies, the ecclesiastical hierarchy in larger ones. Through reference to precedent (the wisdom of the ancestors) and discussion among themselves, the negotiators implicitly decide on the behaviors they want their society to follow and they then seek the gods' endorsement of their ideas. The gods set the rules or courses of action that are indicated to them, along with rewards or punishments for compliance or disobedience. The divine requirements habitually include common standards of morality within the group, and readiness to unite in response to external challenges such as aggression from other societies.

Communities would not gain the social benefits of religious behavior unless people had strong personal motivations to participate. And indeed religion is attractive because it does bring many deep personal satisfactions. It is the source of some of the deepest emotions of which people are capable, such as feelings of awe, of exaltation, of transcendence, of rightness and harmony with the world. It gives people hope in adversity, because the faithful believe that through prayer and ritual they can exert some measure of control over unpredictable disasters like disease or bad weather.

The personal aspects of religious behavior, however, are not all rewards. There is fear of punishment, too, the knowledge that retributive deities are watching for infractions of their rules and will deliver harsh penalties in this world or the next, perhaps for even contemplating a forbidden act. Fear of an omnipresent supervisor is of utmost practical benefit to a group, particularly in primitive societies that lack courts and police forces. Fear of divine retribution keeps almost everyone in line with the prevailing rules and moral code; and these laws, though always attributed to supernatural decree, as recorded by previous generations in sacred sayings or texts, can in fact be shaped by society.

From an evolutionary perspective, therefore, the following definition emerges: Religion is a system of emotionally binding beliefs and practices in which a society implicitly negotiates through prayer and sacrifice with supernatural agents, securing from them commands that compel members, through fear of divine punishment, to subordinate their interests to the common good.

## Cultural Development of Religion

The religion that evolved among hunter gatherers tied a clever knot. It enabled a society to impute to the gods its collective wisdom as to how members should behave so as best to ensure the society's survival; and through initiation rites and communal dancing it induced in everyone the emotional commitment to obey the gods' rules and fear their sanctions. Without a police force or prison guards or judiciary, in any case impossible for hunter gatherers, early societies achieved through religion both social cohesion and effective compliance with the dictates of an invisible government.

Once religion had evolved among early people, it underwent a long and extensive cultural development into the very different forms of religion that are familiar today. The nature of that development, as is laid out in the chapters ahead, can now for the first time be reconstructed, even if only in outline.

The initial step is to infer the general form of early religion from the rites of contemporary hunting and gathering societies whose way of life has not changed for millennia. The appropriate societies can be chosen by genetic criteria that point to their relative degree of isolation. Next, with the help of archaeology, it is now possible to trace the steps by which early religion developed into the forms found in settled societies. Hunter gatherer religions involved the whole community as equal participants in interaction with the gods. In settled societies, a class of priestly officials emerged between the people and their gods. Religious power became more exclusive and began to serve as a pillar of archaic states, which were often ruled by a priest-king. The cohesive power of religion also began to be applied to other tasks requiring collective action, such as the unaccustomed hard labor required by societies first taking up agriculture. The principal rites of these religions were tied to the farming calendar, and these ceremonies were co-opted by the more sophisticated religions that arose in advanced states.

From one of these states, that of the Canaanites and their Israelite descendants who lived in the Near East in the second millennium B.C., the first great monotheism emerged. Scholars can now reconstruct in reasonable detail the historical context in which Judaism was shaped and some of the motivations of its shapers.

As for the second great monotheism, the origins of Christianity are still shrouded in considerable mystery. The religion first flourished among the Greek-speaking Jews dispersed through the cities of the Roman empire. Though the roots of Christianity are Jewish, all its earliest documents and liturgy are in Greek, and in its new linguistic home the religion adopted its distinctively non-Jewish themes. Christianity was so successful that within just over 300 years it had become the state religion of the Roman empire.

Islam, by contrast, did not climb to an imperial role but was born into it. The third great monotheism burst into history as the official sect of the Arab state that inherited the Byzantine empire's holdings in the Near East. Scholars, both Muslim and non-Muslim, have for years assumed that the truth about the origins of Islam can be found somewhere within the rich field of Islamic writings. Only recently has a small band of researchers developed a new premise, that Islamic writings should be regarded primarily as sacred literature, not as history. These revisionists are in the process of constructing an alternative and somewhat surprising history of Islam. Their account has not yet received the attention or the testing it may merit but would, if supported, provide another instance of how the cohesive power of religion can be skillfully adapted to political ends.

These cohesive powers are evident in most collective activities of ancient societies and remain surprisingly visible in modern societies, despite the profusion of secular institutions that have taken over many of religion's former roles. In marriage and reproductive practices, in enforcing standards of morality, in political movements, in generating the bonds of trust essential for commerce, and in warfare, religion continues to play many of its ancient roles as effectively as ever.

THE COMPLEXITY OF RELIGION—its intricate role in human history, the strong mix of emotions it raises in participants' hearts—all seem to some degree explicable in terms of the forces that shaped the emergence of religious behavior during the dawn of human evolution. It is these shaping forces that must now be explored. But before examining religious behavior itself, it is pertinent to consider an essential human faculty that is a pillar of religion, though also separable from it, and that is the moral instinct. At the social level, religion has long been seen as essential to morality and probably still is. For even though individuals can behave morally without religion, most atheists and agnostics take good care to observe the moral standards of their community, which even in highly secular countries are influenced by religion.

Religion and morality share a common feature that reflects their origins as evolved behaviors: both are rooted in the emotions. Religious knowledge is not like knowing the day of the week; it is something a person feels and is deeply committed to. Moral intuitions usually appear in the mind as strong convictions, not as neutral facts. Religious and moral beliefs can be discussed in a rational way, but both have emotion-laden components that are shaped in regions of the brain to which the conscious mind does not have access. Natural selection has tagged them with a compelling quality of which mere facts are free.

Morality is older than religion—its roots can be seen in monkeys and apes—and religious behavior was engrafted on top of it in the human lineage alone. Understanding how the moral instincts evolved makes it easier to see that religious behavior too has an evolutionary origin.

# 2

## THE MORAL INSTINCT

*Man was destined for society. His morality, therefore, was to be formed to this object. He was endowed with a sense of right & wrong merely relative to this. This sense is as much a part of his nature, as the sense of hearing, seeing, feeling. . . . State a moral case to a ploughman & a professor. The former will decide it as well, & often better than the latter, because he has not been led astray by artificial rules.*

THOMAS JEFFERSON[10]

Everyone knows the difference between right and wrong. But where does that sure knowledge come from? From reason, as some philosophers have taught? Or from divine revelation, as theologians say?

In the last few years a startling new idea has been introduced to the age-old debate about the nature of morality. Biologists have come to realize that social animals, in interacting with other members of their community, have developed rules for restraining their self-interest. It is these rules of self-restraint, which are likely to have a genetic basis, that make up the social fabric of a baboon troop or band of chimpanzees.

No one is imputing morality to animals, but observers have found that monkeys and apes show many behaviors, such as empathy and a sense of reciprocity, that could be building blocks of the moral sense that is so evident in people. Humans would have inherited these building blocks from their apelike ancestors and developed them into moral instincts.

Biologists thus began to see that they might be able to construct a new explanation of morality: moral behavior does not originate from outside the human mind or even from conscious reasoning, the sources favored by theologians and philosophers, but rather has been wired into the genetic circuitry of the mind by evolution.

The clearest statement of the new program came from the distinguished biologist Edward O. Wilson. "The time has come," he wrote in his book *Sociobiology*, "for ethics to be removed temporarily from the hands of the philosophers and biologicized."[11] A few years later he confidently predicted that "Science for its part will test relentlessly every assumption about the human condition and in time uncover the bedrock of the moral and religious sentiments."[12]

Both philosophers and psychologists took some time to respond to Wilson's challenge, but a highly interesting investigation is now being undertaken by both groups, working partly in collaboration.

The new view of morality, that it is at least partly shaped by evolution, has not been arrived at easily. Philosophers long focused on reason as the basis of morality. David Hume, the eighteenth-century Scottish philosopher, defied this tradition in arguing strongly that morals spring not from conscious reasoning but from the emotions. "Morals excite passions, and produce or prevent actions. Reason of itself is utterly impotent in this particular. The rules of morality, therefore, are not conclusions of our reason," Hume wrote in his *Treatise on Human Nature*.

But Hume's suggestion only made philosophers keener to found morality in reason. The German philosopher Immanuel Kant sought to base morality outside of nature, in a world of pure reason and of moral imperatives that met the test of being fit to be universal laws. This proposal, Wilson wrote acidly, made no sense at all: "Sometimes a concept is baffling not because it is profound but because it is wrong. This idea does not accord, we know now, with the evidence of how the brain works."[13]

Psychologists too, however, were long committed to the philosophers' program of deriving morality exclusively from reason. The Swiss psychologist Jean Piaget, following Kant's ideas, argued that children learned ideas about morality as they passed through various stages of mental development. Lawrence Kohlberg, an American psychologist, built on Piaget's ideas, arguing that children went through six stages of moral reasoning. But his analysis was based on interviewing children and having them describe their moral reasoning, so reason was all he could perceive.

Even primatologists, who would eventually contribute to the new view of morality, were muzzled because animal behaviorists, under the baleful influence of the psychologist B. F. Skinner, accused anyone of anthropomorphism if they attributed emotions like empathy to animals.

With everyone on the wrong track, and Hume's insight neglected, the study of morality was at something of a stalemate. "It is an astonishing circumstance that the study of ethics has advanced so little since the nineteenth century," Wilson wrote in 1998, dismissing a century's work.[14]

A development that helped break the logjam was an article in 2001 by Jonathan Haidt, a psychologist at the University of Virginia. Haidt had taken an interest in the emotion of disgust and was intrigued by a phenomenon he called moral dumbfounding. He would read people stories about a family that cooked and ate its pet dog after it had been run over, or a woman who cleaned a toilet with the national flag. His subjects were duly disgusted and firmly insisted these actions were wrong. But several were unable to explain why they held this opinion, given that no one in the stories was harmed.

It seemed to Haidt that if people could not explain their moral judgments, then evidently they were not reasoning their way toward them.

The observation prompted him to develop a new perspective on how people make moral decisions. Drawing on his own research and that of others, he argued that people make two kinds of moral decision. One, which he called moral intuition, comes from the unconscious mind and is made instantly. The other, moral reasoning, is a slower, after-the-fact process made by the conscious mind. "Moral judgments appear in consciousness automatically and effortlessly as the result of moral intuitions. . . . Moral reasoning is an effortful process, engaged in after a moral judgment is made, in which a person searches for arguments that will support an already made judgment," he wrote.[15]

The moral reasoning decision, which had received the almost exclusive attention of philosophers and psychologists for centuries, is just a façade, in Haidt's view, and it is mostly intended to impress others that a person has made the right decision. People don't in fact know how they make their morally intuitive decisions, because these are formed in the unconscious mind and are inaccessible to them. So when asked why they made a certain decision, they will review a menu of logically possible explanations, choose the one that seems closest to the facts, and argue like a lawyer that that was their reason. This, he points out, is why moral arguments are often so bitter and indecisive. Each party makes lawyerlike rebuttals of the opponent's arguments in the hope of changing his mind. But since the opponent arrived at his position intuitively, not for his stated reasons, he is of course not persuaded. The hope of changing his mind by reasoning is as futile as trying to make a dog happy by wagging its tail for it.

Haidt then turned to exploring how the moral intuition process works. He argued, based on a range of psychological experiments, that the intuitive process is partly genetic, built in by evolution, and partly shaped by culture.

The genetic component of the process probably shapes specialized neural circuits or modules in the brain. Some of these may prompt universal moral behaviors such as empathy and reciprocity. Others probably predispose people to learn the particular moral values of their society at an appropriate age.

This learning process begins early in life. By the age of two, writes the psychologist Jerome Kagan, children have developed a mental list of prohibited actions. By three, they apply the concepts of good and bad to things and actions, including their own behavior. Between the ages of three and six, they show feelings of guilt at having violated a standard. They also learn to distinguish between absolute standards and mere conventions. "As children grow, they follow a universal sequence of stages in the development of morality," Kagan writes.[16]

That children everywhere follow the same sequence of stages suggests that a genetic program is unfolding to guide the learning of morality, including the development of what Haidt calls moral intuition.

Such a program would resemble those known to shape other important brain functions. The brain does much of its maturing after birth, forming connections and refining its neural circuitry when the infant encounters relevant experience from the outside world. Vision is one faculty that matures at a critical age; language is another, and moral intuition is a third.

Damage to a special region of the prefrontal cortex, its ventromedial area located just behind the bridge of the nose, is associated with poor judgment and antisocial behavior. Neural circuitry in the brain's prefrontal cortex is evidently associated with the cultural shaping of moral intuitions.

The existence of special neural circuitry in the brain dedicated to moral decisions is further evidence that morality is an evolved faculty with a genetic basis. In the well-known case of Phineas Gage, a thin iron rod was shot through Gage's frontal lobe in a railroad construction accident in 1848. Gage, astonishingly, survived the accident but his personality was changed. Previously hardworking and responsible, he was now "fitful, irreverent, indulging at times in the grossest profanity (which was not previously his custom), manifesting but little deference for his fellows, impatient of restraint or advice when it conflicts with his desires," according to a physician who examined him 20 years later.[17]

A more specific damage to moral sensibilities is seen in patients with Huntington's disease. Strangely, they become very utilitarian, making moral judgments by weighing only the consequences and ignoring strong social taboos. Consider a situation where a man's wife has just died. Her body is there on the bed, and he decides to have intercourse with her one last time. Is that OK? Most people will say absolutely not. Huntington's patients see no problem. Their sense of disgust, an emotion that intensifies certain moral judgments, seems strangely relaxed: if shown a piece of chocolate molded in the form of dog turd, most people will lose any appetite for it, but many Huntington's patients will happily wolf it down.[18]

There seem to be neural circuitries for morality and for disgust, since specific damage to the brain can cause a loss of either behavior. But these behaviors, though at their core very similar in every society, are heavily shaped by culture. Because of cultural differences, societies may vary widely in terms of the actions they consider morally permissible. In Western societies, for instance, killing an infant is generally regarded as murder. But among the !Kung San, a hunting and gathering people in the Kalahari desert of southern Africa, it is the mother's moral duty to kill after birth any infant that is deformed, and one of each pair of twins.[19] A !Kung mother must carry her infant wherever she goes, and does for some 5,000 miles before the child learns to walk. Since she must also carry food, water and possessions, she cannot carry twins. So the duty to kill a twin, and to avoid investment in a defective child with limited prospects of survival, can be seen not as any moral deficiency on the !Kungs' part but rather as a shaping of human moral intuitions to their particular circumstances.

Standards of sexual morality vary widely, particularly in regions like aboriginal Australia and neighboring Melanesia where conception is not regarded as dependent on the father's sperm and men are therefore less jealous of sexual access to their partners. Thus at *kayasa,* the festival gatherings held by people of the Trobriand Islands off the eastern end of Papua New Guinea, the sportive element in games was taken somewhat further than is customary in Western countries. "At a tug-of-war *kayasa* in the south," reports the anthropologist Bronislaw Malinowski, "men and women would always be on opposite sides. The winning side would ceremonially deride the vanquished with the typical ululating scream (*katugogova*), and then assail their prostrate opponents, and the sexual act would be carried out in public. On one occasion when I discussed this matter with a mixed crowd from the north and the south, both sides categorically confirmed the correctness of this statement."[20] As Rudyard Kipling had occasion to note, "The wildest dreams of Kew are the facts of Khatmandu, And the crimes of Clapham chaste in Martaban."

But the commonalities in morality are generally more striking than the variations. The fundamental moral principle of "do as you would be done by" is found in all societies, as are prohibitions against murder, theft and incest. Many of these universal moral principles are likely to be shaped by innate neural circuits, while the variations spring from moral learning systems that are more guided by cultural traditions and a society's particular ecological circumstances.

Returning to moral intuition and moral reasoning, the two basic psychological processes that underlie morality, the question arises as to why evolution has so generously equipped us with two processes, when one might seem plenty. The most plausible answer is that the two processes emerged from different stages of human evolution.

Moral intuition is the more ancient system, presumably put in place before humans gained either the power of reasoning or the faculty of language. After the evolution of language, when people needed to explain and justify their actions to others, moral reasoning would have developed. But evolution would have had no compelling rationale for handing over control of individual behavior to this novel faculty, at the expense of the moral intuition that had safeguarded human societies for so long. So the arrangement that evolved was that both systems were retained. The moral intuitive system continues to work beneath the level of consciousness, delivering its snap judgments to the conscious mind. The moral reasoning system then takes over, working like a lawyer or public relations agent to rationalize the moral input it has been given and to justify an individual's actions to himself and his society.

## Moral Intuition and Trolley Problems

Though the moral intuitive system is inaccessible to the conscious mind, some intriguing traces of its presence can be seen in the subtle moral exercises known as trolley problems. First devised by the moral philosopher Philippa Foot, trolley problems have been developed by psychologists interested in probing the invisible moral rules of the intuitive system. The problems are entirely artificial, which avoids real-life complications and purifies the moral decision to be made.

In the typical trolley problem, a trolley or train is barreling down on five people who are rashly walking on the tracks, oblivious to the danger until the last moment and unable to escape because the track runs through an embankment with steep sides. An individual standing between the train and the five people has the power to save them, but only after making a fraught moral decision.

So consider first the case of Denise, who is standing by a switch that can divert the train onto a side-track. However, a hiker is walking on the side-track and he too cannot escape the train. Would Denise be right to pull the switch and divert the train, saving five people but killing one?

Ethicists may debate the correct answer but psychologists are more interested in the practical matter of what answer do most people in fact give. Marc Hauser, a psychologist at Harvard University, posed the question on his Web site. Tallying the results after several thousand people had taken the test, he found 90 percent said it was OK for Denise to pull the switch.

Subjects were next asked to consider Fred's dilemma. Fred is standing on a bridge above the railroad tracks. He can save the five people on the track ahead by throwing a heavy object down in the train's path and slowing it. Just such an object is standing beside him. It's a thick-set man. Can Fred push the man in the train's path, killing him to save the five?

Only 10 percent of the respondents to Hauser's survey thought it was OK for Fred to kill the man.

Then came the interesting question: Why is Denise's action OK but Fred's not, when the practical outcome in both cases is identical—one life lost to save five?

Some 70 percent of the subjects were unable to give any plausible reason for the distinction. "The fact that most people have no idea why they draw a distinction between these cases reinforces the point that people tend to make moral judgments without being aware of the under-lying principles," Hauser writes.[21] He also notes the problem posed by this result for those who think that all morality is taught. For if people cannot articulate the reasons for their moral decisions, how can they teach them?

The beauty of the trolley problems is that they capture moral intu-ition at work in ways for which the moral reasoning process is unable to invent a plausible explanation. This gives a deep insight into the hidden rules by which the moral intuitive process operates.

Hauser and his colleagues have described three of these rules, which they call the contact principle, the intention principle and the action principle. (Philosophers have described them under other names.)

The contact principle is perhaps the most fascinating because it seems the most primitive. It is simply a taboo on causing bodily harm to anyone. It was presumably engraved in the mind's neural circuits long before the invention of spears or arrows that allowed people to be killed at a distance. The contact principle may also underlie the reason why moral situations before our eyes are more compelling than those at a distance. If we see a child injured by the roadside, we know we must stop and help. But if we see an advertisement soliciting funds to repair a child's harelip in faraway places, it's permissible to turn the page.

The contact principle explains part of the reason why in Fred's moral dilemma, people say it's wrong for him to push the thick-set man onto the tracks to save the five. In Denise's dilemma, her actions led to the death of the hiker on the side-track, but there was no personal contact between her and the person killed.

Another insight into the contact principle is to assume, in Fred's

dilemma, that all the people but Fred have been replaced with chimpanzees. Is it OK for Fred to push a fat chimp off the bridge to save five chimps
on the track? Most people say it's OK. The taboo of killing a person with
one's bare hands is no longer evoked. Curiously, when subjects were asked
why they judged Denise's action OK but not Fred's, several mentioned
the fact of physical contact but rejected it as sufficient reason for the distinction. "Subjects were typically able to articulate the relevant principle
used, but unwilling to endorse it as morally valid," Hauser writes.[22]

Another hidden rule of intuitive morality, the intention principle,
can be discerned in Denise's and Fred's dilemmas. Denise foresaw that the
hiker on the side-track would be killed, but didn't intend it. The hiker's
death was a foreseen consequence but not the desired outcome of her
action. Whereas Fred, if he pushes the thick-set man into the train's path,
intends the man's death or, at the very least, must include the likelihood
of the man's death in his intended act. The moral intuitive process clearly
makes a distinction between intended harm, which is not OK, and merely
foreseen harm, which may be justifiable. The complexity of this distinction, which most people cannot articulate, suggests an innate rule at
work, one to which the conscious mind has no more access than to the
rules that generate grammatical sentences.

A third hidden rule, the action principle, is that harms caused by
positive action are deemed worse than those caused by omission, or not
acting. Suppose Fred has a lever that drops the thick-set man onto the
tracks in front of the train. (The lever arrangement is to avoid triggering
the intuitive contact principle.) Then there is Jeff, whose lever does the
opposite—it prevents the thick-set man's otherwise inevitable fall onto
the tracks. Fred's action in pulling the lever, and Jeff's failure to do so,
have precisely the same effect—the thick-set man is killed but the five are
saved. Nonetheless, people judge Jeff's omission far more acceptable than
Fred's action. In this case, however, most subjects can articulate the intuitive principle at work.

The moral intuitive process equips everyone with the neural machinery for making instant moral decisions, without review by the moral

reasoning apparatus. It is easy to see how advantageous such a system would have been in days when our ancestors were hunter gatherers and had to make life-or-death decisions in a split second. This instantaneous process is useful in today's societies too. The social fabric is surely stronger if everyone has immediate knowledge of what is right and wrong.

But doesn't the possession of an instantaneous moral decision-making machinery, inaccessible to the conscious mind, make a person into a contemptible robot? Not really; an individual can always ignore the machinery's prompting. Also, the moral intuitive process, as mentioned above, is shaped by culture, meaning the education and moral instruction a person receives in childhood. Religion plays a central role here, as described in the next chapter. So do a child's peers and parents. All these influences are working to shape a set of innate moral behaviors to each society's particular values.

These values are set by tradition and ultimately by the collective behavior required for each society to survive in its particular environment. They may therefore vary from one society to another. Human nature, generally thought of as being the same everywhere, must depend more on the constant features of every society's moral behavior, and therefore on the innate moral behaviors. What are these behaviors and where do they come from?

## The Origin of Moral Sentiments

Darwin, in his book *The Descent of Man*, published in 1871, devoted two chapters to the evolution of morality. His arguments were long dismissed by many biologists, but they anticipated much of what is current wisdom today.

Darwin argued that sociality arose as a defense against predators, and that animals that banded together for this purpose would need to moderate their behavior toward one another. "All animals living in a body, which defend themselves or attack their enemies in concert, must indeed be in some degree faithful to one another; and those that follow a leader must be in some degree obedient," he wrote.[23]

The social instincts would develop from simple emotions like the parent-child bond, Darwin argued, and any social animal would acquire morality once it had evolved sufficient intellectual powers. He saw no discontinuity between the social instincts in animals and in people but in human societies, he assumed, the instincts would be enhanced by people's desire for the approval of their peers, and the "remorse, repentance, regret or shame" that follows on forfeiting the good opinion of one's peers.

Darwin then raised the problem that an altruistic person who gave his life for his community would leave no children, or at any rate fewer than less heroic people. So how could the inherited character of altruistic behavior ever become more common?

The biologist William Hamilton answered the question a century later, at least for small communities of related individuals. In his theory of kin selection, Hamilton explained that getting your relatives' genes into the next generation was just as advantageous, as far as natural selection is concerned, as passing on your own genes. So since your brother has on average half of the same genes as you do, you could get your genes for altruism into the next generation by saving two brothers' lives just as well as by saving your own.

But Darwin's answer, despite Hamilton's more specific formulation, is still of great interest. First, Darwin wrote that "To do good unto others—to do unto others as ye would they should do unto you—is the foundation-stone of morality." A man who sacrificed his life following this principle would be widely admired and inspire valor in other members of his tribe. "He might thus do far more good to his tribe than by begetting offspring with a tendency to inherit his own high character," Darwin wrote.

The second part of Darwin's answer raised an issue now known as group selection, the idea that genes can become more common if they confer a benefit on groups of people rather than just individuals. Darwin did not know of the existence of genes, so could not have formulated the problem to himself in those specific terms. Nonetheless, he described a process which, if it occurs, shows immediately how the genes underlying morality and other aspects of human sociality could have become common.

But Darwin's insight was dismissed for more than a century because of several intellectual blinders that have begun to fall only in recent years.

First, people did not want to abandon the idea that morality is the bright line that separates people from animals. Darwin's idea that there was a continuum of the social instincts from social animals to man cut right through that line. Even biologists didn't like the idea that morality had been shaped by natural selection. If morality had a genetic basis, it must have arisen as an unintended by-product of some other process, they argued. "I account for morality as an accidental capability produced, in its boundless stupidity, by a biological process that is normally opposed to the expression of such a capability," wrote George Williams, a leading evolutionary biologist, in 1988.[24]

Second, the idea that natural selection works at the level of groups has been rejected by most evolutionary biologists, largely under the influence of George Williams. He argued that selection of genes through the individuals who carry them was far more likely and should be assumed as a matter of principle unless there was strong evidence to the contrary.[25] So though group selection might be theoretically possible, he contended that "group-related adaptations do not, in fact, exist."

Darwin's thesis about the evolution of morality raises a seriously disturbing possibility. He is saying that morality, viewed by some as man's noblest achievement, arose from warfare, the least noble, and that the brisker the pace of warfare the more rapidly would morality have blossomed. This suggests that people were highly aggressive in the distant past, an implication that has raised a third mental block. Many social scientists are reluctant to believe that people were more violent in the past than they are today. Archaeologists, seeking to avoid glorification of war, have contrasted the carnage of modern wars to the peaceable behavior of human foragers before agriculture and the birth of cities. Only recently has a careful survey shown how constant and merciless was the warfare between pre-state societies, much of it aimed at annihilating the opponent.[26]

A fourth obstacle to understanding the evolutionary nature of morality has been the insistence by researchers who study animal behavior that it was fallacious to attribute complex emotions to them, especially positive ones. The primatologist Frans de Waal reports that in his studies of peacemaking among chimpanzees he was instructed to use dehumanized language. A reconciliation, sealed with a kiss, had to be described as a "post-conflict interaction involving mouth-to-mouth contact."[27] Given the evolutionary closeness of humans and chimpanzees, de Waal considered that the two species were likely to have similar emotions. Excessive fear of anthropomorphism had long stifled research on animal emotions, in his view. It also prevented biologists from acknowledging the continuum of social instincts that Darwin recognized between social animals and people.

After decades of neglect because of these various intellectual roadblocks, the evolutionary origin of morality has been slowly resurrected as a fit subject of research. William Hamilton's theory of kin selection explained how altruism could evolve in kin-based societies, like those of the social insects. Another biologist, Robert Trivers, showed how, even in groups of individuals who were not related to one another, natural selection could favor reciprocal altruism—doing someone a favor on the assumption it would be paid back later. These ideas were developed by Edward O. Wilson in his landmark 1975 book *Sociobiology* and extended from animals to people. "The requirement for an evolutionary approach to ethics is self-evident," he wrote.

*Sociobiology*, though intended by its author as merely a synthesis of new biological ideas, posed a political challenge to Marxists and much of the academic left. It showed how the human mind was not a blank slate, on which governments could write whatever ideological prescriptions they wished in order to shape Socialist Man, but was already shaped or predisposed by evolution to behave in certain ways. Wilson's book was assailed by Marxist colleagues at Harvard, such as the geneticist Richard

Lewontin. Students disrupted Wilson's lectures and harassed even Hamilton and Trivers. Researchers dared not use the word *sociobiology*, even if they agreed with its ideas, lest they be caught up in the furor. Sociobiology, as applied to people, is now pursued mostly under the name of evolutionary psychology.

Richard Alexander, after the storm over *Sociobiology* had settled, was one of the first biologists to resume the study of morality. Human ancestors lived in groups, he argued in a book published in 1987, as a defense against other human groups, and warfare had been a major influence in human evolution. Usually predators find it most efficient to live in small groups (wolves, lions, killer whales) while it is prey animals that congregate in large herds for defense. But humans departed from this rule, probably because their most feared enemies were other human groups. Incessant warfare led to selection for greater social complexity and intelligence, and the larger societies required ever greater self-constraint to avoid infringing on other individuals' interests, Alexander argued. "The function or *raison d'être* of moral systems is evidently to provide the unity required to enable the group to compete successfully with other human groups. Only in humans is the major hostile force of life composed of other groups in the same species," he wrote.[28]

The surprising idea that people might be inherently moral was difficult for biologists and others to accept because it conflicted with the usual assumption that human nature is selfish. Even harder to swallow, for those not steeped in the concepts of evolutionary biology, was the assertion that something as precious as morality could have blossomed from the murky soil of strife and warfare.

Alexander's book was largely theoretical. It was a work of practical observation that gave substance to his views. Frans de Waal, now at the Yerkes National Primate Center, had spent many years observing apes and monkeys in captivity. He noticed that each species had its own special protocols for peacemaking and for patching things up after fights.

Why would animals have any interest in peacemaking? Social monkeys and apes, de Waal observed, live in just the conditions specified by

Alexander as conducive to the emergence of morality. In many primate species there are conflicts between rival groups. Chimpanzees are territorial and patrol their boundaries, killing any neighboring male they find. Sometimes chimps conduct lethal raids into their neighbors' territory, trying to kill off male defenders one by one in a systematic campaign. If successful, they then take over their neighbors' property.

Female chimpanzees seem to be aware of the dangers posed by internal strife. If their males kill or maim one another, the community is less well defended against neighboring bands. So it is greatly in their interest to prevent or assuage conflicts between rival males. De Waal observed that in captive chimpanzee colonies the females would sometimes prize stones or sticks out of the hands of males who are about to fight.

The art of reconciliation and peacemaking is one of the building blocks of primate behavior from which human morality later evolved, in de Waal's view. He has found several other such building blocks of morality in monkey and ape societies. A basic one is empathy, the ability to perceive another's emotions. Many social animals seem aware of one another's pain. In a particularly striking experiment, rhesus monkeys allowed to take food only from an apparatus that delivered an electric shock to a companion would starve themselves, for 5 days in one case, for 12 days in another.

But it could be that the monkeys were not trying to help their companion but were personally distressed by their cries. Chimpanzees present a clearer case for empathy. They regularly console the loser of a fight. In distress, they elicit sympathy with a range of very human expressions. "When upset, chimpanzees pout, whimper, yell, beg with outstretched hand, or impatiently shake both hands so that the other will hurry and provide the calming contact so urgently needed," de Waal wrote.[29] Chimps have been known to try to save others from drowning in the moats that sometimes surround zoo colonies. This is a huge risk for them because they cannot swim.

A third moral building block is an ability to learn social rules. Infant monkeys are accorded much license, but as they grow older they learn how to respect the food and space of dominant animals. Monkey and ape societies are organized in hierarchies, in which each individual knows its place. Each species has its own repertoire of signals for communicating who is higher in the hierarchy and who is lower. Among rhesus monkeys an inferior will give a bared-teeth grin to an approaching superior and often present its vulnerable rear quarters. The hierarchy gives the community a structure and an order.

A fourth likely building block of morality is a sense of reciprocity. This is not so far from the human concept of justice. Chimpanzees remember who is a good sharer of food and who isn't, indicating they have a notion of fair treatment. In a fascinating experiment with capuchin monkeys, de Waal trained them to exchange tokens for a food reward, either a grape or a slice of cucumber. When capuchins saw their neighbor get a grape in exchange for a token, but they were given just a slice of cucumber, they seemed outraged by the unfairness of it all. Some refused to eat the slice of cucumber they were handed or even flung it back at the researcher.[30]

So what then is morality? De Waal's definition, from his perspective as a primatologist, is very different from that of rationalist philosophers. "We understand morality as a sense of right and wrong that is born out of group-wide systems of conflict management based on shared values," he writes. "Moral systems thus provide a set of rules and incentives to resolve competition and conflicts within the group in the service of the 'greater good,' that is, benefits (to individuals) derived from resource distribution and collective action. Morality, by this definition, is closely related to social behavior."[31]

By breaking out of the specialist frameworks in which philosophers and psychologists had long imprisoned the study of morality, De Waal established that morality is a biological behavior and that evolution is the only framework in which the origins of morality can be addressed.

## Human Morality

In the terms of Haidt's distinction between people's moral intuition and moral reasoning, it is easy to see how the moral intuitive process could have evolved by slow degrees in the human lineage from the four building blocks described by de Waal in primates—getting along (techniques for reconciliation after conflict), empathy, learning social rules and a sense of reciprocity.

Moral reasoning probably evolved because justifying one's actions to the group would have helped burnish one's reputation, a matter of the greatest importance for survival in small hunter gatherer bands.

People in a small community gossip all the time and maintain elaborate mental dossiers on one another's behavior. Any infraction of social norms may be remembered for years. Guarding one's reputation would have become critical. Hunter gatherer societies don't run prisons or have a penal code. You're either in or you're out, and if you are ostracized your prospects of surviving alone in the wilderness are unpromising. Better learn quickly to fit in and conform.

The fear of disobeying the community's rules could well have solidified into something close to an imperative. Philosophers looking at the primatologists' descriptions of primates' pro-social behaviors like to echo Hume's remark that there is no way of stepping from "is" to "ought." But in social situations in which an individual fears community disapproval if he fails to do something, the "is" lies pretty close to the "ought."

Consider a remarkable human behavior, one seldom hailed as distinguishing people from other animals but quite unique all the same—that of blushing. No other species changes its skin color, against its conscious will, so as to signal to others that it is ashamed or embarrassed. It is hard to reconstruct how blushing evolved. It's good for the social fabric, so perhaps societies full of blushers were more cohesive and successful. Or maybe individuals who blushed seemed more honest and trustworthy, giving them an advantage.

But however the blushing reflex evolved, it shows how acutely attuned humans have become to the necessity of observing social rules, and to their discomfiture when they feel they have transgressed the bounds of accepted behavior. Morality is at the heart of our social behavior. Evolution seems to have inscribed not just the capacity for learning the moral rules of one's community, but a significant part of the content.

There may be a universal moral grammar, as Hauser suggests, a counterpart of the universal grammar machinery that enables children to learn the language of their community. But the moral grammar, unlike that for language, is not content free. Many moral rules are universal and therefore likely to have a genetic origin. The anthropologist Donald Brown, in his survey of universal human behaviors found in societies throughout the world, cites reciprocity as the cornerstone of moral values. "The strong moral feeling attached to reciprocity, and the assiduousness with which reciprocal action and reaction are watched also suggest some degree of innateness," he writes.[32]

The Universal People, as he calls the exemplars of typical human behavior, display other moral behaviors. They care for children and the helpless. They deplore and punish the following actions: killing, stealing, cheating, lying, breaking promises and committing adultery.[33] Causing harm to others is also forbidden, and the three principles uncovered by the trolley problems show how finely grained are the innate moral rules in this category. They distinguish the in-group from the out-group, being more disposed to cooperate with the first.

Moral behavior, on the basis of the findings discussed above, seems very likely to have a genetic basis. The joint ancestors of chimps and humans, who lived some 5 million years ago, were presumably capable of premoral behaviors much like those seen in chimpanzees today. But down the human side of the chimp-human split, individuals were evolving larger brains which eventually reached a volume three times that of chimps.

With the increasing power of the human mind, individuals started to think for themselves and to calculate where their own interests lay.

Their assessments of their self-interest often proved to differ from what their moral instincts told them was in the community's interest. If societies of these cognitively advanced hominids were not to disintegrate, a higher level of social cohesion had to come into play. A new kind of behavior evolved, one that induced individuals to subordinate their own interests to that of the group. This new behavior, the instinct for religion, enforced moral instincts by making people fear deeply the consequences of ignoring them.

# 3

## THE EVOLUTION OF RELIGIOUS BEHAVIOR

*The human mind evolved to believe in the gods. It did not*
*evolve to believe in biology. Acceptance of the supernatural*
*conveyed a great advantage throughout prehistory, when the*
*brain was evolving. Thus it is in sharp contrast to biology,*
*which was developed as a product of the modern age and is not*
*underwritten by genetic algorithms.*

EDWARD O. WILSON[34]

*It is difficult to find a religion which has not, at some stage in its*
*history, inspired in the breasts of at least certain of its followers*
*those transports of mystical exaltation in which man's whole*
*being seems to fuse in glorious communion with the divinity.*

I. M. LEWIS[34A]

The human form has undergone extraordinary changes since its lineage split from that of chimpanzees some 5 to 6 million years ago. Our brain tripled in size, our body hair was shed, we downsized our teeth, shriveled our gut and gained a fine facial appendage for conserving moisture in dry climates—the nose.

Equally radical and transformative, though less well appreciated, have been the changes in human social behavior. In the societies of our apelike forebears, coordination was achieved relatively simply, through a strict hierarchy dominated by the alpha male. Hunter gatherer societies are organized on a very different principle—they are completely egalitarian. It was during the transition from male dominance to egalitarianism that religious behavior emerged.

Many other social innovations developed in the human lineage as this new species, driven by the increasing intellectual capacity of its individuals, experimented with one novel mechanism after another for communicating among members of a group and governing the interactions among them. The surprising gift of music appeared in the repertoire of human faculties. Even more remarkable was language, a wholly novel system for conveying precise thoughts from one individual's mind to that of another. Humans developed or enhanced a skill known to psychologists as theory of mind—the ability to infer what someone else knows or intends. Groups possessing these new skills in various strengths competed furiously with each other in the struggle to survive. All these new faculties were doubtless drawn upon as natural selection searched for an effective solution to the most pressing of all problems for a social species—how to make selfish individuals place society's needs above their own. This departure from self-interest required not just moral self-restraint and social cohesiveness, but an emotional commitment to the group so fierce and transcendent that men would quite readily sacrifice their lives in its defense.

The solution that evolved was religious behavior. It was those who learned to bond to each other through ritual song and dance who developed the most cohesive communities. It was those who believed that the gods or their dead ancestors were seeing into their hearts who hewed closest to their society's rules. It was those who most feared supernatural retribution who built the most moral societies with the strongest social fabric and the resilience to outlast others.

## Common or Universal Features of Religion

The principal evidence for thinking religious behavior is an evolved part of human nature is the fact that religion is universal. Every known society possesses some form of religion. And though there are wide cultural variations—religions across the world are very different from one another—there are also many shared elements. These constant or almost constant features of religious behavior are the ones likely to have a genetic basis.[35]

All religions are centered on rituals, and the rituals include music. Dance is also a regular part of ritual in primitive societies though it has been eliminated from the religion of many settled societies.

All societies have rites of passage, rituals that mark birth, puberty, marriage and death. The music that accompanies these often includes percussive effects, since drums or rhythmic beating are widely held to be a way of communicating with the spirit world. The initiation rites accompanying puberty often involve pain and terror, a way of instilling courage and loyalty in future warriors.

All religions include some way of gaining access to the gods, even though the gods live in a different world, and of influencing their behavior through rituals, sacrifice or prayer, even though eternal beings might seem likely to have little interest in quotidian human concerns.

Access to the supernatural realm may be gained through trance in primitive societies, and through revelation in advanced societies. In some primitive societies, anyone may enter the trance state, either through hour-long dancing or by taking hallucinogenic drugs. In others, trance specialists known as shamans venture out on special journeys to the spirit world. In advanced societies, control of religion often rests with a religious hierarchy which monopolizes access to the supernatural. In some religions, access is confined to the occasions in the distant past when the founding prophet received communications from the deity or his surrogates.

In many societies rules of morality are part of the pact with the super-natural powers, an understanding that elevates moral behavior from an individual to a collective matter. Conformance with the gods' wishes entitles society to their favors. Conversely, if anyone misbehaves and is not punished, the group as a whole stands to suffer divine retribution.

All or almost all religions share the belief that the soul survives after death, and that the gods control both fortunate and unfortunate events.

Even though the gods enjoy eternal lives in their supernatural realm, they are intensely interested in human affairs down to the minutest detail. They are aware of everything and can know a person's thoughts. They may punish remorselessly every infraction of their rules, with penalties meted out in the form of disease, death or disaster in this world or as sanctions on the soul when it joins the supernatural world.

The divine rules include codes of moral behavior, as well as largely arbitrary ritual requirements, such as taboos on certain foods or on speaking certain words.

The gods can be propitiated with appropriate rituals, which usually include sacrifices of various kinds. The prayers that accompany these pro-pitiatory rituals are accompanied with gestures used in human and other mammalian societies to indicate submission—bared throat or chest, kneeling or prostration.

Central to many religions is the idea of sacrifice, of valuable gifts made to the gods to influence their behavior. As in relationships among people, the gifts impose on the divine recipients the obligation of repayment at a later date. The gods are expected to provide the things people need of them, such as good fortune, good health, good harvests, and victory in war or at least the avoidance of defeat. Sacrifice is a principal means of influencing the gods' behavior and, along with prayer, of negotiating the expectations between the gods and society as to how each party should behave.

"Beneath the diverse forms it takes," Henri Hubert and Marcel Mauss wrote in their classic essay, sacrifice "always consists in one same proce-dure, which may be used for the most widely differing purposes. This procedure consists in establishing a means of communication between the sacred and profane worlds through the mediation of a victim, that is, of a thing that in the course of the ceremony is destroyed."[36] Every sacrifice, in their view, is a contractual arrangement based on the principle of *do ut des*—"I give that you may give."

Among the Nuer, for example, a pastoral Nilotic people of the lower Sudan, explicit bargaining negotiations are conducted with the spirits as to how serious a sacrifice is required for their favors. The Nuer spirits, writes the social anthropologist E. E. Evans-Pritchard, "require bloody offerings. And if they are not given animal sacrifices they seize their devotees and make them sick. Nuer, therefore, do not hesitate to bargain with these spirits, speaking through their mediums, in a downright way which astonished me. The sense of the bargain is always the same: if we give you an ox or a sheep or a goat will you leave the sick man alone that he may not be troubled by you?"[37]

The sacrificed animal is the intermediary between the sacrificer in the living world and the gods in the supernatural world. In some religions the sacrificer sacrifices himself, but this, Hubert and Mauss note, can only happen when the sacrificer is himself a god. In Christianity, the sacrifice has become the death of Jesus, and is performed by the priest metaphorically in the communion rite. Jesus was killed by men of ill will "but by a complex transformation this has retrospectively become a sacrifice, in that the murder was willed by God," writes the social anthropologist Edmund Leach. "The sacrifice is now a persisting channel through which the grace of God can flow to the devout believer. The donor of the sacrifice is Christ himself and the priest, in offering the bread and wine to the congregation as 'the body and blood of Christ,' is, by implication, timelessly repeating the sacrifice at the behest of the divine Donor. . . . The Christian Mass, as a whole, is a transformation of the Jewish Passover and the crucified Christ 'is' the sacrificial paschal lamb, 'the Lamb of God.' "[38]

The remarkable variety of the world's religions can thus be seen to depend on a handful of common behaviors. Foremost among them is the belief in the gods as awesome governors of society and enforcers of moral standards. Though the gods are known to live in the supernatural realm, people believe that they closely follow events in this world and can be swayed by prayer, sacrifice and appropriate rituals. Societies whose members embraced such beliefs would have been more cohesive and united in attaining difficult goals, whether in peace or warfare. Because an instinct for faith would have promoted survival, genes that favored such an instinct eventually became universal in the early human population.

## Religious Behavior and Genetics

The universality of religious behavior suggests that, as with language, it is mediated by specialized structures in the brain. Language is known to be supported by neural circuitry in certain regions of the brain because, if these regions are damaged even minutely, specific defects appear in a patient's linguistic abilities. No such dedicated regions have yet been identified with certainty for the neural circuitry that may underlie religious behavior. Excessive religiosity is a well-known symptom of temporal lobe epilepsy and could reflect the activation of neural circuits associated with religious behavior. But there is no agreement on this point, and the search for such circuitry in people who don't suffer from epilepsy is "suggestive but not conclusive," according to the neurologist Steven Schachter.[39] It could be that religious behavior itself does not require a dedicated brain region large enough to be detectable by present methods.

The fact that religious behavior is universal strongly suggests that it is an adaptation, meaning a trait shaped by natural selection. If it is an adaptation, it must have a genetic basis, such as a suite of genes that are activated during development and wire up the neural circuits needed to induce the behavior. Identification of such genes would be the best possible proof that religious behavior has an evolutionary basis. The lack of any progress in this direction so far is not particularly surprising; the genes that underlie complex diseases have started to be identified only recently and funds to support such expensive efforts are not available for studying nonmedical complex traits.

An indirect approach to the genetic basis of religious behavior is through psychological studies of adopted children and of twins. Such studies pick up traits that vary in the population, such as height, and estimate how much of the variation is due to environmental factors and how much to genetics. But the studies cannot pick up the presence of genes that don't vary; genes for learning language, for example, are apparently so essential that there is almost no variation in the population, since everyone can learn language. If religious behavior is equally necessary for survival, then the genes that underlie it will be the same in everyone, and no variation will be detectable.

Religious behavior itself is hard to quantify, but studies of religiosity—the intensity with which the capacity for religious behavior is implemented—have shown that it is moderately heritable, meaning that genes contribute somewhat, along with environmental factors, to the extent of the trait's variation in the population. "Religious attitudes and practices are moderately influenced by genetic factors," a large recent study concludes.[40] Another survey finds that "the heritability of religiousness increases from adolescence to adulthood," presumably because the influence of environmental factors decreases in adulthood (when you leave home you go to church if you want to, not because your parents say so).[41] The aspects of religiosity that psychologists measure include factors like the frequency of church attendance and the importance assigned to religious values. Their studies show that there are genetic influences at work on the intensity of religious behavior, but do not yet reach to the heart of the issue, that of probing the neural circuitry for learning and practicing the religion of one's community.

In the absence of direct evidence about the genes underlying religious behavior, its evolutionary basis can be assessed only indirectly. The effect of cultural learning in religion is clear enough, as shown by the rich variety of religions around the world. It's the strong commonalities beneath the variations that are the fingerprints of an innate learning mechanism.

These common features seem very unlikely to have persisted in all societies for the 2,000 generations that have elapsed during the 50,000 years since the ancestral human population dispersed from its African homeland, unless they have a genetic basis. This is particularly true given the complexity of religious behavior, and its rootedness in the emotional levels of the brain.

To no less an observer than Darwin himself it seemed that religion was like an instinctive behavior, one that the mind is genetically primed to learn as indelibly as the fear of heights or the horror of incest. His two great books on evolution, *Origin of Species* and *Descent of Man,* have nothing directly to say about religion but in his autobiography, written in his old age, he was more explicit about this controversial topic. He wrote, "Nor must we overlook the probability of the constant inculcation in a belief in God on the minds of children producing so strong and perhaps an inherited effect on their brains not yet fully developed, that it would be as difficult for them to throw off their belief in God, as for a monkey to throw off its instinctive fear and hatred of a snake."[42]

To understand how the instinct for religious behavior evolved, it is necessary to explore the circumstances in human development in which it first arose.

## From Male Dominance to Egalitarianism

For most of their existence, modern humans have lived as small bands of hunters and gatherers. Only 15,000 years ago did people begin to settle down in fixed communities, forming the large societies that are commonplace today. Religious behavior evolved in hunter gatherer society, well before settlement. The social structure of these hunter gatherer bands therefore has considerable bearing on the nature of religion.

Five million years earlier, human social structure was very different and probably resembled that of chimpanzees today. In chimpanzee societies everyone knows their precise rank. There is a male hierarchy and below it a female hierarchy. The alpha male rules the male hierarchy and gets most of the mating opportunities, a common arrangement in primate societies. Probably because of chimpanzees' unusual intelligence, the alpha male can rarely rule alone and has to share power by building coalitions with a few close allies who get cut in on the mating system.

Chimps, unlike humans, seem to have changed rather little in the last 5 million years, perhaps because they have always occupied the same forest and woodland habitat, whereas humans had to learn how to survive on the ground and in a range of different environments. Hence the joint ancestor of chimps and people was probably quite chimplike. If so, it would probably have had a chimplike social structure based on dominance by the alpha male.

Fast-forward from the joint ancestor to the first human hunter gatherers, and the social structure has changed completely. To judge by the living hunter gatherer societies studied by anthropologists, the social order would have been fiercely egalitarian. Hunter gatherers have no headmen or chiefs, and no one is willing to give or take orders. Men like power and will seize it if they can. But if they can't rule, their next preference is that no one rule over them.

The egalitarianism of hunter gatherers is not a passive preference but a system that is aggressively maintained because it is under constant challenge. From time to time strong individuals emerge and try to dominate a group. But their efforts invariably provoke a coalition against them. Others in the group will mock them or ignore their orders. If they persist, they will be shunned or even evicted from the group. If they are too intimidating, they will be killed. To avoid blood feuds, the group that has decided to eliminate a domineering leader will often assign one of his own relatives to kill him.

A perennial threat to the egalitarianism of the hunter gatherer band was a skillful hunter who might try to dominate the band through his success. So hunter gatherers impose a rule that all meat must be distributed. Bragging and stinginess are the two social errors that bring instant disapproval. The !Kung decree that an animal belongs to the owner of the arrow that brought it down, who is usually not the hunter. The owner then distributes the meat while the hunter makes light of his achievement.

Primitive farmers too will take steps to kill those who disrupt social harmony. Behavior judged as disruptive can consist of merely causing envy through success or just being hard to get along with. Among the Tsembaga, slash-and-burn farmers of central New Guinea, a man whose pigs and gardens do conspicuously better than those of his neighbors may be betrayed to the enemy so that through sorcery they will be able to kill him in the next battle.

Making too many enemies in one's own village is a bad idea if one is a Tsembaga. "Widespread antagonism toward a member of the group is likely to lead to general agreement that he is a witch," writes the anthropologist Roy Rappaport, "and when such agreement exists, betrayal to the enemy is unnecessary; a man's own clan brothers may kill him." Inquiring about the personalities of the people killed recently for witchcraft, Rappaport learned that the victims were "likely to be bad-tempered, argumentative, and assertive."[43]

The egalitarian approach "appears to be universal for foragers who live in small bands that remain nomadic, suggesting considerable antiquity for political egalitarianism," writes the anthropologist Christopher Boehm, who has studied the transition from hierarchy to a society of social equals.[44]

A critical question in human evolution is how the hierarchy typical of ape societies was transformed into its opposite, the egalitarianism of hunter gatherers. Human brain size started to expand dramatically after the split with chimps. One consequence of this increased cognitive capacity was the invention of weapons such as wooden spears. Weapons are great equalizers, and would have had the effect of flattening out the male hierarchy of a still apelike society, Boehm suggests. Another leveler would have been the cognitive ability of the weak to form coalitions against tyrannical leaders.

But as egalitarianism slowly evolved in the human lineage, it would have exposed a critical weakness in the social structure: with the power of the alpha males eclipsed, how was order to be kept? If no one were willing to defer to anyone else, who would determine the interests of the group? Who would take the personal risk of punishing deviant and antisocial behavior?

The threat of freeloading and anarchy would have become increasingly serious as human cognitive abilities increased. Individuals would have figured out new and better ways to take advantage of the group's protection without contributing anything in return. Nothing is more corrosive to a group's cohesion than free riders. If they go unpunished, the advantage of social living quickly diminishes; others will contribute less, and the group will disintegrate or crumble under challenge from neighbors. Free riders would have gained new power with the advent of language, a perfect instrument with which to deceive, prevaricate and manipulate. Those who were not pulling their full weight had a new means of cloaking their selfishness.

Just as the emerging human societies were being undermined by the freeloaders within, they had to confront a pressing external threat, that of warfare. Like the ability to freeload, warfare became more sophisticated and deadly as cognitive capacity increased. People may not like warfare, but the point needs no belaboring that they are very proficient at it. The skill is an ancient one that reaches far back in the primate lineage, a fact that has come to light from close study of chimpanzees. Though at first thought to be peaceful, chimpanzees in fact occupy territories that are patrolled and defended by bands of males. Through raids and ambushes, they try to pick off the males of a neighboring group one by one until they are able to annex the group's territory and females.

Early humans seem to have inherited the same instinct for territorial defense and warfare. As with chimpanzees, the aggressiveness of hunter gatherer societies was not at first recognized by anthropologists, partly because colonial administrations had suppressed warfare and partly because the style of primitive warfare differs greatly from that of modern societies. It was conducted not with campaigning armies but through ambushes and raids, in which aggressors would seek to kill a few of the enemy at minimum risk to themselves.

Anthropologists at first dismissed these skirmishes as hardly serious, until they recorded causes of male death over many years. They then realized that if you go to war every week, even low casualty rates start to mount. In some tribes up to 30 percent of male deaths occurred in warfare.

War seems to have been the natural state of hunter gatherer societies. "Peaceful pre-state societies were very rare; warfare between them was very frequent, and most adult men in such groups saw combat repeatedly in a lifetime," writes the anthropologist Lawrence H. Keeley in his survey of primitive warfare.[45] He estimates that a typical tribal society lost about 0.5 percent of its population in combat each year, far more than the toll suffered by most modern states—war deaths in the twentieth century would have amounted to 2 billion people had the tribal death rate persisted.[46]

Pre-state societies fought often. About 75 percent went to war at least once every 2 years, until they were pacified, whereas the modern nation state goes to war about once a generation. Adding to the carnage, primitive peoples were not in the habit of taking prisoners, unless to torture them as the Iroquois did, or to fatten them for eating later, as was the practice among certain tribes in Colombia. Otherwise, captured warriors were killed on the spot. "In fact, primitive warfare was much more deadly than that conducted between civilized states because of the greater frequency of combat and the more merciless way it was conducted," Keeley concludes.[47]

Thomas Hobbes's description of primitive warfare was all too accurate. "It is manifest," he wrote in 1651, "that during the time that men live without a common power to keep them all in awe, they are in that condition which is called war. This war is every man against every other man."[48] Some anthropologists and archaeologists have long been reluctant to accept this conclusion. Instead, perhaps with a desire to portray modern warfare as unusually wicked, they have suggested that war is an aberration, or that it started only after the beginning of agriculture some 10,000 years ago.

The anthropologist Raymond Kelly (to be distinguished from Lawrence Keeley, quoted above) argues that there is little evidence of violent death in the Upper Paleolithic period, which lasted in Europe from 45,000 to 10,000 years ago. Since warfare would leave such evidence, he asserts, there can have been little or no warfare during the period. "The 'nightmare past' that Hobbes envisaged in which individuals lived in continual fear of violent death clearly never existed," he writes.[49]

But the people of the Upper Paleolithic were hardly pacifists. They would not have been in Europe in the first place had they not wrested it from the grip of the fearsome Neanderthals and driven them to extinction. The style of primitive warfare—raids and minor skirmishes—would not leave a strong fingerprint in the archaeological record, and the absence of much evidence of warfare at this time cannot be taken as evidence of its absence.

Nor is it at all likely, as Kelly contends, that "war is not primordial but has a definite origin in the relatively recent past."[50] The existence of territorial warfare among chimps, and its practice by people today, suggests that both species inherited the behavior from their common ancestor who lived some 5 million years ago. The frequency of warfare may wax and wane and peaceful societies can always be found, such the Icelanders of today, who have no army, or Sweden, which last went to war in 1815. But given that both peoples are descendants of the hyperaggressive Vikings, no one is likely to accuse them of having pacifism in their genes. Human societies are remarkably well adapted to warfare, but exercise that capacity depending on circumstance and calculation of their own interests.

Modern humans have lived as hunters and gatherers for most of their existence, and the warlike nature of most contemporary hunter gatherer societies can reasonably be assumed to have prevailed throughout the distant past as well. "We need to recognize and accept the idea of a nonpeaceful past for the entire time of human existence," writes the archaeologist Steven LeBlanc. "To understand much of today's war, we must see it as a common and almost universal human behavior that has been with us as we went from ape to human."[51]

Morality, altruism, loyalty and duty are considered high virtues, but policies of aggression and extermination reflect the darkest aspects of human nature. It is not a comfortable thought that both should have been shaped by the same selective pressure, the need for a degree of social cohesion sufficient to withstand the demands of intergroup warfare. Still, as Lawrence Keeley notes, "Warfare is ultimately not a denial of the human capacity for social cooperation, but merely the most destructive expression of it."[52] Human nature, as has often been remarked, is a mixture of contrarieties, with capacities for great good and great evil being interwoven. It is not so surprising that both should be branches of a tree that itself is rooted in deeply ambiguous moral territory, the struggle to survive in a dog-eat-dog world.

Early human societies transitioning away from male dominance thus faced two social problems of the utmost severity—the threat of free riders from within and the threat of hostile neighbors from without. How were the new societies to be fortified against these threats? One solution would have been to build on the premoral systems that had evolved in primate societies: from these emerged the innate moral dispositions of early humans. "There appears to be a universal short list of values that all cultures share: negative ones that proscribe killing, seriously deceptive lying, or theft within the group, and positive ones that call for altruism and cooperation for the benefit of the whole community," writes Boehm.[53]

But moral restraint by itself is not sufficient to deter freeloading or to energize a group to prepare for warfare. Knowing what's right and doing it are two different things. Freeloaders may figure the chances of getting caught are acceptably low. A man may desire deeply to defend his community, but what rational motive could make him sacrifice his life to do so?

A solution gradually emerged to counter the two acute threats of freeloading and of warfare: religion.

Religious behavior addressed these two leading challenges to social order in the evolving human lineage. It both enforced the moral instincts and motivated people to pay any cost in defense of their community. Religion secured a new level of social cohesion by implanting in people's minds a stern overseer of their actions. The Nuer, for instance, believe that "if a man wishes to be in the right with God he must be in the right with men, that is, he must subordinate his interests as an individual to the moral order of society," writes Evans-Pritchard.[54] It was belief in these supernatural supervisors that enabled egalitarian societies to emerge from the dictatorship of the alpha male that primate societies had endured for so long.

Ants, the other evolutionary masters of social living, are distinctive for the high degree of cooperation between members of the same colony. But with ants, just as with people, sociality toward the in-group is combined with relentless hostility toward other ant colonies. Ants are territorial and will fight pitched battles at their borders with neighboring groups. Some species have developed special soldier castes. Victory may lead to the opponents' extinction, their queen being killed, their workers and larvae eaten or enslaved, and their territory and other property annexed. "The greatest enemies of ants are other ants, just as the greatest enemies of men are other men," observed the Swiss myrmecologist Auguste Forel.[55]

It is striking that, with both ants and people, evolution should have made cooperation and warfare two sides of the same coin. Social cohesion is critical to both the ant and human systems. With ants, cohesion is secured by the shared chemical signals that regulate their behavior and by the high degree of relatedness among members of a colony. Neither of these factors is compatible with human physiology. This is why ants don't need religion but people do.

## Religion and the Supernatural

All religions have concepts of the supernatural, whether in the form of gods or the spirits of departed ancestors. These supernatural entities, whether real or not in themselves, exerted a pervasive impact on human societies. To understand religion, it seems essential first to reconstruct how the gods came into the picture and what their primary role might have been.

In the view of nineteenth-century anthropologists such as Edward Tylor, people assumed that the figures seen in dreams were spirits. Speculating about the nature of death, they inferred that after the body was dead, its spirit essence lived on in another world. In dreams, the appearance of particular spirits known to the dreamer proved that this was so. It was a small step from there to assume the existence of greater spirits with supernatural powers, and that in dreams or trances communication could be established with the spirit world.

Though Tylor's proposal that dreams were the source of early ideas about the supernatural cannot be proved, it is significant that dreams are of central importance in many religions. The dreamworld is the central focus of Australian Aborigine religion, in which even conception is accomplished through dreams. In Judaism, Jacob dreamed at Bethel of the ladder of angels ascending to heaven and Yahweh promising him the land of Israel. Joseph had prophetic dreams of ruling his brothers and interpreted the pharaoh's dreams. In Christianity, the Joseph of the New Testament is prepared by angels in a sequence of four dreams to accept his wife's pregnancy, to flee to Egypt to escape Herod's massacre of the newborns, to return to Israel on Herod's death, and then to live in Nazareth. "Throughout history, in cultures worldwide, people have seen their dreams first and foremost as religiously meaningful experiences," writes the dream specialist Kelly Bulkeley.[56]

If the idea of the supernatural first came through dreams, the concept of regular, controllable access to the supernatural realm was perhaps suggested by trances. Trances would have been attained, accidentally at first, during the prolonged dance sessions of early ritual. Because people in trances would expect to see what others had seen, a community would eventually construct a consensus view of the supernatural world and its named inhabitants. This doorway into the supernatural realm was so

compelling that people throughout history have sought different ways
to gain access to it, whether through prolonged exertion, hallucinogenic
drugs or anesthetic gases.

The gods of the supernatural realm may at first have been just a curi-
osity. But they soon acquired an extraordinarily useful occupation. This
insight has emerged from a school of anthropologists and economists
studying the basis of human cooperative behavior. Their explanation is
all the more interesting because it was initially directed not at religion at
all but at the issue of punishment.

People in all kinds of situations are far more cooperative, even with
total strangers, than biologists would expect. This behavior seems deeply
embedded in human nature, but there are few good biological explanations for cooperation other than with a person's close kin.

Scholars from several disciplines have suggested that such a high level
of natural cooperativeness could not arise unless those who deviated
from this expected behavior could count on inexorable punishment.

But the problem then arises as to who would have meted out the punishment. In small societies, the person who takes on the role of enforcer
exposes himself to general resentment, not to mention retaliation from the
miscreant or his relatives. Hunter gatherer societies punish deviants quite
carefully, often by securing everyone's agreement beforehand and preferably getting one of the offender's own kin to kill him so as avoid revenge.

In a series of recent papers the evolutionary psychologist Dominic
Johnson has pointed out that every community possesses a highly effective punishment mechanism in the form of supernatural agents. In
societies throughout the world, the gods or the spirits of dead ancestors
are reputed to be keenly interested in people's observance of prevailing
laws and taboos. The gods punish infractions unfailingly, either in this
world or in the next or both. The religions of advanced societies are no
less emphatic. The Hebrew Bible makes clear that sin will be punished.
Christianity promises admission to heaven for obeying divine law, eternal damnation for defying it. Hinduism and Buddhism prescribe reincar-
nation as a lower species for disgracing oneself as a human.

A system of supernatural punishment carries enormous advantages for a primitive society. No one has to assume the thankless task of meting out punishment and risk being killed by the offender or his relatives; the gods perform this chore willingly and vigilantly.

No legislation is needed: the list of offenses and associated punishments is set out in the religious ritual and kept well in mind by all believers. No police force is required; believers restrain their own behavior, and are consumed by fear of divine retribution for any sin they commit.

That the supernatural punishment may have been imaginary did not destroy its deterrent value as long as people feared it, and there was ample stimulus for such fears. In the belief systems of many primitive societies, the evidence of the gods' retribution is plain for all to see, in the form of disease or disaster. People who suffer misfortune are believed to have incurred it through their own misdeeds. And those who commit some sin fully expect misfortune to befall them.

Belief in moralizing gods would have been a fine solution to the problem of discouraging deviancy. Johnson's proposal accounts well for a puzzling feature of the world's religions: almost all take for granted that the gods in their supernatural realm care deeply about events in the real world. Why should human sexual affairs or dietary preferences matter in the least to immortal beings living in a spirit world? The assumption makes little sense unless the gods are viewed as embodying a society's moral authority and its interest in having all members observe certain rules of social behavior. From this Durkheimian perspective, the gods are of course minutely interested in human moral conduct—it's their raison d'être. Gods die when people no longer worship them.

Many of the rules the gods enforce, such as those concerning tabooed foods or prescribed dress, may be arbitrary in substance but they serve to signal adherence to belief in the prevailing religion. And all religions include rules that affect the social fabric, such as regulation of marriage and the prohibition of murder and theft. Moral obligation, and punishment and reward, are among the religious traits that are "probably found, in some shape or form, in all human societies—or at least are very widespread and historically recurrent," according to the anthropologist Harvey Whitehouse.[57]

Religious belief may have become particularly advantageous as humans developed language and the ability to gossip about one another. Earning a bad reputation in a small society is a poor idea. Even excelling at some skill or another could stir envy and invite accusations of being a witch, with consequent execution. Those who behaved with extreme care, scrupulously following the gods' apparent wishes, could well have left more progeny. Religious behavior could therefore have been favored by natural selection, Johnson suggests. He and psychologist Jesse Bering write: "We have inherited the general template for religiosity because those early humans who abandoned the prospect of supernatural agents, or who lacked the capacity to represent their involvement in moral affairs, likely met with an early death at the hands of their own group members, or at least reduced reproductive success. Those who readily acquiesced to the possibility of moralizing gods, and who lived their lives in fear of such agencies, survived to become our ancestors."[58]

Another quite curious aspect of many religions is that they impute omniscience to their supernatural agencies, including even detailed knowledge of people's thoughts. Several scholars have noted the similarity of this divine faculty with the human capacity, known as theory of mind, for inferring what other people are thinking.

Evolutionary psychologists consider that the brain is not a general-purpose calculating machine but rather a set of neural systems, each of which evolved to solve a specific problem important to survival. People have an extraordinary ability, for example, to see someone's face, perhaps just once, and recall it decades later. A general-purpose memory system would surely get overloaded if it had to remember every image recorded by the retina over a lifetime. It's reasonable to suppose that the brain is not constructed this way. Rather, it has a dedicated face-recognition module which evolved, doubtless early in primate history, because of the extreme importance of being able to recognize other individuals in a small society. The module is superb at recognizing faces and, in conjunction with other brain systems, at deciding which of its memory traces are worth storing.

The "theory of mind" module is another inferred brain circuit for which there is reasonably good evidence. Its utility and survival advantage are evident; almost every social situation requires a forecast of how others may react to one's words or deeds.

Johnson and Bering argue that people, being familiar with their own abilities to infer other people's thoughts, would have assumed the gods too possessed theory of mind capabilities, ones so penetrating that they could read people's thoughts. Gods from Zeus to the Babylonian Enlil are credited with the ability to read minds. "O Lord, thou hast searched me, and known me," says the psalmist. "Thou knowest my downsitting and mine uprising, thou understandest my thought afar off. . . . Search me, O God, and know my heart: try me and know my thoughts: And see if there be any wicked way in me, and lead me in the way everlasting."[59]

People who imputed a thought-reading version of their own theory of mind to the gods inferred that the gods could not be deceived, and came to fear their supervisory powers all the more.

The genetically shaped neural circuits that underlie religious behavior may have stayed much the same since hunter gatherer days but, as the cultural aspects of religion change, the various parts of the behavioral circuitry may be invoked to different extents. Early people may have felt chiefly fear for the gods since they had daily proof of divine vengeance in the form of disease and natural calamities. But for many people today the personal and positive aspects of religion are at least as important as the social and punitive. Religion's harsher beliefs, such as assuming disease is divine punishment for past sins, are no longer held. Faith is now more a source of solace than of fear: there are rituals to control unpredictable forces, prayers to seek success or relief from sickness and danger, and the personal satisfaction of being part of a moral community.

Important as these solaces are, they can have direct evolutionary significance only if they lead to a person's having more surviving progeny, the coin by which evolution measures success. It's hard to make the case that any personal aspect of religion does have such an effect. Many studies have been undertaken of the effect of religion on health but without any decisive result so far. The mild benefits seen in some studies seem unlikely to have any great impact or to lead to someone's leaving more surviving children.

The personal aspects of religious involvement probably matter for an indirect reason. From an evolutionary point of view, religious behavior can be seen as a necessary biological drive, as imperative for survival—at least in hunter gatherer days—as was eating or reproduction. Natural selection makes food and sex highly rewarding or pleasurable because the individuals who pursue them most energetically leave the most progeny.

Eating and reproduction are fundamental drives that appeared at the dawn of animal evolution; natural selection instituted rewards that make people want to do them. Religious behavior is a very recent faculty and its reward system is perhaps for that reason positioned at a far higher cognitive level. Whatever the exact train of cause and effect, the bottom line is that religious behavior had to be perceived as deeply satisfying. Otherwise people would have practiced it insufficiently, or not at all. Many forms of religion are highly demanding in terms of time or effort; few people would adhere to them without a strong personal motivation.

The pleasure of eating makes one eat but is distinct from the evolutionary reason for eating, which is to provide sustenance for the body. The satisfactions of religious belief make people practice religion, but are far removed from the evolutionary function of religion, which is to bind people together and make them put the group's interests ahead of their own.

## Costly Signaling

Belief in punitive supernatural agencies is one universal feature of religion. Another is that most religions impose costs of some kind on membership.

Some religions demand tithes, some require donations of time, others ban certain foods or working on certain days. Why do religions impose such costs? And why do people join very demanding religions, such as Mormonism or Orthodox Judaism, when softer options like the Episcopal church are available?

Religions impose costs on members, it seems, in order to deter people who seek to enjoy a religious community's benefits without contributing to its costs. Free riders can be highly corrosive to a community's cohesion. "Winter Shakers," who took food and shelter from Shakers but departed in the spring, were a heavy burden. But systems to monitor people's level of commitment and enthusiasm tend to destroy the property being measured. A better solution is to make the religion costly to join, whether by fees, donation of time, or requiring distinctive diet and dress.

Economists and anthropologists who have studied the question conclude that these costs serve several critical functions. By raising the cost of entry, a religious community excludes free riders and ensures that its members are committed. A high price of entry also raises the level of trust among its members, because by obeying all the required rules and taboos, congregants signal to one another that they have bought into the religion's moral code and can be relied on to behave accordingly. An extra benefit of distinctive dress or dietary habits is that members find it harder to associate with nonmembers and so devote more time to the community.

"If strictness increases costs, why should anyone join a strict church?" asked the economist Laurence Iannaccone. Many psychologists have sought to analyze strict religious behavior as if it were some kind of mental aberration. Applying the economic approach known as rational choice theory to church attendance in the United States, Iannaccone arrived at a quite different answer. "Strictness reduces free riding," he said. "It screens out members who lack commitment and stimulates participation among those who remain. Rational choice theory thus explains the success of sects, cults and conservative denominations without recourse to assumed abnormalities, irrationality, or misinformation."[60]

There is an optimum level of strictness, Iannaccone observes. Many sects are too strict and fail. Others are not attractive to outsiders, and thrive only if they maintain high fertility and accommodate sufficiently to change. The Amish, an Anabaptist order with settlements in Ohio, Pennsylvania and Indiana, are an example of the latter strategy. They have high fertility and retention. They ban most new technology but allow telephones in public places, though not in homes, and let cars be hired but not owned.

For an injudicious adjustment of strictness, Iannaccone offers the example of the Catholic church, which relaxed many of its distinctive rules after the Second Vatican Council of 1962 but adhered to hard-line positions on birth control and the celibacy of priests. "The Catholic church may have managed to arrive at a remarkable, 'worst of both worlds' position—discarding cherished distinctiveness in the areas of liturgy, theology and lifestyle, while at the same time maintaining the very demands that its members and clergy are least willing to accept," Iannaccone writes.[61]

The anthropologist William Irons came to much the same conclusion about the virtues of costliness. A religion, he noted, is "basically a commitment to behave in a certain way without regard to self-interest." The costly rituals enable members of a community "to monitor one another's commitments to the community and its moral code, thereby facilitating the formation of larger and better united groups."

A high degree of commitment was vital to the survival of groups that were locked into fierce competition with one another. Because religious commitments are more powerful than any other kind, "evolution has built into human beings a strong propensity to seek a religious orientation toward life and to hold this orientation to be of the highest value," Irons wrote.[62]

Biologists who study animal signaling have noted that cheap signals can be imitated and thus lose their value. Trustworthy signals are those that are very costly to produce and cannot be counterfeited. Only very healthy peacocks can afford to grow a magnificent tail, so peahens can rely on this signal in choosing mates. When Thompson's gazelles spot a leopard, some will jump up and down in a conspicuous movement known as stotting, instead of just running away. This true signal of fitness advertises to the leopard that it needn't waste its time and would do better to hunt some less healthy gazelle.

Religious behavior too serves as a true signal because religions are learned only in arduous initiation rites and demand a heavy commitment of time. The signals are important to other members of the community. They cannot watch an individual's movements all the time, but they can assess his sincerity in the ritual.

The signals, it should be noted, are symbolic, and they convey their message far more effectively than could mere words. A man may say "You can trust me!" but greatly more credible is his participation in whatever rituals are required by the group's religion.

The members of a Jewish sect in Israel known as the Haredim continue to wear the thick black coats and fur hats of their eastern European homeland. "By donning several layers of clothing and standing out in the midday desert sun," writes the anthropologist Richard Sosis, "these men are signaling to others, 'Hey! Look, I'm a Haredi Jew. If you are also a member of this group, you can trust me because why else would I be dressed like this? Only a lunatic would spend their afternoon doing this unless they believed in the teachings of Ultra-Orthodox Judaism and were fully committed to its ideals and goals.'"

Because of trust among group members, not only is the problem of free riders eliminated, but members benefit from mutual help. During his study of Haredi communities, Sosis notes, he often saw Haredi travelers being offered free meals, lodging and rides by Haredi hosts who did not know them. "On several occasions I witnessed cars being loaned to complete strangers, and interviews revealed a surprising number of interest-free loans offered and accepted between people who had previously not known each other."[63]

Trust and cooperation of this strength are invaluable. It is easy to imagine that cohesiveness of this kind could make a critical difference for small groups constantly at war with one another. Irons, for one, believes that this aspect of religion has been too little appreciated by skeptics because of their focus on religious texts and beliefs rather than on ritual. He writes, "The theory of religion as it applies to commitment emphasizes the vital importance of religion to most human communities and the fundamental [role] that religion plays in the lives of most human beings. The theory also suggests that the core of religion is not belief (which most scientists and intellectuals are prone to criticize), but rather, for the most part, commitment to socially constructive behavior."

Given the costliness of religious behavior, and its salient role in determining a primitive society's ability to deal with foes both internal and external, the forces of natural selection seem very unlikely to have ignored it. If religious behavior offered no benefit, groups that wasted time and resources this way would have been eliminated by groups that did not bear such a handicap in the struggle for survival.

## Is Religion Adaptive or Just a By-product of Evolution?

Despite the strong likelihood that religious behavior has helped people survive, several biologists deny that it has emerged because of natural selection.

Most of the few biologists who have written on the subject of religion seem to agree that it has an evolutionary origin. But some contend that religious behavior is merely an accidental by-product, dragged into existence in the wake of some other feature favored by natural selection. By this account, religious behavior arose as an inadvertent consequence of some other process and not because it conferred any evolutionary advantage. In other words religious behavior, in biologists' parlance, is nonadaptive, meaning it was not favored by natural selection.

The anthropologist Scott Atran, for example, argues that people use their theory of mind module, together with the brain's system for detecting unseen agents, to infer the existence of supernatural agents. The agency detection system, always on the alert for potential predators, especially of the human kind, is easily triggered. "The evolutionary imperative to rapidly detect and react to rapacious agents encourages the emergence of malevolent deities in every culture, just as the countervailing evolutionary imperative to attach to caregivers favors the apparition of benevolent deities," he writes.[64]

A similar idea has been advanced by another anthropologist, Pascal Boyer. "Concepts of gods and ancestors with whom you can interact require a minor but consequential 'tweaking' of standard theory of mind," he says.[65] Both he and Atran view religious behavior as an accidental consequence of the way the brain works and hence as nonadaptive.

How can something be specified by the genes yet not be adaptive? One example is the redness of the blood. Natural selection did not favor individuals with red blood over those with blood of some other color. It favored an efficient method of transporting the respiratory gases between the lungs and tissues. That method employs the hemoglobin family of molecules which, because each contains four atoms of iron, are a vivid red when carrying oxygen. The redness of the blood is accidental, a mere by-product of the trait that was selected for; hence red blood, though genetically specified, is regarded as nonadaptive.

Now a biologist who argues religious behavior is adaptive must then concede that it confers some significant benefit, in the form of whatever caused it to be favored by natural selection. But from the nonadaptive position, religion can be derided as an evil or useless pursuit, with no redeeming feature.

Two well-known biologists who advocate the nonadaptive view are Steven Pinker and Richard Dawkins. Both, it so happens, are trenchant critics of religion.

Pinker considers and dismisses three reasons for thinking religious behavior is adaptive and then offers a hypothesis of his own as to why religion is universal. Pinker is a distinguished psychologist and author whose views merit respect, but there is room to differ with his position that religion confers no evolutionary advantage.

The three dismissible adaptive arguments, in his view, are that 1) religion is a source of intellectual comfort in facing death or uncertainty; 2) religion brings a community together; and 3) religion is a source of moral values.

Pinker is probably right to dismiss the first argument; it is hard to see how mental comfort could translate into leaving more progeny, the only measure that natural selection cares about. The third argument Pinker derides by stating that the Bible "is a manual for rape and genocide and destruction." The good book, he says, "contrary to what a majority of Americans apparently believe, is far from a source of higher moral values. Religions have given us stonings, witch burnings, crusades, inquisitions, jihads, fatwas, suicide bombings, gay bashers, abortion-clinic gunmen, and mothers who drown their sons so they can happily be united in heaven."[66]

But excesses in suppressing the schisms with which established religions are regularly challenged do not alter the fact that religion is nevertheless a source of moral values. Almost all religions encode some form of the golden rule, that of "do as you would be done by," as well as other moral restraints, and these will be adaptive if they enhance the social fabric.

In countering the second argument, that religion could be adaptive because it fosters group cohesion, Pinker concedes that "religion certainly does bring a community together," but says this could be achieved by other means. He asks, "Why, if there is a subgoal in evolution to have people stand together to face off common enemies, would a belief in spirits or a belief that ritual could change the future be necessary to cement a community together? Why not just emotions like trust and loyalty and friendship and solidarity? There's no a priori reason you would expect that a belief in a soul or a ritual would be a solution to the problem of how you get a bunch of organisms to cooperate."

But however strange religious behavior may seem, this is the means that evolution has found effective. For much of history, emotions like trust and loyalty have generally grown out of a shared religion. And belief in punitive gods, as discussed above, is highly effective at getting people to cooperate for the good of society. There is every reason to suppose the cohesion thus attained would be highly adaptive in the struggle for survival against competing societies.

If religious behavior is not adaptive, as Pinker argues is the case, how did it get to be universal? The explanation he offers is that religion flourishes because it is good for priests, however bad it may be for people. This may be true but stumbles on the fact that religion became universal long before priests existed. Hunter gatherer societies, as noted above, were egalitarian. They had religion but no religious officials, with the possible exception of shamans in certain tribes. Their rituals were communal, with everyone on an equal footing.

Pinker suggests that a trait or behavior should meet three tests before being considered adaptive. The first is that it should be shown to be innate, for example by being universal in its species and developing reliably across a range of environments. Speaking, for instance, meets this criterion but reading does not, since children learn to read only when taught to do so. Religious behavior too would seem to meet the criterion quite well, given that religion is universal and the propensity to learn it appears reliably in every culture around the age of adolescence. Children may be exposed to religion starting from much younger ages but it is rites around the age of puberty that induce an emotional commitment to supernatural beliefs.

Pinker's second criterion is that the trait should have improved survival in the past, such as during hunter gatherer days. Religious behavior meets this criterion too. It strengthened social cohesion, and thereby a society's moral fabric and military strength. It evidently enhanced survival so efficiently that societies which failed to inherit the behavior all perished, leaving religious behavior a universal trait of all the survivors.

The third criterion is that the trait should have engineering functionality—it should be something evolution has worked hard to perfect, like the design of the human eye or ear, even if by methods very different from those a human engineer might choose. But religion meets this criterion with flying colors. With nothing but rituals and symbols, it deftly induces members of a community to lay aside their self-interest and make an emotional commitment to the common good, including with the sacrifice of their lives if necessary. By what conceivable means, if not by religion, could such a goal be attained?

Dawkins is another well-known biologist who argues that religious behavior is nonadaptive. Like Pinker, he agrees with the proposals by Boyer and Atran that belief in supernatural agents is a nonadaptive by-product of other brain modules. He begins by conceding that religion is ubiquitous and acknowledging that "universal features of a species demand a Darwinian explanation."[67]

Dawkins raises one possible explanation, that religious behavior could indeed have been selected for when the societies with religion wiped out those without it. This raises the question, about which biologists have differing opinions, of whether natural selection can operate at the level of groups, rather than on individuals, an issue discussed further below. All that need be noted here is that Dawkins argues group selection could occur, but not to any significant degree. Hence religion could not have become adaptive through intergroup competition, in his view.

He then notes that people die and kill for their religious beliefs, behavior which he compares to the misfiring of a moth's navigational system when it flies into a candle flame. Since the moth's behavior is nonadaptive, so too is religion, Dawkins argues. So what, he asks, "is the primitively advantageous trait that sometimes misfires to generate religion?" His hypothesis is that "There will be a selective advantage to child brains that possess the rule of thumb: believe, without question, whatever your grown-ups tell you." Religious belief, in his view, spreads like a virus from parents to impressionable children, a cycle that is repeated every generation. Religion, therefore, is the accidental by-product of children's propensity to believe what their parents tell them.

This argument seems a little stretched because nonsensical information is not of great help in the struggle for survival and seems unlikely to have been passed on for 2,000 generations in every known human society since the dispersal from Africa. Religion can impose enormous costs, just in the amount of time it takes up, as is evident from the rites of Australian

Aborigines. Had religion no benefit, tribes that devoted most of their time to religious ceremonies would have been at a severe disadvantage against tribes that spent all day on military preparations.

Dawkins does not seem highly confident in his gullible child theory because he stresses it is "only an example of the kind of thing that might be the analogue of moths navigating by the moon or the stars." But without offering any more plausible explanation he insists that "the general theory of religion as an accidental by-product—a misfiring of something useful—is the one I wish to advocate."

Dawkins's gullible child conjecture, like Pinker's manipulative priest proposal, seems to be driven less by any particular evidence than by the implicit premise that religion is bad, and therefore must be nonadaptive.

## Religious Behavior and Group Selection

But if religious behavior is adaptive, how did it evolve? Religion, as has been argued above, is primarily a social behavior, meaning one that exists to benefit the group. But there is a serious general problem in accounting for the evolution of social behaviors. Biologists have not yet resolved the issue, so it cannot be resolved here, but the problem is easy enough to describe. Any individual who behaves so as to benefit his group will put himself at a disadvantage with respect to other individuals who behave selfishly. This altruist, by spending time and resources to benefit others, will leave fewer progeny and his genes for altruistic behavior will soon be eliminated from the population. How therefore could altruism or other forms of self-denying, pro-social behavior ever have evolved or be maintained?

The answer that occurred to Darwin was that natural selection could take place at the level of a group of people, not just at the individual level. A society full of altruists, say of men ready to sacrifice their lives in battle, would be very likely to prevail over a less well-motivated group. Just as some individuals within a group will be more successful than others and leave more progeny, so it is in the struggle between groups. The more unified societies, those whose members contain a larger proportion of pro-social genes than do their rivals, will prevail over others, and pro-social genes will become more common in the population as a whole.

Despite Darwin's authorship of the idea, selection at the level of groups, known as group selection for short, is controversial among evolutionary biologists. It has recently drawn the support of notable champions, such as David Sloan Wilson and Edward O. Wilson, but they are at present in a minority. Most evolutionary biologists believe that although natural selection could in theory operate at the group level in special circumstances, its principal operation takes place at the level of individuals.

The argument that follows shows how group selection, if it has occurred in human evolution, could account well for the evolution of religious and other social behaviors in early human groups. Human social behaviors, such as the deeply ingrained moral instincts described earlier, exist and must have evolved somehow. If they did not do so through group selection, then it was through some other evolutionary process, but group selection, despite the uncertainties surrounding it, is the process presented here.

Here is how Darwin said group selection would work:

"It must not be forgotten that although a high standard of morality gives but a slight or no advantage to each individual man and his children over the other men of the same tribe, yet that an increase in the number of well-endowed men and an advancement in the standard of morality will certainly give an immense advantage to one tribe over another. A tribe including many members who, from possessing in a high degree the spirit of patriotism, fidelity, obedience, courage, and sympathy, were always ready to aid one another, and to sacrifice themselves for the common good, would be victorious over most other tribes; and this would be natural selection. At all times throughout the world tribes have supplanted other tribes; and as morality is one important element in their success, the standard of morality and the number of well-endowed men will thus everywhere tend to rise and increase."[68]

This deep insight carries political implications that some biologists and others have found unwelcome. It could be extended to imply that might is right, that victorious nations are more virtuous than those they vanquish, or that the rule of colonial powers is justified. But Darwin neither said nor implied any of the above.

Whether or not with extraneous political reasons, many evolutionary biologists have looked askance at the idea of group selection. They still embrace the position put forward by George Williams and others that group selection might occur to some small account, but its contribution will always be minor compared with individual selection.

Biologists developed several more specific reasons for thinking they could do without group selection to explain human social behaviors such as altruism. One was the theory of inclusive fitness, or kin selection, produced by William Hamilton, who argued that altruism could spread among groups of closely related individuals. Even if an individual perished, genes identical to his own would survive, on average, in the children and siblings for whom he laid down his life.

Hamilton's theory seemed at first to explain how sociality arose in social insects like ants and bees in whose colonies the workers, by a quirk of insect genetics, are more closely related to their sisters than to any daughters they might have. But recent research has shown that social insects are in some cases not as closely related as thought. And in any case, kinship seems to have limited power in explaining the sociality of human societies.

Researchers have recently noted several special features of human behavior that might have made group selection significant in people, even though it seems to play little role elsewhere in the animal kingdom.

The most serious objection to group selection has to do with the balance between the forces favoring people with altruistic genes and the forces opposing them. A hunter gatherer group with many self-sacrificing, altruistic heroes might, as Darwin suggested, destroy a group less fortunately constituted, and genes for altruism in the population as a whole would increase. But within the victorious group, as time went on, the nonaltruists would devote their resources to their own families, raising more children, and the genes for altruism would become less common. Skeptics of group selection say the second process, the within-group selection against altruistic behavior, will always proceed faster than the between-group process favoring it and hence will overwhelm it.

The proponents of group selection agree that the balance between the two forces is the crux of the issue. "Selfishness beats altruism within groups. Altruistic groups beat selfish groups. Everything else is commentary," say David Sloan Wilson and Edward O. Wilson in a recent article.[69]

There are two significant behaviors that may have made humans far more strongly affected by group selection than are most other species. One was the fierce conformist pressures within hunter gatherer groups that reduce the heavy disadvantages of altruism. The other was intense warfare between groups that accelerated the rate of group selection.

A major point made by the two Wilsons is that selfishness within groups is likely to have been limited by a crucial event in human evolution—the emergence of egalitarianism in early hunter gatherer societies, as discussed at the beginning of this chapter. Successful hunters are forced to share their catch with everyone else. They cannot resist sharing, and cannot put on airs, because stinginess and bragging are the two behaviors that incur the most opprobrium in hunter gatherer communities.

Hunter gatherer egalitarianism was no mere principle; it was rigorously applied. And the conformity that ensued would have greatly reduced the natural variability in human social behavior. The mighty hunters, the power seekers, the philanderers and any who stood out and made themselves a subject of gossip, all found it difficult to thrive. If everyone had to behave alike, within-group variation would have been suppressed and differences between groups would have taken over as the principal driver of evolutionary change, at least in terms of social behavior.

For a modern example of just how rigorously small communities can secure conformity, consider the case of Toby Greenberg, a young mother in the Orthodox Jewish village of Kiryas Joel in New York state. Because of minor infringements of the dress code approved by her Hasidic sect, the tires of one of her cars were slashed and a message in Yiddish, "Get out, defiled person," was painted on the window of the other. She and her husband filed a complaint with the police accusing the rabbinically appointed modesty committee of orchestrating the harassment. A member of the committee, David Ekstein, denied it had any involvement but told a reporter that in the case of people who defy social mores, "If we find they have a TV or a married woman won't wear a wig, we invite them to speak with us and try to convince them it's unacceptable, or next year we will not accept their children into the school system."[70]

If this is how nonconformity is stamped out in twenty-first-century New York, imagine how efficiently materially primitive people in earlier centuries could have erased any behavioral deviation from some equally arbitrary norm, especially given the almost total lack of privacy in hunter gatherer societies. People who rejected orthodoxy or even expressed strange ideas would have been ejected from the band, which in hunter gatherer days meant death, unless they could find another band that would take them in. Over the generations, cultural suppression of novel behavior could well have retarded genetic novelty, especially in a small group whose members were already highly interrelated.

Because of egalitarianism, the two Wilsons write, "Suppressing fitness differences within groups made it possible for between-group selection to become a powerful evolutionary force. The psychological traits associated with human moral systems are comparable to the mechanisms that suppress selection within groups for other major transitions [in the history of life]. The human major transition was a rare event, but once accomplished, our ability to function as team players in coordinated groups enabled our species to achieve worldwide dominance, replacing other hominids and many other species along the way."

A second powerful influence favoring group selection, besides conformity within groups, is warfare between them, especially wars as frequent as those in pre-state societies. The more cohesive or altruistic group is likely to win, diminishing or eliminating its opponent. The importance

of warfare as an evolutionary force has been demonstrated in mathemati-
cal models of the group selection process constructed by Samuel Bowles,
an economist interested in evolution. Using an equation developed by
George Price for tracking genetic variation within and between groups,
Bowles has devised a model that shows how intimately altruism and warfare are related, a theme discussed earlier in relation to morality.

Altruism and war coevolved, Bowles concludes. "The group-oriented
behaviors that make cooperation for mutual benefit possible among
humans also make large-scale lethal warfare possible," he writes. "And
frequent warfare . . . may have been an essential contributor to the evolution of precisely the altruistic traits that facilitate war making."[71]

The insight explains why human nature is so contradictory, capable
both of the most sickening cruelty and of the most self-denying care for
others: the roots of altruism and of aggression are inextricably intertwined in evolutionary history.

Bowles has recently tried to make his model more realistic by feed-
ing into it data from hunter gatherer groups relating to group size, the
genetic variation between groups, and the frequency of conflict. He finds
that death due to warfare makes up a sizeable fraction of all deaths among
foragers—13 percent according to archaeological data, 15 percent according to ethnographic reports. To understand just how heavy a toll this is,
consider the percentage of deaths due to warfare in the United States and
Europe during the twentieth century, the epoch of two world wars: less
than 1 percent of male deaths.[72]

Bowles argues that periods of intense conflict are likely to have ensued
toward the end of the Pleistocene ice age when world climate fluctuated
violently. The encroaching glaciers that rolled down over Europe and
East Asia during the Last Glacial Maximum, which lasted from 20,000 to
15,000 years ago, would have diminished livable areas and pitted groups
against one another in a conflict for survival.

A high mortality in conflict would explain a paradox that has long
puzzled demographers. Hunter gatherer groups can increase by more
than 2 percent a year, yet global human population grew at less than

0.1 percent until the advent of agriculture 10,000 years ago. Heavy attrition through warfare and climatic change would have driven group selection to significant levels. "Genetic differences between early human groups are likely to have been great enough so that lethal intergroup competition could account for the evolution of altruism," Bowles concludes.

One expression of altruism is in religious behavior. By devoting time and resources to religious activities, rather than looking after his own family, an individual contributes to behavior that benefits the group. The evolutionary shaping of religious behavior has been explored by David Sloan Wilson. After reading a passage by a seventeenth-century Hutterite author comparing the community of the faithful to a beehive, he was struck by the possibility that group selection, in which he had long been interested as a matter of evolutionary theory, might explain the emergence of religion. In his book *Darwin's Cathedral* he argues, with the help of several case studies, that group selection can indeed explain many features of religion.

His thesis is that human groups function as units subject to natural selection when behavior within the group is regulated by a moral system or religion. Supernatural agents are an essential part of the moral system because they operate as the sanction that enforces it. Well-functioning groups coordinated by such a moral system out-compete other groups. The social coordination provided by the moral system enables groups to secure resources and other items of value that would be beyond the reach of individuals.[73]

Wilson's concept draws on several works already described here, such as Durkheim's theory of religion as the embodiment of society and Boehm's description of egalitarianism among hunter gatherers, as well as his own research on group selection. He distinguishes between what religion achieves—the social coordination for which religious behavior was selected—and what its practitioners feel, which he acknowledges is entirely different. "Since writing *Darwin's Cathedral*, I have spoken with many religious believers who feel that my focus on practical benefits misses the essence of religious experience, which is a deeply felt relationship with God," he writes.[74] But there is no necessary connection, he points out, between an end that evolution has favored and the means it has arrived at to get there. People fall in love in part to have children, he notes, "but that doesn't remotely describe the subjective experience of falling in love." Similarly, the experience of communing with the deity is one of many benefits that make people practice a religion.

Wilson rejects the view of many social scientists and others that belief in the supernatural and nonrational elements of religion should be seen as some kind of mental aberration. To the contrary, religious belief "is intimately connected to reality by motivating behaviors that are adaptive in the real world—an awesome achievement when we appreciate the complexity that is required to become connected in this practical sense."

One of the ways in which religion connects to reality is through its use of sacred symbols. These symbols evoke emotions, and emotions are ancient, evolved mechanisms for motivating adaptive behavior, often doing so beneath or partly beneath the level of consciousness. "Sacred symbols organize the behavior of the people who regard them as sacred," Wilson notes.

It's this organization—not the implausibility of certain elements in a religion's sacred narrative—that should be seen as the criterion of a creed's effectiveness. The adaptedness of religious beliefs "must be judged by the behaviors they motivate, not by their factual correspondence to reality," Wilson says.


## How Religious Behavior Emerged

Complex organs like the eye or ear emerge step by step in evolution, and the same would be true of a complex behavior like religion. But there is as yet little evidence to help trace the steps by which religious behavior came into being. One question is whether religion existed before language. If belief in supernatural beings is an essential feature of religion, it is hard to see how such beliefs could have been shared before language.

But it's possible that some proto-religious behavior existed before language, based on communal dancing and such information as can be shared through grunts and gestures. Without the use of language, an alpha male chimp, for instance, can conduct all the politics necessary to keep himself in power.

Rhythmic activity, such as dancing or marching, can induce strong feelings of togetherness in members of a group, as is discussed further in the next chapter. And humans for some reason have acquired the ability, not possessed by chimpanzees, of entraining their movements to a common beat. It seems quite possible that this ability emerged because communal dancing fostered group cohesiveness. If so, some kind of wordless community dancing may have been the first element of religious behavior to have been favored by natural selection.

Once language had developed and people were able to share precise thoughts with one another, a second element would have emerged— belief in the supernatural. There is considerable plausibility in Tylor's argument that early peoples attached great significance to dreams, and particularly to dream time encounters with dead relatives. It would have been easy to assume that people's ancestors had continuing existence in a supernatural world from which they exerted godlike influence on the everyday world.

Natural selection might have favored groups or individuals who practiced ancestor worship if in fact their beliefs about godlike ancestors led them to behave in ways conducive to their society's survival. A relationship with the ancestors might have developed through the concept of reciprocity—I give you this, you owe me that in return—which is deeply rooted in the primate heritage. Reciprocal relationships with the ancestors may have seemed quite natural to early societies.

But what did the ancestors, being dead, want or need from the living? Early people had many needs, for fertility, health, good hunting, success in warfare, all of which were assumed to lie in the ancestors' power to grant. So humanlike needs were imputed to the ancestors, whether for social respect, or for prized food such as meat. Special forms of respect—prayer and worship—were developed for the ancestors' benefit. For donations of food, the idea of sacrifice developed. We will give the ancestors this precious gift, and they in return will grant our prayer for successful hunting, a bountiful harvest, victory in tomorrow's battle. The gifts, if living, evidently had to be killed in order to assure immediate delivery to the supernatural realm.

Sacrifice, prayer and ritual all have the same basic purpose, that of influencing the gods' behavior. It is easy to see how negotiation with the gods would have become a potent way of harnessing a society's energies to achieve common goals. The gods will grant our wishes if we behave as they have commanded. But what are their wishes? Those who interpreted the gods' intent, whether the hunter gatherer band, or the priests and rulers of settled societies, gained the power to unite their society in a common purpose, whether in standards of morality or in battle against neighboring tribes.

People and groups who were inclined to believe in the supernatural would have formed more cohesive societies and left more progeny than those who did not. A propensity for supernatural belief could therefore have been favored by natural selection.

Other genetically shaped behaviors could then have accreted around a basic belief in the supernatural, enhancing its value for survival. These would have included a propensity to fear that the gods would punish infractions of their rules and a willingness to yield one's life in society's defense.

This handful of behaviors provided an extraordinarily economical and effective way of evoking in early people a deeply felt allegiance to their group or tribe. The groups that made most effective use of this new human faculty prevailed over others, and the genes supporting the faculty became universal. The time course in which each behavior was added to the growing complex cannot at present be constructed. All that is known is that by 50,000 years ago, the date that modern humans dispersed from Africa, all the elements of religious behavior were in place and were inherited by all descendants of the ancestral human population.

That is the genesis of religion. But there is one essential component of religious behavior, perhaps the most magical and mysterious of all, that requires closer attention—the faculty of music. And closely allied with music is sacred dancing, and the rhythmic muscular exertions that induce trance.

# 4

---

# MUSIC, DANCE
# AND TRANCE

*[Bach's] St. Matthew Passion of 1729 . . . probably brought
religion home to many more souls than the words of a thousand
curates. At times doctors of music have been nearer than doctors of divinity to God.*

OWEN CHADWICK[75]

In the ancestral religion of hunter gatherers, people bound their
communities together in emotionally compelling dramas of music,
chant and dusk-to-dawn dances. The marathon rituals ended for some
in exhaustion, for others in a state of trance that opened doors, for them
and their community, between this world and that of the supernatural.

Little by little, the ancestral religion was suppressed in the settled
societies that began to emerge 15,000 years ago and has survived only
among the handful of hunter gatherer tribes that endured into the modern era. The new settled societies adopted a structured form of religious
practice, one in which priests controlled the ritual and monopolized
interaction with the supernatural. The communal dances ceased. The
songs were silenced. The shamans were marginalized as witch doctors or
sorcerers.

But the ancestral religion was woven too deeply into people's behavior to disappear entirely. The vase was shattered, but its shards endured. It required an intuitive leap to recognize the pieces, see how they had once been assembled and figure out what the vessel's purpose had been. That leap was made not by any anthropologist or archaeologist, but by a distinguished military and world historian, William McNeill.

McNeill's epiphany came when he was drafted into the U.S. Army in September 1941 and set to marching about for hours on a patch of Texas plain. It was hot and dusty, and the exercise seemed worse than useless, given that marching in close formation on a modern battlefield within range of machine guns would have been suicidal. But all that aside, McNeill writes, marching about in step with the others somehow felt good. "Words are inadequate to describe the emotion aroused by the prolonged movement in unison that drilling involved. A sense of pervasive well-being is what I recall; more specifically, a strange sense of personal enlargement; a sort of swelling out, becoming bigger than life, thanks to participation in a collective ritual."[76]

McNeill's insight was that rhythmic muscular movement in unison had a strange and powerful effect on the emotions: it created both a sense of exhilaration and a feeling of solidarity with other participants. Group cohesion, though not well understood by many civilians, is a matter of the greatest concern to military commanders. A poorly trained group will dissolve and run when 10 percent of its men have been killed; a cohesive force will not break until just 10 percent of its members are left alive. This is a difference that decides battles.

Why should military organizations be able to evoke, by suitable training, this strange behavior of group cohesion, one that routinely prompts soldiers to the biologically irrational act of risking their lives? McNeill realized that this must be an aspect of human behavior left over from the ancestral religion. Military drill, like the religion of hunter gatherers, involves rhythmic muscular movements, performed by a small community. The transcendence of self, achieved by ritual dancers, or in the heat of battle, or to a lesser extent by hours of drilling, is somehow induced by sustained rhythmic movement. "Drill, dance and battle belong together," McNeill writes. "All three create and sustain group cohesion; and the creation and maintenance of social groups—together with resulting rivalries among groups—constitute the warp and weft of human history."

The strange power of strenuous rhythmic movement to bind a group together may be hard to imagine for any who have no personal experience of the effect. But there is no reason to doubt that it does so. Alfred Radcliffe-Brown's description of how the Andaman Islanders of the Indian Ocean achieved group cohesion is worth quoting at length because it shows how people enjoy the dancing, despite its strenuous demands, and come to experience a state of "ecstatic harmony" with the rest of their community:

> The Andaman dance, then, is a complete activity of the whole community, in which every able-bodied adult takes some part. . . . In the dance the individual submits to the action upon him of the community; he is constrained, by the immediate effect of the rhythm as well as by custom, to join in, and he is required to conform in his own actions and movements to the needs of the common activity. The surrender of the individual to this constraint or obligation is not felt as painful, but on the contrary as highly pleasurable. As the dancer loses himself in the dance, as he becomes absorbed in the unified community, he reaches a state of elation in which he feels himself filled with energy or force immensely beyond his ordinary state, and so finds himself able to perform prodigies of exertion. This state of intoxication, as it might almost be called, is accompanied by a pleasant stimulation of the self-regarding sentiment, so that the dancer comes to feel a great increase in his personal force and value. And at the same time, finding himself in complete and ecstatic harmony with all the fellow-members of his community, experiences a great increase in his feelings of amity and attachment towards them.[77]

Not a bad way to build esprit de corps, a quality that may seem far removed from everyday life today but would have been highly relevant in small groups that fought frequently with their neighbors. McNeill is a historian, not an evolutionary biologist, but he gives weight to a factor that biologists have often ignored—the role of warfare in shaping human evolution. Early human groups that instilled better cohesion in their members through ritual dancing would have survived better than their adversaries. This suggestion ties in well with the condition for group selection mentioned in the previous chapter—a high level of conflict between groups is required if group-level selection in favor of pro-social behavior is to outweigh the within-group selection against it.

McNeill also draws attention to the central issue of communication. It's the sharing of information that binds a group of individuals together. This can be spoken information, but more important than words in the binding process is emotional information. This is conveyed by different, and probably much older, forms of communication than language. The vehicles of emotional information are gesture, such as dance, and evocative sounds, such as music, including wordless chanting and drumming.

It might seem that complex information can be conveyed only in the form of words, because that is the only way with which we are familiar. But consider the complexity of the task faced by the alpha male of a chimpanzee group. At any time he can be overthrown by a coalition of other powerful males. Yet by sound and gesture, he somehow manages to divide his adversaries and bind his allies so successfully that his reign may last many years—16 years is the longest reign on record. Evidently chimps can conduct sophisticated coalitional politics without uttering a single word.

Humans have a sound and gestural repertoire analogous to that of chimpanzees but in addition have developed three other modes of social communication. These are very relevant to understanding the evolution of religious behavior, which makes use of all three. They are dance, music, and language.

Dance and music should in many respects be considered together because, in many cultures, they seem to be inseparable. Both are found universally. Among hunter gatherers, one cannot dance without music, and if there is music there is dance. Some cultures use the same word for both. Among the Blackfoot Indians the principal word for music, *saapup*, means singing, dance and ceremony all rolled into one.[78] The ancient Greek word *mousikē*, from which the English word *music* is derived, means any art over which the Muses presided, hence included dance, music and recited poetry.

Even the Taliban, who banned most forms of music in Afghanistan, allowed men to sing a cappella.[79] Music and dancing give participants a vigorous sense of community. The shared emotions evoked by the rhythmic activity create feelings of exaltation that bind the group to a common purpose. The origin of music has long been mysterious, but its social role, as a pillar of ritual, may have been the reason that natural selection has made sensitivity to music a universal property of the mind.

Both dance and music are very social activities and underlying their social nature is a simple behavior we take for granted but which no other primate possesses. People in groups can synchronize their movements, whether in stamping or clapping or any other rhythmic sound-making activity, and do so spontaneously. Chimpanzees have never been observed to synchronize their calls or drumming, and there is only one report of bonobos in captivity doing so.

The ability to synchronize dance and music would have been of great value to human groups, given the role of sustained rhythmic movement in promoting cohesion. Therefore it would seem to be an adaptive behavior, meaning one shaped by natural selection because of the survival advantage it conferred. But this raises a wider question, that of whether music itself is adaptive.

It was obvious to Darwin that music, being a universal behavior of all known human societies, should be considered as having been shaped by natural selection. But what selective advantage did it confer, given that its only function seemed to be that of giving pleasure? "As neither the enjoyment nor the capacity of producing musical notes are faculties of the least use to man in reference to his daily habits of life," Darwin wrote in a well-known passage, "they must be ranked amongst the most mysterious with which he is endowed."[80]

Curiously, Darwin as a young man witnessed an event that could have suggested to him how music had come to play so essential a role in human existence. In 1836, when his ship the *Beagle* stopped in King George's Sound in southwest Australia, he attended an aboriginal rite. From his description, it seems evident that the performance was an enactment of an event in the Aborigines' dreamtime mythology. But ethnographers had not at that stage appreciated Aborigine religious ideas, and barely understood that they had any religion at all. Then as now, as Barbara Ehrenreich argues in her book *Dancing in the Streets*, the practice of attaining collective emotional bonding through dancing was unfamiliar to Western observers. With their emphasis on self-control and the psychology of the individual, they viewed with incomprehension and horror the wild dance rituals of the primitive peoples with whom their colonial administrations came in contact, and particularly the trances into which the dancers often fell. "Western psychology was disabled from comprehending the phenomenon of collective ecstasy," Ehrenreich writes, in part because anything that required the loss of self was regarded as pathological.[81]

Darwin, not yet the destroyer of Victorian certitudes, saw only a rite he could not understand, two totemic clans performing the emu dance. "When both tribes mingled in the dance, the ground trembled with the heaviness of their steps, and the air resounded with their wild cries," he wrote. "Every one appeared in high spirits, and the group of nearly naked figures, viewed by the light of the blazing fires, all moving in hideous harmony, formed a perfect display of a festival among the lowest barbarians."[82]

Writing his *Descent of Man* thirty-five years later, Darwin neglected to wonder if the "hideous harmony" might have offered some insight into the origin of music. A major purpose of his book was to advance the idea of sexual selection—that the choice of males by females and the competition for females between males were far reaching forms of natural selection. It was sexual selection—the singing of men and women to impress one another in courtship—that he proposed as the driving force of human music.

Song has evolved many times independently among vertebrate species—in songbirds, parrots, hummingbirds, whales and seals, as well as primates. Singing doesn't necessarily have the same purpose in all these species. In some, such as whales, it seems to have arisen for reasons of communication. In birds, song may be a way of defending a territory or to attract a mate. Noting the song of gibbons, which perform very impressive duets, Darwin wrote that "it appears probable that the progenitors of man, either the males or females or both sexes, before acquiring the power of expressing their love in articulate language, endeavored to charm each other with musical notes and rhythm."[83]

Darwin's thoughts on the origins of music are the starting point for many discussions today because his insights were keen and biologists are further than ever from agreeing on whether music has an evolutionary purpose.

Steven Pinker, for instance, says music shows clear signs of not being an adaptation, meaning it was not shaped by natural selection. "I suspect that music is auditory cheesecake, an exquisite confection crafted to tickle the sensitive spots of at least six of our mental faculties," he writes.[84] Obviously the liking for cheesecake confers no survival advantage that might allow genes for cheesecake consumption to become more common through natural selection. What has happened, Pinker argues, is that a liking for fat and for rare sources of sweetness like honeycombs conferred a survival benefit on our foraging ancestors, and cheesecake happens to stimulate the taste and odor detection systems that evolved for that purpose.

Pinker's argument is that the love of music too is an accidental by-product of faculties that exist for different purposes. Music may trick the language system into thinking there is meaning in some string of notes, or hit the auditory system with natural resonances it is primed to focus on for other reasons, Pinker suggests. But this argument seems like examining each part of an elephant in isolation and dismissing each as pointless, without asking what they might all do together.

In fact, there are substantial reasons to suppose that music is adaptive. It is found in every known society, a strong indication of being shaped by natural selection. And the faculty of music perception is acquired very easily, like learning a language, and at a very early age. Sandra Trehub, a psychologist at the University of Toronto, has found that babies as young as 6 months have advanced musical abilities, being able to tell the difference between a changed melody and one that has merely been shifted by some musical interval. "The rudiments of music listening are gifts of nature rather than products of culture," she concludes.[85]

So why did nature confer this gift? Two leading proposals are sexual selection, which was Darwin's choice, and group cohesion. The sexual selection theory has been ingeniously developed by the evolutionary psychologist Geoffrey Miller. He notes that musical ability is an excellent indicator of the brain's fitness. So women may have preferred men with good musical abilities as the fathers of their children, leading to the genes underlying the faculty becoming more common. The rock guitarist Jimi Hendrix, Miller writes, "did have sexual liaisons with hundreds of groupies, maintained parallel long-term relationships with at least two women, and fathered at least three children in the United States, Germany and Sweden."[86]

Miller rejects the idea that music conferred an advantage by bonding people; such an approach, he argues, depends on group selection, and group selection is a grisly matter of one group wiping out another: "Group selection models of music evolution are not just stories of warm, cuddly bonding within a group; they must also be stories of those warm, cuddly groups out-competing and exterminating other groups that do not spend so much time dancing around their campfires."[87]

This of course is an irrelevant argument because moral or political preferences have no place in trying to understand the evolutionary process. But Miller's politically tinged objection may well explain part of the resistance of other academic researchers to the idea of group selection. Group selection does indeed assume that some groups survive at the expense of others. The evidence of frequent warfare between hunter gatherer groups suggests that just this kind of pressure has operated throughout the human past, and was at least as intense among foraging peoples as among their descendants who adapted to settled life.

Could sexual selection have been the driving force behind the emergence of the human appreciation of music, as Miller argues? It may have played some role: male musicians seem not to lack for young female admirers, though whether they in fact father more children has yet to be proved. But sexual selection seems unlikely to have been a major force in shaping the music faculty because most features shaped by sexual selection are highly dimorphic, meaning that they differ between male and female. The peacock has a gorgeous, iridescent tail; the peahen is drab and dowdy. Male deer have elaborate antlers; the females of most species do not. The appreciation of music, however, is not at all dimorphic; both men and women seem equally skilled. In terms of generating music, there may be more male than female rock stars, but this affects a handful of people, not the population as a whole. "Based on current data, the assumption that music is a sexually selected trait complex is unjustified," concludes Tecumseh Fitch, a psychologist at the University of St. Andrews, Scotland, in a recent review.[88]

The highly social nature of music, notably the fact that it is performed for others to listen to, seems the strongest clue to its purpose, or at the least one that no theory can ignore. True, drawing people together for a feel-good jam session may not seem to carry any overwhelming survival advantage. But it is probably an error to consider music in isolation from the context in which it is played. The context relevant for its evolution is not the modern concert hall but the hunter gatherer societies in which music first came to prominence.

Music, particularly that made with percussive instruments like drums, rattles and bells, is in evidence at many ordinary social occasions, such as healing, hunting, warfare and funerals, observes the social anthropologist Rodney Needham. "Percussion," he adds, "is typical of a remarkably wide range of other situations such as birth, initiation, marriage, accession to office, sacrifice, lunar rites, calendrical feats, declaration of war, the return of head-hunters, the reception of strangers, the inauguration of a house or a communal building, market days, sowing, harvest, fishing expeditions, epidemics, eclipses, and so on." All these events, he notes, mark transitions from one state to another. And percussion is the constant accompaniment of these important ritual occasions.[89]

Among hunter gatherers, music is inseparable from two other behaviors. First, where there is music, there is dance. Second, where there is dance and music, there is ritual. In this context, it is clear why music confers an advantage in survival: it is an essential component of religious behavior, the catalyst of social cohesion.

Besides music and dance, two other components of ancient religious behavior remain to be examined—language and trance.

## Music, Language and Belief

Modern religions like Judaism or Christianity emphasize creeds and intellectual belief over rituals and emotional engagement. Language is essential for expressing religious concepts, but it may be less so for engaging in rituals, where chants or wordless songs would often suffice. For example the *n/um* songs sung by the !Kung people of the Kalahari at their principal ritual "have titles but few if any words," the anthropologist Lorna Marshall reports.[90] One of their best songs, meaning that it could cure any sickness according to the !Kung, is called the =*Kowa Ts'i N!a*, which means Giraffe Song Great. But the lyrics are short on specific meaning, being mostly a string of vowels and nonsense syllables. (The odd punctuation marks represent various kinds of clicks in the !Kung language.)

It seems possible, therefore, that there could have been a proto-religion that developed before language, or at least before language had assumed its present degree of articulacy. This proto-religion, even though based on dance, music, and wordless chants, could have been effective enough at securing group cohesion and coordination and therefore, to the extent it promoted the group's survival, would have been favored by group selection.

The evolution of language is a rich and complex subject which linguists have largely avoided and on which other experts have reached little agreement. But it seems more than likely that the context in which language evolved was affected by dance, music and religion, the other systems of communication that were emerging in our distant ancestors. These four kinds of social communicative behavior may in some way have coevolved.

The details of this complex four-way interaction are entirely unknown, though they may one day come to light as the genes underlying the relevant neural circuits are identified. The evolutionary processes that brought each faculty to birth would have lasted over many generations and probably overlapped extensively.

Dance, being mostly just rhythmic movement, seems the most ancient. Music too would seem to reach far back in the human lineage, given that its rudiments can be seen in the singing of other primates. Because dance and music are inseparable in primitive cultures, it seems likely they coevolved, soon being joined by the first forms of religious behavior.

A new version of a gene may take many generations to sweep through a population, though fewer generations are needed if the population is small or the selective advantage very great. Complex behaviors like music perception presumably depend on a large number of genes to set up the appropriate neural circuitry, so several hundreds or thousands of years may be required to put such faculties in place. The evolution of behaviors like dance, music and religion would have taken many generations, with considerable opportunity for improvements in one form of communication to spur greater sophistication in the others.

So where does language fit in? Many observers from Darwin onward have noted the similarities between music and language. Both require the generation and perception of sound. Both have the essential quality of recursiveness, that of being able to embed one phrase within another. Both are vehicles of communication, even though music communicates principally at the emotional level. Darwin suggested that music was in some way a precursor of language. "We must suppose that the rhythms and cadences of oratory are derived from previously developed musical powers," he wrote. "We can thus understand how it is that music, dancing, song, and poetry are such very ancient arts. We may go even further than this and . . . believe that musical sounds afforded one of the bases for the development of language."[91]

In support of Darwin's idea, there is wide variation in people's musical abilities, but everyone speaks with much the same degree of competence. From the geneticist's perspective, this is a sign that language is under tight selection, meaning that any genes that degrade or disrupt it are quickly eliminated from the population. Music, in contrast, being evolution's first attempt at a human auditory communications system and now no longer essential for that purpose, is free of exacting constraints on its perception and production and so can absorb considerable genetic variation.[92]

Also favoring the view that music is more ancient than language is the fact that it speaks more strongly to the emotions than to the mind's purely cognitive faculties.

If language provides a powerful enhancement of ritual but is not in fact essential to it, as argued above, then it was perhaps a latecomer to the emerging complex of behaviors that underlie religion. This raises the interesting possibility that language in fact emerged in the context of ritual. Language is so powerful that if it had evolved early, it would surely have dominated religious behavior. The fact that it seems to have been almost an optional ingredient in the mix suggests it was a late arrival. So a tentative sequence of events would be 1) dance, 2) music, 3) proto-religion based on ritual, 4) language, 5) religion based on shared beliefs about the supernatural. In such a staging there would doubtless have been copious overlaps between the evolutionary initiation and completion of each faculty.

The archaeological record at present holds little evidence to help set dates on the emergence of music, language and religion, all of which must have been in place before the modern human exodus from the African homeland 50,000 years ago. The oldest known musical instruments are a pair of flutes, made from the wing bones of a swan. Found in Geissenkloesterle in Germany, they are some 36,000 years old. This is a minimum age for instrumental music, which is presumably far older. Instruments like drums and rattles are made of perishable materials that leave no trace in the archaeological record. Authorities generally agree that the oldest musical instrument of all is the human voice, and it seems likely that song predated language.

There is one significant clue to the date of language, and that is the exodus of modern humans from Africa. Their behavior, as judged by their appearance in Europe fairly shortly afterward, is far more sophisticated than that of the anatomically modern humans who started to appear in the archaeological record some 200,000 years ago. It looks as though some neural development has brought about a quantum leap in their cognitive powers. Since few faculties could be of greater value to a social species than language, it seems possible that language, although it must have been generations in development, did not attain its modern form until 50,000 years ago, and that this development was what allowed behaviorally modern humans to break out of Africa, escaping the encircling Neanderthals who had long penned them into their ancestral homeland.[93] If this scenario is correct, then language would have been perfected as the last in a series of communicative behaviors.

The final form of communication that is part of religious behavior is one designed for dialogue not between people, but between people and gods. This special channel is the trance.

## Visiting with the Gods

At the culmination of their ritual dances, primitive peoples would fall into trance states in which they communicated with their gods. The trances didn't affect everyone, just a few of the dancers. But their experiences allowed others to witness a supernatural power inhabiting the body of the affected dancer.

The evidence for these practices comes from observations of hunter gatherer religions, as well as from remnants of the behavior visible in today's cultures, from the spirit possessions of voodoo rituals to the crowd frenzy at rock concerts.

Trances are hard for people today to understand because like other aspects of ancient religion they were mostly suppressed long ago. With the advent of settled societies, priests appointed themselves official intermediaries with the supernatural world and had no wish to see people communicate directly with their gods.

Trances seem to have been a central feature of the ancient religion. In a survey of almost 500 small-scale societies the anthropologist Erika Bourguignon found that 90 percent had rites in which regular trance states occurred, data for the other 10 percent being insufficient to know whether or not this was the case.[94] Trance is a state resembling hypnosis, in which a person has limited sensory awareness, and no memory afterward of what happened. The symptoms may also include trembling, convulsions, foaming at the mouth, paralysis, rasping breathing and a fixed stare. "Trance always manifests itself in one way or another as a transcendence of one's normal self, as a liberation resulting from the intensification of a mental or physical disposition, in short, as an exaltation—sometimes a self-mutilating one—of the self," writes the ethnomusicologist Gilbert Rouget.[95]

It was through these trances, perhaps, that the gods were first discovered. People would have surmised the existence of a supernatural world through dreams, in which they saw relatives and acquaintances who were dead. But dreams are personal and cannot be directly shared. Through the trances induced by prolonged dancing, early people came to believe that they had acquired a means of entering the supernatural realm at will. The trances proved that the supernatural world existed. It would have been a small step from there to reconstructing the nature of the gods who might inhabit this strange, parallel world of primitive peoples' imaginings.

Physiologists do not understand how the trance state is brought about, but music, especially drumming, and strenuous dancing are conducive. Drumming can affect the body directly with its vibrations, as well as through the ear's perception of sound. "If one nears one of the extremely large drums the Yoruba beat at their secret *oro* ceremonies," writes Rouget, "one will hear the sounds through one's abdomen—which vibrates in sympathy—as much as through one's ears."

Despite the drum's reputation as an instrument of frenzy, Rouget concludes that "there is no valid theory to justify the idea that the triggering of trance can be attributed to the neurophysiological effects of drum sounds."[96] A different view is held by Mickey Hart, a percussionist for the Grateful Dead, who has explored shamans' use of drums to enter the trance state. "For myself," he writes, "I know that it's possible to ride the rhythms of a drum until you fall into a state of receptivity that can be construed as the beginnings of trance. When I'm drumming, I like to get as close to this state as I can, yet I also know that I can't let myself go completely because if I do, my drumming will deteriorate and I will quickly lose the state. There have been many times when I've felt as if the drum has carried me to an open door into another world."[97]

A common belief in societies that practice trance is that the person who falls into a trance is either possessed by a supernatural entity, or is traveling out of his body to meet with such agents. Different cultures have many variations on this central belief. Shamans, trance specialists first recognized among the Tungus and other peoples of Siberia, will take an out-of-body journey to meet the spirits of the underworld. Among the Azande, a people of north central Africa, witch doctors enter trance for purposes of divination. Here is a description of a witch doctors' dance by E. E. Evans-Pritchard, one of the most careful of anthropological observers:

> Sometimes at these meetings the performers dance them-selves into a state of fury and gash their tongues and chest with knives. . . . I have seen men in a state of wild excitement, drunk with the intoxicating orchestral music of drums and gong, bells and rattles, throw back their heads and gash their chests with knives, till blood poured in streams down their bodies. Others cut their tongues and blood mixed with saliva foamed at the cor-ners of their lips and trickled down their chins where it was car-ried away in a flow of sweat. When they have cut their tongues they dance with them hanging out of their mouths to show their art. They put on ferocious airs, enlarge the whites of their eyes, and open their mouths into grimaces as though contortions, due to great physical tension and exhaustion, were not grue-some enough. The dance of Zande witch-doctors is . . . weird and intoxicating.[98]

The trance state may sometimes be faked but for the most part it seems a real phenomenon, even if no precise scientific description is available as to how it is induced, maintained or recovered from. Why did trances play so central a role in the ancient religion? A plausible explana-tion has been developed by McNeill. He suggests that early peoples' beliefs about the supernatural were drawn principally from dreams. But dreams are an unreliable channel of communication with the other world and are not adaptable to public ritual. Trances, on the other hand, can reliably be induced by strenuous communal dances. There is no need for every-one to enter trance; just a few susceptible individuals in trance can serve as a doorway for everyone to peer into the supernatural.

The trance state, with its strange tremblings and altered breath-ing, naturally suggested that the person was possessed by a good or evil spirit, or that their spirit had gone wandering in the supernatural realm. This interpretation made trances a compelling public confirmation of a supernatural world, existing in parallel with the real one. "Important new meanings were attached to the extreme trance state that dancing can induce. This, indeed, became one of the important growth points for the enormously influential complex of rituals and beliefs that we call religion," McNeill writes.[99] Trance dancing became the most reliable way of entering into communication with the spirit world. Believing they had opened a channel between the realms of the natural and supernatural, early people devised an elaborate array of rites and ceremonies for manipulating the gods of the supernatural world into bringing about desired ends in the real world.

Dancing for hours on end was an arduous way to gain access to the supernatural. Early peoples discovered a variety of other ways to alter brain chemistry and lightly distort the sensory gates of the conscious mind. In appropriate contexts, these transcendental experiences could be interpreted as communications with the supernatural. Some species of plant contain mind-altering drugs which were taken by shamans to help their travels into the spirit world. The Aztecs used the hallucinogen found in the peyote cactus, and made ritual use of the family of mushrooms that generate psilocybin. Soma, the sacred brew mentioned in the Rig Vedas of ancient India, may have been the psychoactive mushroom known as fly agaric. The Eleusinian mysteries, held at Athens for some 2,000 years starting in 1700 B.C., involved drinking potions that may have contained hallucinogens of some sort.

The oracle at Delphi, on the other hand, was based on the inhalations by the prophetess of a subterranean gas, recently identified as probably ethylene. The Pythia, as she was known, fell into a gas-induced trance and her mind was possessed by the god Apollo. Her utterances, generally not very comprehensible, were interpreted by priests, and carried considerable political influence in the ancient Greek world.[100]

The Pythia may have been the first to experiment with anesthetic gases but she was not the last. "Nitrous oxide and ether, especially nitrous oxide, when sufficiently diluted with air, stimulate the mystical consciousness in an extraordinary degree," wrote the psychologist William James. "Depth beyond depth of truth seems revealed to the inhaler. This truth fades out, however, or escapes, at the moment of coming to; and if any words remain over in which it seemed to clothe itself, they prove to be the veriest nonsense. Nevertheless, the sense of a profound meaning having been there persists; and I know more than one person who is persuaded that in the nitrous oxide trance we have a genuine metaphysical revelation." That person may have been himself; James tried nitrous oxide and was persuaded that there exist other forms of consciousness that may provide different and valuable insights.

Naturally occurring mystical religious experiences often include such feelings as stepping outside oneself, transcending space and time, a sense of knowing ultimate truths, a sensation of sacredness and a deeply felt positive mood. In an experiment of 1962, later known as the Good Friday experiment, Walter Pahnke gave psilocybin, a hallucinogenic drug, to 10 Protestant divinity students, and a placebo to 10 others, with neither himself nor his subjects knowing who had received which. He sat all 20 in the basement chapel beneath Boston University's Marsh Chapel while they listened to the Good Friday church service being held above them. His goal was to see if psychedelic drugs could facilitate a mystical experience in religiously inclined volunteers who took the drug in a religious setting.

Pahnke scored his subjects on nine elements of mystical religious experience, including the 5 listed above. He found the subjects who received psilocybin scored significantly higher than those who didn't. In a follow-up 25 years later, most of the subjects who could be reached reported largely positive memories of the experience.[101]

Are natural mystical experiences and those induced by drugs the same? "The two experiences appear to be very similar or identical," conclude the neuropharmacologists David Nichols and Benjamin Chemel. They suggest that the normal flow of sensory information to the brain's outer cortex, the seat of consciousness, is somehow reduced or cut off. But instead of shutting down, as a computer might, the cortex "will fill in or extrapolate missing information, creating sensory constructs where none exist," they write. Alternatively, as the usual torrent of sensory information from the outside world is shut down, the cortex may become unusually sensitive to interior information of a more introspective kind.[102]

Consciousness itself is so little understood that it is impossible to interpret the abnormal state of it from which subjects report mystical experiences. People using hallucinogens sometimes report frightening sensations, not the mystical experiences felt by Pahnke's subjects. This suggests that subjects are to some extent cued by their surroundings as to how to interpret the experience. Is there some module in the brain that is attuned to communication with the supernatural and which comes to the fore in mystical experiences, whether natural or drug-induced? What seems more likely is that all the methods of achieving the trance state distort the usual data processing system of the conscious brain, and that these distortions are experienced as unusual, sometimes deeply affecting, states of mind. When suitably primed, the subjects, or those who observe them, view their experiences as communications with the supernatural realm, and interpret them in the context of their particular religious tradition.

It's easy to see how a society might manipulate its rites and ceremonies, even at an entirely unconscious level, so as to secure desired social goals, such as observing agreed moral standards, punishing cheaters, and preparing people to sacrifice their lives in the community's defense. If everyone believed that a supernatural agency would punish theft, for example, high standards of honesty would prevail. Religion emerged as an effective means for an egalitarian community to govern itself. The rituals and ceremonies established agreed rules of desirable behavior, and the supernatural agencies secured compliance with them. It was a remarkable solution to the problem of getting highly intelligent primates to put an abstract goal—the good of society—ahead of the self-interest they could all now calculate so finely.

In a state of constant warfare, such as prevailed through much of the hunter gatherer era, societies that used religion to best advantage would have prevailed over others. Probably through the mechanism of group selection, the essentials of religious behavior became engraved in the human genetic repertoire. These would have included a propensity to commit to the religious practices of one's society, starting around the age of puberty; a liking for group rituals and the sense of community they generated; and a tendency to believe in punitive supernatural agents.

The genes that shape religious behavior provide merely an inclination to such behaviors. Each society specifies its own religious culture, shaping its religious tradition so as to fit its political and ecological circumstances. It is now time to trace the steps by which the earliest forms of religion, brought into being by the evolutionary forces described above, were transformed over the last 50,000 years into the very different religions that are familiar today.

# 5

---

# ANCESTRAL RELIGION

*Let us realize that in primitive conditions tradition is of
supreme value for the community and nothing matters as much
as the conformity and conservatism of its members. Order and
civilization can be maintained only by strict adhesion to the
lore and knowledge received from previous generations. Any
laxity in this weakens the cohesion of the group and imperils its
cultural outfit to the point of threatening its very existence.*

BRONISLAW MALINOWSKI[103]

Cathedrals, sacred music, the aroma of incense, theological trea-
tises, matins and compline—the religions of today are enriched
with the cultural accretions of many centuries. None of these
adornments seems a plausible advantage in the struggle for survival. But
run the clock back to the earliest forms of religion from which today's are
derived, and the survival value of religion becomes much clearer.

The earliest religion seems to have taken the form of sustained communal dancing that invoked supernatural powers and promoted emotional bonding among members of the group.

All known human societies have some form of religion and so too,
almost certainly, did the ancestral population of modern humans which

evolved in northeast Africa and was confined in its ancestral homeland there until some 50,000 years ago.

It would be of the greatest interest to know the religious practices followed by these ancestral people. But the ancestral human population of 50,000 years ago has left no direct trace of its existence, and there is no good archaeological evidence of whatever religion may have been practiced by its forebears. Only later, in the Upper Paleolithic age that began in Europe around 45,000 years ago, does the first copious evidence appear of art and of burials, both of which imply ritual process.

The nearest one can get to the religious practices of the people who lived 50,000 years ago is through studying the rites of living hunter gatherer peoples, or at least those whose way of life was recorded before the encroachment of more powerful cultures. The hunting and gathering way of life has remained essentially unchanged for 50,000 years and, assuming that religions are shaped to the societies they serve, their religion may have retained the same general form.

Of course culture can change quite significantly between generations—witness the change in the English language since Chaucer's day—and some 2,000 generations separate people today from the ancestral population. Still, there are two reasons why some hunter gatherer religions may still reflect the ancient forms.

One is that many preliterate or primitive peoples place great importance on carrying out rites exactly as their forebears did. The justification of their rituals is that this is how they have always been performed. So religious practice is handed on with as much fidelity as possible. Among the Klamath and Modoc Indians of the northwest coast of America, certain myths may be recited only in the presence of three people who know the story and can check the rendition for accuracy, and the myths may not be told by children lest they garble them. These rules are reported to keep the myths intact over many generations.[104]

A second reason is that new genetic evidence has established surprisingly direct lines of descent between the ancestral population and certain long-isolated groups, such as Australian Aborigines. Anthropologists long assumed that several waves of migration had reached Australia at various times since its original founding. But a new genetic analysis has shown that, until modern times, no one but the original founders reached the continent. Having traveled from Africa to the Arabian peninsula and along the coastlines of southeast Asia, they were established in Australia by 45,000 years ago, and presumably managed to fight off any later visitors.

This finding, if confirmed, means that Australian aboriginal culture is home grown, without significant outside influences. So aboriginal religious practices probably reflect a very ancient tradition, one that derives from the ancestral population without intervening influences.

Another long-isolated people with a possible claim to a very ancient religious tradition are the Andaman Islanders studied by Radcliffe-Brown. The Andaman Islands lie in the Bay of Bengal, some 120 miles off the coast of Burma. Their inhabitants have dark skins, suggesting that they are descendants of the original migration from Africa to Australia. Their genetics, too, fit with the idea of an ancient origin. Since at least A.D. 871, the Andaman Islands have had a fearsome reputation among sailors. The Islanders routinely killed the survivors of the many ships that shipwrecked on their islands, and burned the victims' bodies so that their spirits would not return to haunt them. The practice suggests they did not particularly welcome outside influences on their culture.

A third very ancient and somewhat isolated people are the !Kung San bushmen of the Kalahari desert in southern Africa. The ancestral human population had split into three branches before the exodus from its homeland. These three branches, identified by the genetic element known as mitochondrial DNA, are designated L1, L2 and L3. Everyone in the group that left Africa is descended from daughters of the L3 lineage. The !Kung San belong to L1, the most ancient branch point of the mitochondrial tree of descent, and as hunter gatherers they may have been quite isolated ever since.

Contributing to that isolation was a remarkable technology that long helped them resist encroachment from other peoples. The San discovered how to poison their arrows with toxin from the pupae of chrysomelid beetles. A single arrow carried enough poison to kill a large antelope within 6 to 24 hours. Their lightweight hunting bows were also effective in warfare. They fought regularly with their pastoralist Bantu neighbors, killing their cows and fending off counterattacks with their poisoned arrows. The southern San held off the better armed and mounted Boers for 30 years until overwhelmed by the Boers' greater numbers.[105]

The religious practices of these three ancient people—Australian Aborigines, the Andaman Islanders and the !Kung San—are probably as close as one can come to reconstructing the religion of the ancestral human population. And though the religions of these three peoples may have absorbed foreign cultural influences, the features they all share can reasonably be assumed to stem from a common source: the religion practiced before modern humans dispersed from Africa 50,000 years ago.

From the accounts written by anthropologists, it is clear that the religions of these three hunter gathering peoples differ greatly from religions familiar in Western countries. Primitive religions have no priests or ecclesiastical hierarchy. They are practiced by the community as a whole, with no distinctions of rank. No separate organization such as a church is recognized—the entire community is the church.

A second special feature of these three hunter gatherer religions is that their rituals, as noted in the previous chapter, are characterized by rhythmic physical activity, with singing and dancing that may go on for 8 hours or longer. These dance marathons, with everyone moving in time together, evoke intense emotion and bind together all who are present with a sense of community and shared exaltation. The focus of their rituals is communal activity and needs, not individual psychic satisfaction.

Third, the sacred narratives of primitive religions convey moral or practical lessons of relevance to the community's survival, just as do those of Western religions. But the sacred narratives are integrated with the rituals and ceremonies and are not the focus of religious practice.

Fourth, primitive religions are little concerned with matters of theology. They focus on practical issues such as initiation rites and on problems of survival that include healing, hunting, and control of the weather. Another practical goal, of the greatest importance for maintaining the group's social cohesion, is that of settling feuds between people in dispute and wiping the slate clean of enmity.

The distinctive aspects of primitive religion are more easily appreciated by considering the specific practices of the !Kung San, the Andaman Islanders and Australian Aborigines.


## The Ritual Healing Dance of the !Kung San

The !Kung ritual healing dance, as practiced by the Nyae Nyae !Kung who live in the Namibian part of the Kalahari desert, has several features typical of these three religions. The dance is the !Kung's principal religious rite. It bears very little overt resemblance to a routine service in a church or synagogue, where a sedate audience gathers at a fixed time every week to watch a priest chant the words of a sacred text. In the !Kung dance, everyone participates. Anthropologists have named the rite a healing dance because it incorporates some of the concepts and gestures used by healers when treating individuals. But in the ritual healing dance, few people are actually healed.

The dance has a larger purpose, that of healing the community. The !Kung do not call it a healing dance but a *n/um* dance, *n/um* being a supernatural force. (The /, like !, indicates one of the many click sounds in their language; others used below are // and =.) A dance may be held at moments of crisis or to ease tensions with a neighboring group. Or the dance can also occur as a celebration, such as after a successful hunt, when it serves to soften the tensions that may arise after the distribution of meat. Following is an account based on the description by the anthropologist Lorna Marshall, who observed 39 such dances between 1952 and 1953.[106]

The *n/um* dance is an intricate interplay of physical movement, music and song. It is physically and emotionally demanding, and so intense that many of the men go into a deep trancelike state, achieved naturally and entirely without drugs. Many of the healers do attain trance and perform their rituals in that state, but trance is not necessary for healing. Any of the men can become healers, though some are better than others.

The dance may start around 9 P.M., after the evening meal. The first sign that one is about to happen occurs when a woman carries a burning branch to light a small fire in the middle of the dancing space. Soon other women join her. They sit close around the fire, squeezed together with shoulders and knees touching. There is no special clothing for the dance. The women wear their usual skin cloaks. They start to sing in high register, often quite loudly.

Then the men turn up and start to dance in a circle around the women. Their feet soon tread out a large circular groove in the sandy desert soil. The women in their singing circle begin to clap in coordination with the stamping feet of the men. The claps are of a special kind, with the fingers held back so that the rims of the palm catch a small pocket of air, making a high-pitched popping sound.

The women clap in two rhythms simultaneously. The basic line, called !gaba, matches the rhythm of the men's stamping feet and that of the song. Most of the women do the !gaba line but some clap the =ku line, an off-beat improvisation that weaves in between the !gaba line. The women clap with great skill and precision, aided by the fact that they are touching one another and can feel as well as hear each other's clapping.

The men contribute to the percussion, both with the stamping of their feet and with strings of soft-sounding rattles, called /khonisi, which are wound around their legs. The rattles are made of moth cocoons from which the pupa has been extracted and replaced with small stones or fragments of ostrich egg shell. Some 80 or 90 of the cocoons are threaded together on a string a yard long, and the string is wound round a man's leg. Because the cocoons are made of silk, the sound of the /khonisi is not harsh but more like a loud swish, which adds a third layer of texture to the percussive sound of the dancing feet and clapping hands.

The heart of the performance is the women's chorus, much of it sung in yodeling style. The women sing what are called *n/um* songs. *N/um* is a powerful supernatural essence, possessed by people, animals and things, which may be either harmful or protective. The healers use their own *n/um* to heal people. The *n/um* songs are sung polyphonically, with some women singing the basic melody, and others shortening or prolonging the rhythmic intervals. !Kung songs are usually sung softly, but in the healing dance the *n/um* songs are belted out, the men's voices interweaving with the women's. The songs are accompanied with instruments such as stringed hunting bows and a four-stringed instrument known as a *//gwashi*.

The dance is broken into periods of 10 to 15 minutes, between which there are brief pauses for rest during which people walk around and chat. After the dance begins, the men prance in a circle around the women for two or three dance periods. The men are naked, apart from their usual breechclout, but the dance is without overt sexual overtones. Then at some point the leader of the line of male dancers slowly moves out of the rutted path around the women and leads his line right through the circle of seated women, past the fire, and out on the other side.

With the women's line penetrated, the men dance a figure of eight, going clockwise around one half circle of women, counterclockwise around the other. Up to 90 people may be engaged in the performance. A cascade of sights and sounds now assails the senses. The interweaving lines of dancing bodies shimmer in the firelight against the background of the starlit desert sky. The air is thick with the clapping of the women, the stamping of the men, the rhythmic swish of the men's rattles and, rising above the rich percussive beat, the women's powerful singing of the ancient *n/um* songs with descant voices soaring above the chorus.

After an hour or two of dancing, the men begin to go into trance. A person going into trance will look preoccupied, then begin to stare fixedly and stagger slightly. At this point, whether in trance or not, the men who are healers will start the healing ritual. They lean over one of the seated women, and briefly flutter their hands on her back and chest while uttering special cries.

The intensity of the dance increases and some of the healers enter a deeper level of trance. A man may start to breathe heavily, staring ahead without seeing while his whole body shudders. "He may throw back his head, yelling '//*Gauwa* is killing me,'" Marshall writes, referring to the great god who lives in the !Kung's western sky. "He may stagger around and lurch into the fire, trample on the women, fall headlong into their circle, somersault over them, or crash full-length onto the ground and lie there rigid as a stick. The men say that the strength of their *n/um* overwhelms them. They lose their senses. Things appear to be smaller than normal and to fly around. The fire appears to be over their heads."

Others will look after the men in trance, pulling them to their feet or dragging them out of the fire if they fall into it. The healers feel their power is at its height. Several rush out into the darkness, hurling invective at //*Gauwa* and the surrounding //*gauwasi*, the spirits of the dead. It is //*Gauwa* and the spirits who afflict people with serious sickness. The !Kung are not perplexed by theodicy, the problem of justifying a good and omnipotent deity who permits evil; //*Gauwa* is omnipotent, the !Kung say, and therefore sickness, and everything else, must come from him. One day he will protect a man, on another let him step on a puff adder or be savaged by a leopard.

After these sorties into the darkness, the healers' trance may deepen. They are convulsed, sit down, shudder, stream with sweat or froth at the mouth. One may rush into the fire, heaping embers on himself until dragged out by the women. Reaching the deepest stage of the trance, men fall unconscious, their limbs rigid and clammy, their eyeballs rolled back to the whites. In this state, which the !Kung call half-death, a man's spirit temporarily leaves the body. He may encounter //*Gauwa*. The greatest healers may even meet =*Gao N!a*, //*Gauwa*'s counterpart who lives in the eastern sky.

A healer in half-death is in grave peril since his wandering spirit may be seized by the //*gauwasi*. Other healers flutter their hands over him, exhorting his spirit to return. They rip off his rattles and shake them to show the wandering spirit where its body is. After a period, often up to 20 minutes or so, those in half-death are revived.

Meanwhile the dance and the singing continue. The intensity of the performance waxes and wanes throughout the night but reaches a climax toward sunrise. As dawn breaks, the women break into a *n/um* song known as the Sun song. The dance may continue for several hours into the day, but the dawn is its emotional crest.

The benefit of the healing dance is the social cohesion it generates. "People bind together subjectively against external forces of evil, and they bind together on an intimate social level," Marshall writes. "The dance draws everybody together. . . . Whatever their relationship, whatever the state of their feelings, whether they like or dislike each other, whether they are on good terms or bad terms with each other, they become a unit, singing, clapping, moving together in an extraordinary unison of stamping feet and clapping hands, swept along by the music. No words divide them; they act in concert for their spiritual and physical good and do something together that enlivens them and gives them pleasure."

A very similar conclusion was reached by another anthropologist, Megan Biesele, who studied a nearby group of !Kung at Dobe, in Botswana, some 15 years later. "The trance dance," she wrote, "is thus not only an art form in which all can participate, but a concerted effort of the entire community to banish misfortune. The fact that all members of a group participate personally in this effort accounts for much of its psychic and emotional efficacy. The dance is perhaps the central unifying force in Bushman life, binding people together in very deep ways which we do not fully understand."[107]

This is religion raw, before it was tamed by the busy life and cooler tastes of cities.

!Kung religion has many other facets—people pray, receive treatment from healers, and explain windfalls, disasters and other events beyond their control in terms of supernatural intervention. These behaviors doubtless provide substantial psychological benefits, such as building confidence in the face of danger, but none seems likely to provide a significant evolutionary advantage, meaning one that enables a person to raise more surviving progeny. The healing dance, on the other hand, clearly enhances the viability of the !Kung group. It raises the quality of the society by drawing people together and dissolving quarrels. It fosters group cohesion against external threats, whether supernatural ones like the //gauwasi or real foes such as other human groups. People belonging to such a society are more likely to survive and reproduce than those in less cohesive groups, who may be vanquished by their enemies or dissolve in discord. In the population as a whole, genes that promote religious behavior are likely to become more common in each generation as the less cohesive societies perish and the more united ones thrive.

## The Dance of the Andaman Islanders

The !Kung provide one example of religious behavior that benefits the community. The Andaman Islanders furnish another. They bear an ancient signature in their mitochondrial DNA that suggests they are one of the populations derived from the original modern human migration from Africa to Australia.[108] These relict populations are called Negritos because they have dark skin and are small, generally less than 5 feet in stature. They have survived only in remote places, such as the forests of Malaya and the Philippines, where they could avoid being overwhelmed by later populations practicing agriculture.

The Andaman Islands were another such Negrito refuge. During the last ice age, when sea level was more than 200 feet lower than today, the islands were probably only 40 miles from the coast of Burma and reachable by boat by the first modern humans. When sea level rose after the end of the last ice age 10,000 years ago, the islands' distance from the mainland tripled. Adding to their inaccessibility was the inhabitants' reputation for discouraging visitors. Marco Polo wrote that the islands' inhabitants "are idolaters, and are a most brutish and savage race, having heads, eyes, and teeth resembling those of the canine species. Their dispositions are cruel, and every person, not being of their own nation, whom they can lay their hands upon, they kill and eat."

In fact the Islanders looked no more canine than anyone else and their reputation for cannibalism was probably undeserved. But they did kill anyone who landed on their shores. And they did better than they knew to burn the bodies of those they killed. When the Andamans were eventually settled by the British rulers of India, the tribes of the main island quickly died of imported diseases like measles and syphilis. But before they perished, their way of life was studied by the anthropologist Alfred Radcliffe-Brown, who visited the islands between 1906 and 1908.

As with the !Kung San, the central element in the Andaman Islanders' religion was the dance, always accompanied by sacred songs. The dances would start at night and last 5 or 6 hours or longer. The women clapped and sang the chorus while the men danced to the beat of a sounding board. The Andaman dances are intense emotional experiences. The style of the dance, with the legs bent and the body bent at the hips, is highly energetic, with almost all the body's muscles under tension. The dancer's physical and mental activities are all directed toward one end, and he gains energy as he surrenders to the rhythm. "This effect of the rhythm," Radcliffe-Brown writes, "is reinforced by the excitement produced by the rapid movements of the dancers, and the loud sounds of the song and clapping and sounding-board, and intensified, as all collective states of emotion are intensified, by reason of being collective; with the end result that the Andaman Islanders are able to continue their strenuous dancing through many hours of the night."[109]

The purpose of the dance is to bind participants together. "The dance produces a condition in which the unity, harmony and concord of the community are at a maximum, and in which they are intensely felt by every member. It is to produce this condition, I would maintain, that is the primary social function of the dance," Radcliffe-Brown says. "The well-being, or indeed the existence, of the society depends on the unity and harmony that obtain in it, and the dance, by making that unity intensely felt, is a means of maintaining it."

Before setting out for a fight, an Andaman village would hold a dance to increase everyone's sense of unity. The dance would also "intensify the collective anger against the hostile group" and "produce a state of excitement and elation which has an important influence on the fighting quality of the Andaman warrior."[110]

Andaman religion operated in several other ways to bolster the notion of community and the individual's awareness of his dependence on society. In initiation rites, youths were made to endure punishing deprivations of food and sleep before they could resume eating two prized items of the Andaman diet, turtle and wild pig. During these periods they were not allowed to join in the communal dances, a symbol of exclusion from social life.

The hunting of turtle and pig are activities seen as full of danger, but performance of the approved rites can protect the hunter. The taboos involved in both initiation rites and hunting serve to impress the moral force of society on the individual. It is only by following social rules that a person may eat and hunt safely.

Andaman religion also protected society against the numerous *Lau*, the spirits of the forest, and the *Jurua*, the spirits of the sea, both of which are in effect ghosts of the Andaman dead. "The Andaman Islander, through the ceremonies and customs of his people, is made to feel that he is in a world of unseen dangers,—dangers from the foods he eats, from the sea, the weather, the forest and its animals, but above all from the spirits of the dead,—which can only be avoided by the help of the society and by conforming with social custom," Radcliffe-Brown writes. "So the belief in the spirit world serves directly to increase the cohesion of the society through its action on the mind of the individual."[111]

The practices of the Andaman Islanders show how central a part religion played in their daily lives and how intimately in their belief the real world and the supernatural world were entwined. But for preoccupation with religion, few societies can rival those of Australia before colonization.

# Religious Practices of the Australian Aborigines

The third people whose religion sheds light on that of the ancestral population are Australian Aborigines. New genetic evidence shows that, contrary to previous belief, the Aborigines appear to have been truly isolated for 45,000 years ever since reaching Sahul, the now foundered continent that then included Australia, New Guinea and Tasmania. Australian religious practices seem therefore likely to have been derived in a direct line of descent from that of the ancestral human population, without outside influences.

Anthropologists had long believed that several later groups of invaders also arrived in Australia, bringing other cultural influences. One reason was that the early skulls unearthed in the continent are of two different shapes. Another was the presence of the dingo, a semidomesticated dog; dogs were domesticated from wolves only 15,000 years ago, and dogs almost always travel with their masters. But a genetic survey of Australian Aborigines and Papuan speakers in Papua New Guinea (both part of Sahul during the last ice age) shows that all are descended from a single founding stock. Although people speaking Austronesian languages settled around the coast of Papua New Guinea in recent times, it seems that the Aborigines managed to keep Australia to themselves until the arrival of Europeans.[112] Any subsequent invaders were either killed or left no presently visible contribution to the population's genetics. The differently shaped skulls must have arisen from adaptations within the aboriginal population to different local conditions. How the dingo arrived, apparently without masters, or with too few to have left any genetic trace, remains a puzzle.

Aboriginal religion is complex and it is not clear how much of it was properly recorded before native societies were changed and undermined by colonization. Nor is it easy to generalize because religious practice varied widely from one tribe to another, although similar themes are found throughout most of Australia. In Arnhem Land, in northern Australia, mortuary ceremonies are of major importance, whereas in central Australia the emphasis is on fertility rites and rites of initiation.

A salient feature of aboriginal religious practice, which also distinguishes the !Kung San and Andaman Islander religions, is the emphasis on song and dance, together with the emotional intensity of the proceedings, and their extraordinary duration.

In Protestant churches Sunday service may last an hour, and there is grumbling if the minister's sermon goes on too long. But many aboriginal ceremonies lasted for days, with hours of singing through the night. An initiation ceremony performed by the Arunta tribe of central Australia in 1896 to 1897 "commenced in the middle of September, and continued till the middle of the succeeding January, during which time there was a constant succession of ceremonies, not a day passing without one, while there were sometimes as many as five or six within the twenty-four hours. They were held at various hours, always one or more during the daylight, and not infrequently one or two during the night, a favorite time being just before sunrise," say Baldwin Spencer and F. J. Gillen, two anthropologists who observed the proceedings.[113]

The initiation rights were searingly intense experiences that would begin when a boy was kidnapped from his home and subjected to a series of deprivations and taboos. During mostly nighttime performances he would see the sacred narrative acted out and be taught the secrets of the male cult. Among the Arunta, a boy was put through three of these ceremonies before being considered an adult member of society. The first, called *Lartna,* lasted 10 days and nights, culminating in the boy's circumcision with a flint knife on the tenth night. Some six weeks later, when his wound had healed, he underwent a second rite, called *Ariltha* or subincision, a severe operation to the penis. Many years later, perhaps at age 25 or so, groups of young men underwent the final rite, called *Engwura*, the four-month marathon mentioned above.

*Engwura* was a long series of rites involving the totem animals of the people in each of the tribe's various localities and culminating in an ordeal by fire in which the men lay for five minutes at a time over burning embers, protected only by a layer of leaves. People would assemble in one place from all regions of the tribe's territory, which occupied an area in central Australia stretching 300 miles north to south and 100 miles east to west. The effect of the ceremony, according to the Arunta, was to impart courage and wisdom and make its subjects "more kindly natured and less apt to quarrel."[114]

The *Engwura* involved all-night singing sessions, elaborate body-painting and costumes and performances of relevant parts of the *Alcheringa*, the Aborigines' principal sacred narrative. One night's program indicates the physical exertions involved, and the emotions elicited by the religious symbolism may have been equally intense: "During the evening close by the *Parra* [ceremonial mound] a dense group was formed with the older men standing in the centre, and the younger ones on the outside. In this way, as closely packed as possible, they sang together for some two hours, the group as a whole swaying backwards and forwards without ceasing. Then towards midnight they all sat down, and in this position, still closely packed together, they continued singing until between one and two o'clock, when the old men decorated the heads of the younger men with twigs and leaves of an Eremophila shrub."[115]

The ordeal by fire, repeated several times over, marks the fourth phase of the *Engwura* ceremony. The young men, considered now to be fully initiated, paint themselves with ochre for a nighttime ceremony. As they are sitting by the fire, Spencer and Gillen report, "A number of young women, who have been waiting out of sight of the fire, come near. Each one is decorated with a double horse-shoe shaped band of white pipe-clay which extends across the front of each thigh and the base of the abdomen. A flexible stick is held behind the neck and one end grasped by each hand. Standing in a group the women sway slightly from side to side, quivering in a most remarkable fashion, as they do so, the muscles of the thighs and of the base of the abdomen. The object of the decoration and movement is evident, and at this period of the ceremonies a general interchange, and also a lending of women takes place, and visiting natives are provided with temporary wives, though on this occasion in the Arunta tribe the women allotted to any man must be one to whom he is *unawa*, that is, who is lawfully eligible to him as a wife. This woman's dance, which is of the most monotonous description possible, goes on night after night for perhaps two or three weeks, at the end of which time another dance is commenced."[116]

Spencer and Gillen may have found the women's dances "monotonous," but the young initiates, after their four months of deprivations and ordeals, possibly entertained a different opinion.

The *Engwura* and other ceremonies served to impress on participants the details of the aboriginal sacred narrative in which the creators brought the present world into being. The creators did good things and bad, and were punished for transgressions such as incest or witnessing sacred rites reserved for the other sex. As with religions elsewhere in the world, the sacred narrative served as a source of moral instruction and a justification of sanctions for breaking the tribe's moral code. "The religious system of the *dingari* is also a system of morality," writes the anthropologist Ronald Berndt, referring to the version of the sacred narrative held by the people of the northwestern desert.[117]

Besides encoding morality, aboriginal religion also provided for reconciliation between quarreling parties within a group. The Warramunga people of northern central Australia held a *Nathagura* or fire ceremony which was designed to bring all conflicts to an end. The ceremony lasted for 14 days. It began with a phase of practical jokes and insults, in which everyday customs and forms of respect were violated, without anyone taking offense.

After several days of further proceedings, which included a dramatic mock battle between the men's and women's groups, the ceremony culminated in a final rite lasting most of a day and night. All parties who had a serious unresolved dispute with each other were expected to engage in a symbolic duel with blazing firesticks, after which the matter was never to be referred to again. When darkness fell, the plaintiffs daubed themselves from head to toe with mud, then covered the mud with a thick layer of white pipe clay until they resembled "a weird, ghoul-like model of a human being." Adding to the effect, they tied on elaborate headdresses and covered their faces with down.

The aggrieved parties, twelve on this occasion, were then given ritual wands, inflammable poles made from a gum tree and called *wanmanmirri*, which they thrust into a fire and set ablaze. "The performance opened," Spencer and Gillen continue, "with one of the men charging full tilt, holding his *wanmanmirri* like a bayonet, and driving the blazing end into the midst of a group of natives in the centre of which stood a man with whom, a year before, he had had a serious quarrel. Warded off with clubs and spear-throwers, the torch glanced upwards. This was the signal for the commencement of a general melee. Every *wanmanmirri* was blazing brilliantly, the men were leaping and prancing about, yelling wildly all the time; the burning torches continually came crashing down upon the heads and bodies of the men, scattering lighted embers all around, until the air was full of falling sparks, and the weird, whitened bodies of the combatants were alight with burning twigs and leaves. The smoke, the blazing torches, the showers of sparks falling in all directions and the mass of dancing, yelling men with their bodies grotesquely bedaubed, formed altogether a genuinely wild and savage scene of which it is impossible to convey any adequate idea in words."

Several more rituals followed throughout the night, and the performance concluded just after sunrise, 18 hours after it began. The men wearily removed their headdresses and rubbed the down from their faces. The last act of the fire ceremony was over. Of the meaning of the various rituals, Spencer and Gillen could find little explanation. "All that the old man who had charge of the series could tell us, and all, apparently, that they knew was, that it had been handed down to them from the far past just as it used to be performed by their Alcheringa ancestors, and that its object was to finally settle up old quarrels, and to make the men friendly disposed towards one another."[118]

But the old man had surely given all the explanation that was needed: the purpose of the fire ceremony was to patch up divisive disputes in an emotionally decisive way and thus repair the social fabric; the precise form was arbitrary. The extraordinary physical effort and emotional intensity that the Warramunga invested in the ceremony is proof of the importance they attached to reconciliation and social cohesion. Religion was the means whereby they attained these goals.

The reports by Spencer and Gillen were a principal source on which Durkheim based his analysis of religion. Several aspects of Durkheim's thesis have been criticized, notably his argument that people divide the world into the sacred and the profane. Many primitive peoples, the Aborigines chief among them, seem to make no such distinction. Almost every aspect of their daily lives has religious significance or is subject to some religious constraint. The distinction between what is sacred and what is secular seems to be principally a European notion which springs most naturally from the Western separation of church and state. Durkheim cited the Aborigines' clan structure, as described by Spencer and Gillen, in support of his central argument that religion embodies the moral power of society, but later observers have taken issue with some of Spencer and Gillen's interpretations, undermining part of the empirical support for Durkheim's theory.

Nonetheless, Durkheim's central insight that religion unites people into a single community seems to have been correct, both for Aborigines and for other peoples. "As for the social implications of primitive religion," writes the sociologist Robert Bellah after a discussion of Aborigine beliefs, "Durkheim's analysis still seems to be largely acceptable. The ritual life does reinforce the solidarity of society and serves to induct the young into the norms of tribal behavior."[119]

From a biological perspective, aboriginal religion confers many obvious benefits on a group. It binds the men with terrifying but emotionally cohesive initiation rites. (Women have separate initiation rites, about which less is known.) It stipulates a moral code and sanctions in the form of the sacred narrative in which everyone is indoctrinated at initiation rites and other ceremonies. It provides a conciliation mechanism for erasing quarrels and enhancing the quality of society.

These benefits do not come without cost. Religious ceremonies seem to have occupied an extraordinary amount of everyone's time. The initiation ceremonies carried a risk of infection and death. And the sacred narrative imposed or supported two counterfactual beliefs with far-reaching consequences.

One was that natural causes were not accepted by the Aborigines as a cause of death, meaning that no one was considered to have died of old age. People died because of sorcery, and their relatives did not rest until the guilty party had been identified and if possible killed. This was a perpetual source of social strife.

Another costly belief, at least for individuals, concerned conception. Aboriginal religious theory held that a woman became pregnant after a spirit-child, extremely small but fully human, had entered her body, usually when she went near special localities. True, intercourse was required to open up the body for conception but could not be sufficient, in the Aborigines' view, because most acts of intercourse were without effect. Anthropologists have argued endlessly about whether the Aborigines were genuinely unaware of the father's role in conception, some contending that aboriginal religious views no more implied actual ignorance of paternity than did the doctrine of the virgin birth among Christians.

The issue is clouded because the Aborigines seem to have shifted their views after contact with Western explanations of conception. But the earliest accounts suggest there was no difference between their religious and their practical views, as might have been predicted given the overwhelming governance of their everyday life by religious belief. "Adult male attitudes on the subject of procreation allow only for spiritual explanations and actively oppose consideration of semen as a relevant factor," concludes Robert Tonkinson after exploring the views of Western Desert Aborigines.[120] According to a leading expert on aboriginal religion, the anthropologist W. E. H. Stanner, "The means, by which, in aboriginal understanding, a man fathers a child, is not by sexual intercourse, but by the act of dreaming about a spirit-child. His own spirit, during a dream 'finds' a child and directs it to his wife, who then conceives."[121]

The spirit-child theory of conception is certainly a beautiful belief, and one that demonstrates the complete unity in aboriginal religion of the dreamworld and the real world. It explains another otherwise puzzling feature of Aborigine life, the men's willingness to share their wives with others in a range of situations. In most other societies men go to extreme lengths to secure exclusive sexual access to their wives, imposing some-times draconian restrictions on women's freedom of association so as to ensure their paternity. However harsh and nowadays unacceptable these measures may seem, they make perfect sense from a biological point of view, given that a man who invests his resources in raising another man's child has in effect reduced his Darwinian fitness to zero.

The Aborigines divided their tribes into clans and obliged a man to choose a wife from a clan other than his own, regarding it as a crime tan-tamount to incest to have sexual relations with a woman of his own clan. But after a man had chosen a wife from the permissible clan, all the other women in that class remained eligible for sexual intercourse on certain occasions, even if married to someone else. "At times a man will lend his wife to a stranger as an act of courtesy, always provided that he belongs to the right class, that is, to the same as himself," Spencer and Gillen observe of the Arunta.[122] In a large number of tribes all of a woman's tribal broth-ers have access to her. When men from other tribes visit to prepare for a ceremony, often staying for a fortnight, their guests will make women available to them. Among the Urabunna tribe, party invitations were sent out with an RSVP that doubtless made recipients less likely to forget the date. When summoning distant groups to a ceremony, it was customary to dispatch both a man and a woman. After the man had delivered the message, all the men of the group being summoned had intercourse with the woman to signal their acceptance of the invitation, but spurned her if they decided otherwise.[123]

Under these circumstances, paternity for an Aborigine man would have been decidedly uncertain, although his group as a whole may have benefited by the vigorous influx of genes from neighboring groups. In terms of Darwinian fitness, it is very expensive for a man to let his wife bear children by other men, diminishing his own contribution to the next generation. The heavy cost imposed by the Aborigines' doctrine of dream-driven, nonspermatic conception is worth noting in assessing the evolutionary origin of religion, because behavior that bore such costs is likely to have been eliminated by natural selection unless it conferred offsetting evolutionary advantages.

LOOKING BACK AT THE three religious systems described above, those of the !Kung San, the Andaman Islanders and Australian Aborigines, they appear to have several common features, despite the fact that their observers were writing at different times and from very different perspectives. With all three peoples, religion was a major part of their daily lives. Religious practice involved all-night ceremonies with vigorous singing and dancing and intense emotional involvement. The emphasis was on ritual rather than belief. The justification of the religion was that it was practiced exactly as it had been handed down by the present generation's forebears. And the central purpose of the rites in all three groups was to bind the community together and fortify the social fabric.

Given these distinctive commonalities, it seems more likely that the three peoples inherited them from the ancestral human population rather than that each developed them independently. If so, religious practice of 50,000 years ago would have consisted of vigorous singing and dancing, conducted in all-night ceremonies. The focus of these ceremonies could have been healing, or initiation rites or celebration of a successful hunt. But whatever the specific theme, the effect of the ceremonies would have been to raise or maintain group cohesion, resolve disruptive feuds, reaffirm the sacred narrative and its moral prescriptions, and energize the group for warfare.

The evolutionary advantages of religion are far clearer among primitive groups than in modern societies, in which religion has undergone profound cultural transformations. Before tracing these transformations, it is worth a short detour to understand why many anthropologists have come to regard questions about the origin of religion as an exercise in futility, and what has led them to such unnecessary despair. It was social anthropologists, after all, who recorded the religious practices of hunting and gathering peoples and invested considerable effort in understanding them, so why have so few of them recognized that religion might be an evolved behavior?

## Anthropologists and the Origin of Religion

In the nineteenth and early twentieth centuries, scholars developed a serious interest in the origin of religion. Europeans were becoming familiar with the religions of people under their colonial rule, and were at the same time developing doubts about their own religion under the influence of Darwin's *On the Origin of Species*, published in 1859, and the historical criticism of the Bible's text pioneered by German scholars of the nineteenth century such as Julius Wellhausen. The first ethnographers, noticing that preliterate or primitive societies lacked the technology and material progress of Europeans, assumed that the primitive peoples' thought processes were also backward. Thus they could trace the evolution of religion, they believed, by comparing primitive religion with that of civilized societies.

Edward B. Tylor argued in his book *Primitive Culture*, published in 1871, that religion began when primitive peoples connected death with the human images they saw in dreams. They inferred that when people die, a spirit leaves them but has continued existence without the help of a body. The appearance in dreams of people known to be dead seemed to confirm the existence of such spirits who, when not troubling people's dreams, presumably lived in a supernatural realm. Our ancestors extended this idea to the natural world, imputing spirits to animals and plants, and then assuming the existence of especially powerful spirits whom they considered to be gods. Animism, the belief that spirits dwell in every living and inanimate object, was the origin of religion, in Tylor's view.

James G. Frazer then took up Tylor's approach, arguing in his monumental work *The Golden Bough*, published between 1890 and 1915, that there had been a steplike progress of cognitive thought from magic to religion to science. Magic was the characteristic mode of thought of primitive peoples, science that of advanced ones. Frazer and other writers assumed there was an early cultural origin of religion, which then evolved through successive stages, similar to those described by Darwin for the biological world.

A later generation of anthropologists repudiated this whole approach. Under the influence of Bronislaw Malinowski, the Polish-born scholar who founded modern social anthropology, it became accepted that to understand other societies one had to live among the people for many months and learn their language. Anthropologists trained in the new tradition of fieldwork found unacceptable the airy theorizing of their predecessors, who had gathered their information from reports by travelers, administrators and missionaries. It was all very well for scholars like Tylor or Frazer to imagine how primitive peoples might have thought, but how could they possibly know for sure, given that they had never lived among them and lacked any historical evidence to support their conclusions?

With a dig at both the methods and upper-class origins of these early pioneers, the social anthropologist E. E. Evans-Pritchard derided them as armchair scholars. "I am sure that men like Avebury, Frazer and Marett had little idea of how the ordinary English working man felt and thought, and it is not surprising that they had even less idea of how primitives, whom they never had seen, feel and think," he wrote.[124]

Evans-Pritchard was the author of two much-admired pieces of anthropological fieldwork. In his *Witchcraft Among the Azande*, he showed that for this African people witchcraft, far from being a mere superstition, embodied a logical system of thought and was used as a method of conflict resolution. He then turned to the Nuer, a pastoral Nilotic people of the lower Sudan, and uncovered by diligent fieldwork that they had a highly sophisticated system of religious beliefs.

"The great advances that social anthropology has made in and by field research have turned our eyes away from the vain pursuit of origins, and the many disputing schools about them have withered away," Evans-Pritchard wrote in 1965 in his influential book *Theories of Primitive Religion.*[125]

Evans-Pritchard included Durkheim in his criticism of the armchair theorists, even though he had a much greater respect for Durkheim's insights than for those of Tylor and Frazer. Like Frazer, Durkheim had never lived among primitive people. He sought evidence for his theory that religion reflects the authority of society in totemism, largely that practiced by the Arunta tribe of Australia. Totemism is a system of classification in which a clan is associated with a sacred animal or object. Evans-Pritchard wrote that Durkheim's thesis is "brilliant and imaginative" and right in seeing religion as part of something greater than the self. But he said the Arunta's practices do not prove Durkheim's point. "Totemism could have arisen through gregariousness, but there is no evidence that it did," Evans-Pritchard declared. "It was Durkheim and not the savage who made society into a god," he said elsewhere.[126]

But what he really seems to hold against Durkheim's thesis is that it sought to explain the origins of religion. Evans-Pritchard converted to Catholicism at the age of 42.[127] It's hard to avoid the impression that he had no desire to see an analysis like Durkheim's undermine his faith. The flaws in Durkheim's theory, he wrote, were "due mainly to his pursuit of the genesis, the origin, and the cause of religion."[128]

After Evans-Pritchard's critique, few anthropologists dared to seek the origins of religion through analysis of culture. Evans-Pritchard was probably correct in dismissing the approach as futile: without historical evidence, there was no way to tell whether one aspect of religion had developed before or after another.

But that left biology. Why could anthropologists and sociologists not have explored the evolutionary roots of religion? A practical reason is that evolutionary biologists have only recently established some of the principles that underlie human social organization. But there was a theoretical reason too. Darwin's idea of the survival of the fittest produced some ugly implications when applied by others to human societies, such as that might was right, or that government should not exert itself to help the poor. Colonial powers claimed they had a right to rule the tribal peoples they conquered. The eugenics movement of the first half of the twentieth century spawned a clutch of mistaken social policies in both Europe and the United States. The National Socialists in Germany persecuted Jews and other minorities on genetic grounds, asserting their own racial superiority.

In their disdain for the abuses of Darwin's theory, many social scientists mistakenly threw out the theory as well. "After a brief and somewhat superficial flirtation of social science with the idea of evolution . . . there developed among social scientists a sharp reaction against the idea of evolution," wrote the sociologist Talcott Parsons. As a result, "for an entire generation most of the comparative research was carried out by anthropologists, whose thought was militantly anti-evolutionary."[129]

In reaction against the claims of racial differences based on evolutionary arguments, social anthropologists emphasized the role of culture in differentiating human societies and played down the arguments based on genetics. Franz Boas, a German refugee who became the founder of anthropology in the United States, declared it was morally preferable to assume people's minds were shaped by culture, not heredity, unless the facts showed otherwise. "Unless the contrary can be proved, we must assume that all complex activities are socially determined, not hereditary," he wrote.[130]

Boas did not intend to evict evolution from the anthropologists' sources of explanation. But in his emphasis on culture, writes Steven Pinker, "he had created a monster. His students came to dominate American social science, and each generation outdid the previous one in its sweeping pronouncements. Boas's students insisted . . . that *every aspect* of human existence must be explained in terms of culture."[131] One of Boas's students, the anthropologist Alfred Kroeber, is said to have stated that "Heredity cannot be allowed to have acted any part in history."[132]

For social scientists to have excluded heredity, genetics and evolutionary biology from any explanatory role in human affairs, however well intentioned in the circumstances of the time, was scientifically unjustifiable, and no more helpful to their inquiries than it would be for chemists to reject Mendeleyev's periodic table of elements. Evolution is the bedrock theory of biology and people belong inseparably to the biological world. Culture is not autonomous, as many of Boas's students came to insist. Genetics and culture interact with one another over a timescale that extends to the most recent periods of history. Human nature is not a blank slate on which only culture can write. Many aspects of human nature and behavior are shaped for survival by the hand of natural selection, just as is almost every feature of the body. Darwin had already shown that some human behaviors, such as facial expressions of emotion, were constant from one society to another and therefore likely to be shaped by nature, not culture. There is now strong evidence, explored in chapter 2, for thinking that intuitive morality is wired into the brain's genetic circuitry.

A disposition against studying evolution and human nature still persists in anthropology graduate schools, according to Christopher Boehm, an anthropologist at the University of Southern California. Despite the better prospects now available for studying human nature, "much of the resistance comes from long-standing, inadequately examined biases of cultural anthropologists," he writes. "In my view, these attitudes derive from a subtly (or not-so-subtly) politicized tradition in many graduate training programs, a tradition that stems from humanistic biases about 'evolutionism.' "[133]

In retrospect, anthropologists and sociologists tackled the problem of the origin of religion too early, before more fruitful conceptual approaches were available, and then through historical accident shut themselves out of exploring the roots of religion from an evolutionary perspective.

Nonetheless, it was the achievement of social anthropologists to have recorded and analyzed many features of primitive religion before they were eroded by Western culture. With their work in mind, it is time to trace how the religion of hunter gatherer groups was adapted to the very different needs of the settled societies that began to emerge some 15,000 years ago.

# 6

---

# THE
# TRANSFORMATION

*Ancient villagers conceived of dance as the most significant
cultic activity, whose essence as a religious experience was
expressed by the circle of dancers. The uniformity of the figures
in the circle gives ideological expression to the equality of the
members of the community. . . . Dancing together creates
unity, provides education, and transmits cultural messages from
one generation to the next.*

YOSEF GARFINKEL, *Dancing at the
Dawn of Agriculture*[134]

The religions of today differ considerably from the ancestral religion practiced by hunter gatherers such as the !Kung San, the
Australian Aborigines and the Andaman Islanders. The profound transformation from which modern religions developed came
about because society itself changed and therefore religion had to change
in response.

Hunter gatherer societies, as already noted, were egalitarian structures in which a coalition of the weak constantly thwarted would-be
leaders. But this system became much more difficult to maintain once

people settled down and started living in communities larger than the usual hunter gatherer band. The hierarchical side of human nature reasserted itself and powerful men established chiefdoms. A process of profound social and cognitive change began.

In these larger communities people began for the first time to acquire property and status. No longer being constantly on the move, or restricted to owning no more than they could carry, people were able to generate surpluses of crops and of goods. These items could be traded, marking the beginning of commerce. Concepts novel to foragers, such as commodity, price, number, quantification, value, capital, became part of everyday life.

Gone were the days when all men were hunters and all women gatherers. These more complex settled societies required a specialization of labor. Managers were needed to store and distribute the surpluses, or trade them with neighboring groups. Gradations of wealth emerged. The new societies became hierarchical, with leaders and led. But how were the new leaders to establish their legitimacy and persuade those they ruled to abandon the age-old principles of egalitarianism?

A central element of the solution was to co-opt religion, the time-honored source of authority and cohesion in hunter gatherer societies. Priesthoods were instituted, and these sacerdotal officials began to control rituals and to separate people from direct communication with their gods. Religious dancing was gradually suppressed. Though the new societies and the archaic states constructed civil institutions, such as bureaucracies and armies, they still depended on religion as an instrument of rule. Even the bureaucracies were at first run from temples, at least in Babylonia, so were religious rather than civil institutions. Many leaders of archaic states asserted that they had been appointed by the gods or, at the least, that they ruled with divine approval. Some assumed the office of chief priest. Leaders found this custom so useful that it has persisted throughout history. Roman emperors declared themselves *pontifex maximus*. Even in the United Kingdom today, the monarch is still supreme governor of the Church of England. Many rulers have claimed even more intimate associations with divinity. The emperors of Japan asserted into the modern age their descent from the goddess Amaterasu. Others, like the pharaohs of Egypt, were held to be living gods. Roman emperors generally had the modesty to postpone deification until they were dead. "*Vae, puto deus fio*—Drat, I think I'm becoming a god," the emperor Vespasian joked on his deathbed.

The institutions made possible by religious behavior would have been invaluable to the first archaic states. Civil authority was rudimentary. Brute force was available, but highly inefficient. Religion was the solution, an accepted and traditional way of coordinating people's motives. "The virtue of regulation through religious ritual," writes the anthropologist Roy Rappaport, "is that the activities of large numbers of people may be governed in accordance with sanctified conventions in the absence of powerful authorities or even of discrete human authorities of any sort. As such, it is plausible to argue that religious ritual played an important role in social and ecological regulation during a time in human history when the arbitrariness of social conventions was increasing but it was not yet possible for authorities, if they existed at all, to enforce compliance."[135]

As a result of the new social forces operating in settled societies, hunter gatherer religion underwent several major changes before attaining a form more characteristic of today's religions.

As noted, the ancestral hunter gatherer religion was focused on ritual, chiefly implemented through music and dance. Modern religions, in contrast, are centered on belief, and many have regulated music and banned or sharply curtailed physical movement.

In the ancestral religion people performed their own rituals. There were no priests or church: the community was the congregation. Modern religions have an often elaborate ecclesiastical structure and make a sharp distinction between the priesthood and the laity.

In the ancestral religion people communed directly with the supernatural world through dreams and trances, not through the mediation of priests. They asked their gods for practical help, such as good hunting, children, or health. In many modern religions priests direct people's attention toward an afterlife, with instructions to focus their present lives on deeds that will secure rewards beyond the grave. In short, adherents of the ancestral religion sought to secure survival in the real world; those of modern religions are more focused on salvation in the next.

Given that a religion reflects its society, it is not surprising that the ancestral religion should have changed as people made the far-reaching transition from mobile to settled societies. The innate propensity to learn religious behavior would have remained much the same but the cultural content of religion could be adapted by each society to its needs. The cultural form of religion can be pushed only so far, however, without straining its genetic template. As is described below, the cultural transformation of religious behavior was so extreme that it set up a constant tension, which has surfaced periodically throughout history, between the ecstatic norms of hunter gatherer ritual and the restraints imposed by ecclesiastical rule.

## The Transformation of Religion in the Oaxaca Valley

Some of the best evidence for the transformation of religious practice comes from a remarkable series of excavations undertaken over 15 years in the Oaxaca Valley of southern Mexico by Joyce Marcus and Kent V. Flannery of the University of Michigan. It can be difficult for archaeologists to reconstruct the religion of a long-gone people, and they have sometimes been mocked by anthropologists for describing every item of unknown purpose as a ritual object. But in this case, Marcus and Flannery have uncovered a series of buildings that have an undoubtedly religious purpose. And the structures span a period of time—some 7,000 years—during which people's social organization passed from the hunter gatherer stage, to small settled societies, to village chiefdoms and eventually to an archaic state. This unusually long and complete record has enabled them to describe quite precisely how religious practice changed as social structure developed.

These transformations in religious and social behavior occurred much later than the equivalent processes in the Old World—the first known settlements there, in the Near East, are 15,000 years old whereas village life in the Oaxaca Valley began only 3,500 years ago. But the religious changes in Oaxaca may have been fairly typical of those elsewhere, given that they accompanied the same general process, the transition from hunter gatherer society to archaic state, that occurred independently in many regions worldwide.

The earliest structure excavated by Marcus and Flannery looks like a hunter gatherers' dance floor.[136] The ground has been swept clean of stones and two sides are marked by parallel rows of boulders. The area is part of a campsite used by some 30 people and dated to around 7000 B.C. In a nearby cave, inhabited during the same era, there are remains of people who seem to have been beheaded, cooked and cannibalized, along with baskets of harvested wild plants. This could have been a ritual associated with harvest seasons and marks an early appearance of the human sacrifices that later became widespread in Mesoamerican cultures like that of the Aztecs.

By about 1500 B.C., maize had been sufficiently domesticated that people could plant crops and store enough food to live in villages all year. At least 19 such villages have been located in the Oaxaca Valley. People dwelled in houses whose walls were made of wattle—intertwined sticks daubed with clay. Each house had a pit for storing maize. The villages also had structures known as men's houses. San José Mogote, a fortified village of more than 1,000 people, had several of them.

The ritual purpose of the men's houses is evident from their orientation; all face 8 degrees north of east, suggesting that they were aligned with the sun's path at the equinox. Assuming they were used like similar buildings in contemporary societies, they would have belonged to a group of families who claimed descent from a common ancestor. Only men who had passed tests and been initiated into secret rites would have been allowed to enter the houses.

The men's houses mark a decisive step away from the communal religious practice of hunter gatherers. An important part of ritual life was no longer open to all but had become exclusive to a small group of men.

By about 1100 B.C., the social structure of San José Mogote included a new class—a hereditary elite who lived in multistoried houses, wore jade ornaments, and deformed their children's skulls, a practice then fashionable among the nobility. As for developments in religion, the men's houses began to be phased out and were replaced with temples, oriented in the same direction. The temples were probably run by part-time priests, marking a further increase in the exclusivity of the religious leadership. In the largest temple the archaeologists found obsidian stilettos which were used for ritual bloodletting, and the remains of two people who had been sacrificed.

From 650 to 450 B.C. there were some 80 villages in the Oaxaca Valley, and intervillage warfare reached a peak, as judged by the number of burn marks on the wattle housing. The main temple at San José Mogote was consumed in an intense fire. Sometime beforehand, however, many of the inhabitants had moved to a more easily defended site in the valley called Monte Albán, which was to become the first major city of the New World.

Stone monuments at Monte Albán show that its leaders measured time with two calendars, a 260-day ritual calendar and a 365-day solar calendar. The two calendars came into conjunction once every 52 years. Like other Mesoamerican peoples, including the Aztec, the leaders of Monte Albán assigned great importance to this interval, as shown by the fact that at least some of their temples were rebuilt every 52 years.

By 450 B.C., the Oaxaca Valley held a population of some 10,000 people and had become divided first into three warring states, and eventually two, Monte Albán and its rival Tilcajete. The temples at both centers had grown more elaborate with the addition of a second room, probably added so that priests could live in the temple.

With the emergence of full-time professional priests, a career often followed by the nobility who were not in line for the throne, the privatization of the ancestral religious behavior was complete. Control of religious practice was no longer exercised by the community but by a caste of religious officials.

As religion became more exclusive, and governable by an elite, warfare in the Oaxaca Valley became more intense. At Tilcajete, leaders built a civic-ceremonial plaza with a different astronomical orientation from that of Monte Albán. The plaza was burned in 280 but the leaders of Tilcajete built a new one on a nearby ridge, with the same orientation as their first. But the war was relentless. The Monte Albán army destroyed Tilcajete a second time around A.D. 30, and this time its rival did not recover. The leaders of Monte Albán now controlled the entire Oaxaca Valley, and founded the polity known as the Zapotec state.[137] Over the span of 7,000 years, the communal religion of hunter gatherers had been developed into a priestly hierarchy that was a principal instrument of state governance.

## The Fading of the Ancestral Religion in the Old World

The progression from hunter gatherer religion to that of the archaic state was completed by A.D. 30 in the Oaxaca Valley but had taken place much earlier in the Old World. The first settlements, those of the Natufian culture of the eastern Mediterranean, appeared 15,000 years ago, and the great city states of Mesopotamia had emerged by shortly before 5,000 years ago.

By 10,000 the Natufians had developed a disconcertingly intimate cult of the dead. They buried the bodies but kept the heads around in their houses. The heads were given new faces, made out of plaster, with shells for the eyes. This ancestor cult was widespread: "In view of their common occurrence in excavations, there can be little doubt that thousands of dead people were brought back to the world of the living in this manner, suggesting that the ancestors were crucial in the making and maintenance of the Neolithic communities," write the archaeologists Peter Akkermans and Glenn Schwartz. The heads are found in stable villages where people lived for generation after generation, indicating strong ties to the past. The purpose of the ancestor cult could have been to motivate people—all the ancestor's descendants—to work together for the good of society. Agriculture, which had only just begun, required forms of shared labor that were quite alien to hunter gatherer societies. The cooperation induced by the ancestor cult was "essential in the small communities that became increasingly reliant on farming, where people had to draw on each other's labor for survival," Akkermans and Schwartz suggest.[138]

There is no continuous archaeological record in the Near East, equivalent to that of the Oaxaca Valley, to show the stages in which the religious behavior of hunter gatherers was transformed to that of settled societies. But an unexpected insight into the process has been gained through the careful work of the archaeologist Yosef Garfinkel.

Scanning archaeological collections from throughout the Near East, dating from 8000 to 4000 B.C., Garfinkel noticed that spread among the artifacts of the period, on wall and floor paintings, stone slabs, stamp and cylinder seals, and above all on pottery, were numerous figures of people dancing.

He collected 396 depictions of dancing figures, drawn from 170 archaeological sites, and began to notice certain patterns. In each picture, the dancers were all the same or dressed alike, indicating that these were communal dances with no one outranking anyone else. Men and women were usually shown dancing separately. The dancers were often depicted wearing masks or costumes or body paintings. There were no signs of buildings, suggesting the dances were being held out in the open. And many of the figures are in silhouette, suggesting the dances depicted are being held at night.

Since all these features matched the ethnographic data on hunter gatherer dances, Garfinkel concluded that his shards of pottery depicted the same thing—hunter gatherer dances that continued to be held after people settled down in villages and started to practice agriculture.

The practical role of the dances was social cohesion, he believes: "The major strategies used by the early farmers of the Near East and southeast Europe from the eighth to the fourth millennium BC to promote the bonding of individuals into communities, and of individual households into villages, were public assemblies for religious ceremonies."[139] Dancing not only encouraged unity but also served to pass on knowledge from one generation to the next.

Many of the depictions show people dancing in circles, a practice Garfinkel believes held great symbolism for early agriculturalists struggling to march to the rhythm of the seasons and, on pain of starvation, to plant and harvest their crops at the right time. The hunter gatherer trance dance became entrained to festivals determined by the agricultural calendar. The echoes of this linkage are enduring. In Judaism, Sukkot originally marked the end of the fruit harvest and the time for plowing and sowing for the next season. Passover once heralded the beginning of the barley festival, Shavu'ot, the end of the wheat harvest. In the Christian liturgical calendar, Passover has been converted to Easter and Shavu'ot to Pentecost or Whitsun.

These festivals, Garfinkel says, became a means of transferring messages to the community about the correct timing of agricultural activities. The masks and body decorations, the music and rhythmic movement combining to induce trance, attracted the greatest awareness and attention from the whole community. "The high supernatural powers," Garfinkel says, "also became involved in the process, as the circle of dance is the actual place where contact is made between this and the other world." These encounters with the supernatural ensured, in the participants' minds, a successful agricultural season and, on a more practical level, helped them accomplish it by informing everybody that it was time to clear the land or sow or harvest.

The dancing depicted on the pottery shards lasted for 4,000 years—longer than the existence of any modern religion. It began to disappear after 3500 B.C., just as the first city states of Mesopotamia were coming into being. Perhaps the priesthood that emerged after the first settled societies had little use for ad hoc dances and sought to confine dancing to the official festivals that they controlled. Perhaps dancing became associated with the rural poor and was looked at askance by the new city dwellers. Perhaps the priests, with their important administrative roles in the first city states, finally gained the power to suppress dancing. In any event, the record of the ubiquitous pottery shards collected by Garfinkel is unambiguous: by the time of the city states, the dancing floors had fallen silent. The ancestral form of religion was dead.

The new religions developed so as to match the needs of hierarchically organized societies. But they bore two critical legacies from their predecessor, one to do with genes, the other concerning the supernatural.

The neural circuitry that predisposed hunters and gatherers to learn the religion of their community remained the basis of religious behavior. However much the priesthood might suppress the ecstatic aspects of the ancestral religion, a propensity to follow the ecstatic behaviors of dance and trance was built into people's minds and provided consistently fertile ground for revolts against established religion. The tension between the ecclesiastical and the ecstatic has persisted throughout history and is a major driver of religious change.

The second legacy of the ancestral religion was a preoccupation with the supernatural that many societies would later take to costly extremes. In the circle of dance where spirits from a parallel world seemed to seize those who fell into trance, hunter gatherers had found what seemed to them a window into the realm of the supernatural. Through the window, it seemed, they could communicate with the spirit beings that controlled vital matters in the world of the living, such as the gift of children, or fair weather and fine harvests, or fortune in war. They seem not to have considered the possibility that the beguiling magic surface might have been no window, just a distorting mirror.

## The Church's Struggle with Ecstatic Religion

The ancestral religion left a vexing legacy to the hierarchical religions that succeeded it, that of people's ingrained desire to communicate directly with their gods. Established religions are seldom fully secure: their priests' assertion of exclusive access to the gods is often subject to question. Their leadership is frequently challenged from within, by movements or sects that may first insist on reform and then threaten to break off on their own. If these sects are not suppressed, the religion may be split. The schism may revitalize the culture or seriously weaken it.

Challenges to orthodoxy often follow a similar pattern: upstarts evoke the ecstatic methods that the priesthood has moderated or suppressed so as to bring the people under its control. The ebb and flow of the tussle between ecstatic and ecclesiastical forces has been described by the anthropologist I. M. Lewis: "So if it is in the nature of new religions to herald their advent with a flourish of ecstatic effervescence," he writes, "it is equally the fate of those which become successfully ensconced at the centre of public morality to lose their inspirational savour." Inspiration becomes institutionalized and individual trances or possession experiences are discouraged and if necessary declared to be a satanic heresy.

"This certainly is that pattern which is clearly and deeply inscribed in the long history of Christianity," Lewis says.[140] Christian sects such as the Pentecostalists and the Charismatic Movement represent modern attempts to revive ecstatic means of communion, such as speaking in tongues.

Ancient Greek culture was a wellspring of rational thought. The philosopher Zeno declared that the human intellect was the true temple and no others were needed. But the classical era of Greece was punctuated with outbursts of maenads and bacchants, throngs of people who danced themselves into frenzy. The frenzies culminated in rending apart and eating a living animal or even a human being. Greek vases depict the dances as being accompanied by flutes and kettledrums. "To the Greeks these were the 'orgiastic' instruments *par excellence*: they were used in all the great dancing cults, those of the Asiatic Cybele and the Cretan Rhea as well as that of Dionysus," writes the classical scholar E. R. Dodds. The cult of Dionysus may have been an attempt by authorities to channel these frenzies into an organized rite that took place once every two years.[141]

The prophets of ancient Israel also came from a tradition of ecstatic song and dance, though the allusions to it in the Bible are often brief and disapproving. When Saul was being prepared for the kingship by the prophet Samuel, he was told to go to a place where he would meet "a company of prophets coming down from the high place with a psaltery, and a tabret, and a pipe, and a harp, before them; and they shall prophesy: and the Spirit of the Lord will come upon thee, and thou shalt prophesy with them, and shalt be turned into another man." But the sight of Saul prophesying shocked his friends, who exclaimed to one another, "What is this that is come unto the son of Kish? Is Saul also among the prophets?"[142]

King David too, a musician, was associated with the ecstatic tradition. When the ark was brought into the City of David, he "danced before the Lord with all his might" wearing only a linen apron. Saul's daughter Michal caught sight of him through a window and "despised him in her heart." She chided him sarcastically on his return to the house: "How glorious was the king of Israel today, who uncovered himself today in the eyes of the handmaids of his servants, as one of the vain fellows shamelessly uncovereth himself!"[143]

By the time of the early Christians the texts of the scripture, not trances and prophecy, had become the principal source of religious truth. Still, there are hints that, like the other mystery cults that swept through the Roman world, the early Christians sometimes practiced ecstatic forms of religion. In Paul's first epistle to the Corinthians—his letters are among the earliest authentic Christian documents—he addresses the subject of speaking in tongues (glossolalia), a form of possession that, like trance dancing, could reliably be made to appear in a ritual setting. Speaking in tongues, says the historian Wayne Meeks, "occurred within the framework of the assembly, performed by persons who were expected to do it. It happened at predictable times, accompanied by distinctive bodily movements, perhaps introduced and followed by characteristic phrases in natural language. It did what rituals do: it stimulated feelings of group solidarity (except, as at Corinth, for those nonspeakers made to feel excluded). . . ."[144]

A Christian sect of the mid-second century, that of the Montanists, was marked by ecstatic outbursts which it regarded as the central focus of Christianity. Charismatic preachers like Montanus threatened to drown the church's unifying voice in a cacophony of personal prophecies. The Montanists, with their emphasis on personal connection with the supernatural, posed a serious challenge to the early church, particularly when they were joined by the leading theologian and antiheretic Tertullian, who refused to accept that contact with the deity could be conducted only through official church channels.

Montanus was declared a heretic around A.D. 170 and his sect was suppressed by the church. His doctrines were not heretical, but too much enthusiasm—the original Greek word *enthousiasmos* means to be possessed by a god—was regarded with suspicion by the church authorities. "As the early Christian community became the institution of the Church," writes Barbara Ehrenreich in her history of ritual dancing, "all forms of enthusiasm . . . came under fire. And when the community of believers could no longer access the deity on their own, through ecstatic forms of worship, the community itself was reduced to a state of dependency on central ecclesiastical authorities. 'Prophesying' became the business of the priest; singing was relegated to a special choir; and that characteristic feature of early Christian worship—the communal meal or feast—shriveled to a morsel that could only tantalize the hungry. But it was to take many centuries before large numbers of Christians came to accept this diminished form of Christianity."[145]

Like other structured religions, the Christian church found itself in a running tactical competition with its ecstatic rivals in terms of just how much dance, music and trance to allow. If it gave the congregation too much leeway, people would think they could communicate directly with the supernatural and might come to regard the priesthood as a mere obstruction. But if the church outlawed dance and music altogether, its priests would be unable to stir the necessary emotions and the flock would drift away to the rival cults of Cybele and Attis, Isis, Adonis or Dionysus.

Lacking an ideal solution, the church tacked and trimmed as seemed best in the circumstances. Basil, a fourth-century saint who succeeded the church historian Eusebius as bishop of Caesarea, approved dancing in circles in imitation of the dance of the angels. Ambrose, who became bishop of Milan in A.D. 373, made major innovations in church music and dance, largely to combat the Arians who held a different theological position on the nature of the Trinity. Ambrose introduced antiphonal singing, employed professional choristers, and even trained the congregation. He was of the opinion that celestial harmony drove out demons.[146] He also encouraged dancing, which he said would help carry souls to heaven.

But his protégé, the church father Augustine, looked askance at dancing. "In time, Augustine's views prevailed," writes the historian William McNeill. "Busy ecclesiastical administrators feared popular excitement of every kind, and since congregational dancing did indeed excite warm and even ecstatic emotions, it fell under increasing suspicion when, after 312, Christianity ceased to be a persecuted sect and, before the end of the century, became the established religion of the Roman empire." Bishops ceased to lead sacred dances. Participation by the congregation in services was discouraged. The new alliance between throne and altar "had the effect of gradually throttling enthusiastic forms of dance and song in Christian worship, and banished popular dancing to the churchyard and other public spaces."[147]

The Catholic church had relatively few challenges to its authority during the Dark Ages but was troubled by numerous Montanist-style heresies during the period of the crusades. From one perspective, the crusades did not spring from the pope's sudden desire to conquer the Holy Land but rather from the need to manage large bodies of people seized with religious frenzy. By unleashing them on the Near East, where almost all eventually perished, they became someone else's problem. "The central problem of the institutional church," writes Paul Johnson in his history of Christianity, "was always how to control the manifestations of religious enthusiasm, and divert them into orthodox and constructive channels. At what point did mass piety become unmanageable, and therefore heresy? It was a problem as old as the Montanists. . . . Naturally, where antinomian mobs were liable to sweep away church institutions, established authority was anxious to get them out of Christendom—preferably to the East, whence few would return."[148]

Ecstatic religion has continued to threaten established churches, but usually with more fortunate outcomes than that of the crusades. Movements like those of the Shakers, the Quakers and, in the twentieth century, the Pentecostalists, all challenged the established order, emphasizing physical movement or ecstatic outbreaks as their points of difference. The Shakers would dance together all night in ecstatic agitation, with trembling, shouting, and speaking in tongues. But rules requiring more decorous behavior were instituted in 1845 and the sect, which favored celibacy, soon dwindled. Among the early Mormons too, frenetic dancing was practiced until the church authorities brought it under control.

The Quaker movement, founded in seventeenth-century England, was built on George Fox's idea that people should be able to experience God directly. But enthusiasm can be hard to sustain. Even within Fox's lifetime, the Quakers had curtailed individual expression and begun to resemble a structured church.

In almost any church that seeks to return to its religious roots, music seems likely to play a prominent role. Music is a particular feature of African American religious practice. "When white Christians attend black worship services," writes the historian Frank Lambert, "they often comment on the power of the music and the 'mystical, ecstatic experience' that transports the singers to the very throne of God."[149]

Solid evidence of established churches' fear of ecstatic religion and people's innate desire to communicate directly with the deity is visible in

a form too familiar to excite much comment: the pew. Providing somewhere to sit through the parson's sermon is only the secondary purpose
of pews. They were placed in European churches from the sixteenth century onward to stop people dancing. The introduction of pews, McNeill
writes, "restrained spontaneous muscular responses to the most fiery of
preachers and, by isolating one person from another with wooden barriers, introduced a new quiescence into public worship."[150]

Music combined with communal dance or bodily movements is the
recipe that leads groups toward the dangerous experience of ecstasy. Once
the church had restricted bodily movements, it had less fear of music,
which was allowed to develop, though in a form not conducive to dance.
The Western tradition of sacred music has been one of Christianity's fin-
est cultural contributions.

In Islam, the situation is somewhat the reverse. Music, especially
instrumental music, is looked on with suspicion. In the strictest forms
of Islam, only unaccompanied singing is allowed. But rhythmic bodily
movement by the congregation is allowed. Rhythmic bowing in unison
may have created the same emotional solidarity brought about by military drill and perhaps contributed, McNeill suggests, to the early success
of Islam.

An outgrowth from the rhythmic movement of the mosque was
that of the dervish orders, which attained mystic union with the deity
by chanting sacred formulas to music, or by dancing until they fell into
trance. The dervishes believed their path to mystic union superior to reason and words. The ideas that flowed from this form of piety spurred the
military expansion of the Islamic world but later handicapped it in deal-
ing with the rise of Europe. The words of the Qur'an were only part of
what united Muslims. "Keeping together in time," McNeill writes, "along
with music, song, and chant, also played its part, arousing primitive,
inchoate, and powerful sentiments of solidarity that allowed them to act
more energetically and effectively than words and doctrine by themselves
could have done."[151]

## Interpreting the Supernatural

The religions of settled societies may have managed ecstasy, with vary-ing degrees of success, but they have had greater trouble with the other legacy of hunter gatherer religion, that of presumed access to the super-natural world.

The window that hunter gatherers believed they had gained into the supernatural world, in the form of trance dances or the dream journeys of their shamans, would have provided only a reflection of their own images, a kind of Rorschach test in which people could see whatever their imaginations might suggest to them. But these assumed commu-nications with the other world would not have been without constraints. First, to make sense, they had to be compatible with the society's existing religious beliefs. One couldn't just invent a new god who had appeared in a trance; to be credible, a trance dancer needed to report on the doings of gods with whom the community was already familiar.

Community agreement would have been a second constraint on the shaping of religious beliefs. In hunter gatherer societies, religion couldn't be captured by a small group who reinterpreted the gods' will for their own benefit. There was no church or priesthood, just all the members of a small community.

But in settled societies the hunter gatherer religion became pro-gressively more exclusive as society became more hierarchical. Religion came to belong to the priests who controlled it. And without democratic restraint, the priests would have had a much freer hand in interpreting communications with the supernatural world.

These interpretations could easily run to excess because there was no readily available mechanism to counteract extremism. The idea of sacrifice, for instance, is common to many religions. Among the Nuer, a cattle-herding people of the southern Sudan, it was often necessary to sacrifice a cow, but if none were available, it was OK to sacrifice a small

plant called a cow cucumber as a temporary expedient.[152] Such modera-
tion was by no means the rule. Priests conferring with the supernatural
world evidently decided that much larger sacrifices were expected. A *heca-
tomb* is the name for a sacrifice in which 100 oxen are killed at the same
time. But soon word came that cattle were not sufficient; the gods desired
human blood. The Carthaginians sacrificed children. Abraham was fully
prepared to sacrifice his son Isaac. The chief purpose of the Aztec state
was to capture and sacrifice as many captives as possible to keep their sun
god nourished with rivers of human blood.

These horrific practices were based on fantastical interpretations of
what the gods required. A hunter gatherer community could ensure
that the messages from the supernatural world were interpreted in a
way generally acceptable to the community; a priesthood had fewer
restraints in imposing alleged demands from the supernatural side on
the congregation.

Communication with the supernatural world emerged as a problem
of increasing difficulty as people in settled societies became more sophisticated and, with the invention of writing some 5,000 years ago, more
literate. Dreams and trances were still consulted, especially on an individual basis, but became less convincing as the basis for state religions.
Instead, whole systems of divination were developed as a means of reading the intentions of the beings in the supernatural world.

In the Shang dynasty in China, which lasted from 1570 to 1045 B.C.,
diviners prepared oracle bones by applying intense heat to the shoulder
bones of cattle or to turtle shells. The king would then make a divination about the intentions of Di, the Shang dynasty's high god. But the
later kings seem to have given up on worrying about Di's intentions,
according to the tens of thousands of Shang oracle bones that have been
preserved. "Di's virtual disappearance from the record," writes the historian David Keightley, "suggests either the increasing confidence with
which the Shang kings relied on the power of their ancestors, their
increasing indifference to Di's existence, or their increasing realization

that Di's will was so inscrutable that it was fruitless to divine about his intentions."[153]

Divination in the West was focused more on entrails than on bones. The Babylonians believed the will of the gods could be discerned from examining sheep's livers, each portion of which represented a different deity. The Etruscans carried this system to Italy where it was adopted by the Romans. The *haruspices*, the priests who did the divining, were still practicing their trade in A.D. 410 when the Goths under Alaric besieged Rome. They are said to have offered their services to Pope Innocent I, who accepted them by one account, rejected them by others. In either event, Rome fell.

Divination clearly had limitations as a means of communicating with the supernatural. What replaced it in serious religions was a throwback to the hunter gatherer shamans and their direct communings with the supernatural. The prophets and patriarchs of Israel spoke directly with their deity and recorded his words. With the advent of literacy, religious narratives could now be written down and studied. The sacred text became an increasingly prominent part of religious practice, matching the shift in emphasis from ritual to belief.

Direct revelation became the accepted form of communication with the supernatural world. But in an increasingly educated world, this channel had to be used sparingly. At the initiation of a new religion, such as in the case of Christianity, Islam or Mormonism, the founding prophet would receive the sacred message or text from the supernatural world and the channel would then fall silent. This made possible a period of stability during which followers could shape the sacred texts in various ways and then declare them closed to further revision.

The new religions were very different from the old and, perhaps, less satisfying. Among hunter gatherers, religious behavior called for the full mental and physical involvement of all members of the community, in intensive rituals that could last through the night. The religions of settled societies were much more cerebral, with an emphasis on points of doctrine spelled out by the priests, often with threats of coercion against dissidents or heretics. The priesthood also tried to suppress ecstatic forms of religion, recognizing their threat to the established system. They usually succeeded, but each failure was the seed of a new religion. Because of this process of continual change, there is not a single religion in the world but many different branches. It is time to consider the tree from which they spring.

# 7

# THE TREE OF RELIGION

*Suddenly, from the island of Paxi was heard the voice of someone loudly calling . . . and the caller, raising his voice, said, "When you come opposite to Palodes, announce that the great god Pan is dead."*

PLUTARCH, *The Obsolescence of Oracles*

*The former gods are growing old or dying, and others have not been born. . . . It is life itself, and not a dead past, that can produce a living cult. But that state of uncertainty and confused anxiety cannot last forever. A day will come when our societies will once again know hours of creative effervescence during which new ideals wil again spring forth and new formulas emerge to guide humanity for a time.*

ÉMILE DURKHEIM[154]

There is, in a sense, only one religion. Or, to put it more exactly, all religions are related to one another because all belong to the same family. This is not a widely held perspective, because people are much attached to the particular features of their own faith and are more likely to dwell on its differences with other creeds than with its commonalities. The focus on differences is evident in the significance attached to the mere word *filioque* in the Nicene Creed, which ultimately split the Orthodox church from Rome, or the furious contests in fourth-century Christendom between the homoousians and the homoiousians, who differed as to whether Jesus was made of the same or a similar substance as God.

But a glance at the history of religions suggests that, as cultural forms, they bear several significant similarities with languages. And just as present-day languages probably all stem from the same tree of descent, so too may religions.

The ancestral human population at one time dwindled through some disaster to perhaps a mere 5,000 people,[155] who may have spoken a single language. Since everyone in the world today is a descendant of that village-sized population, all today's languages are very possibly derived from a single language spoken by these early people.

If so, one could, at least in principle, draw up a tree of descent that included all the world's living languages. Its trunk would be the mother tongue of more than 50,000 years ago. Its major branches would be the 14 or so language super-families now in existence, like Indo-European, Altaic or Afro-Asiatic. The twigs on these branches would be the 6,000 languages spoken in the world today.

Such a tree is generated by the fact that languages keep changing, but each is derived from a predecessor. It should be possible, again in principle, to draw up a similar tree for all the world's religions, because religions too emerge by slow degrees from their predecessors. A totally novel religion has little chance of success. The easiest way for a new religion to start is as a sect of an existing one. Converts are most easily found among the members of the church from which the sect is seceding. The leader of the sect may evoke ecstatic aspects of religion and fault the established priesthood for having strayed from its founding precepts. He may base his teaching on a new revelation from the vantage point of which he offers a reinterpretation of the sacred texts. This is the approach taken by the followers of Jesus, by Montanus, by Muhammad and by Joseph Smith, the founder of the Mormon faith.

Such challengers, unless co-opted by the guardians of religious orthodoxy, either will be suppressed or will break away from the founding
church and survive as a new sect. And if this is the general mechanism by
which new sects arise, then every sect is derived from a predecessor, and
all religions are branches of the same tree.

But religions are shaped not just by their path of descent; like languages, religions may borrow material from others, often quite heavily.
The most important religious ritual of the Christian church is Easter,
which celebrates the resurrection of Jesus. How surprising, therefore,
that the word *Easter* should derive from Eostre, an Anglo-Saxon goddess
of the dawn. The Anglo-Saxon word for April was *Eostur-monath*, a month
which probably then started on March 25, a date that falls close to the
vernal equinox. Spring festivals are ancient rituals, probably observed in
all religions that have existed since the birth of agriculture. These festivals have been co-opted both into Judaism—Passover, or Pesach, marked
the beginning of the barley harvest—and into Christianity.[156] It is striking that these pagan festivals are not just minor items in the ritual calendars of Judaism and Christianity but in fact mark the date of their central
rites, almost as if the two monotheisms had been constructed around
them but with the imposition of different sacred texts to explain their
importance. Judaism, it seems, seized the agricultural year's spring festival and adapted it to a central religious tenet, the deliverance of the Israelites from Egypt, while the Christians linked it to the principal focus of
their religion, the resurrection.

In bringing heathen tribes into the fold, the early church found it
expedient to co-opt their temples and festivals rather than force them
to embrace an alien faith outright. An explicit statement of this policy
occurs in a letter written by Pope Gregory the Great in 601 to the Abbot
Mallitus who was en route to visit Bishop Augustine in Canterbury. Tell
the bishop, Gregory wrote, "that I have long been considering with myself
about the case of the Angli; to wit, that the temples of idols in that nation
should not be destroyed, but that the idols themselves that are in them

should be. . . . And since they are wont to kill many oxen in sacrifice to demons, they should have also some solemnity of this kind in a changed form. . . . For it is undoubtedly impossible to cut away everything at once from hard hearts, since one who strives to ascend to the highest place must needs rise by steps or paces and not by leaps."[157]

Religions are composite cultural creations in that they generally consist of a core of beliefs or rituals derived from a preceding religion, combined with new material. The new component may be supplied by the founding prophet's revelation, or by borrowing and co-opting material from the religions of neighboring or conquered peoples.

Religions can seldom, if ever, be entirely new because of the way they are learned. People commit to religion during the formative years of puberty, often during emotionally searing initiation rites. In these rites a young man is taught, says the anthropologist Bronislaw Malinowski, "the sacred traditions under the most impressive conditions of preparation and ordeal and under the sanction of Supernatural Beings—the light of tribal revelation bursts upon him from out of the shadows of fear, privation and bodily pain."[158]

Modern religions have reduced the element of pain in initiation rites but their procedures ensure that the sacred texts and symbols that are taught at that time have lasting significance throughout a person's adult life; it is this sense of emotional familiarity that makes one's own religion feel so natural, whereas most other religions seem far-fetched or deluded. Although conversions do of course occur, though usually between similar religions, most people are very unwilling to abandon the religion they learned in childhood and adolescence. This is also likely to be the religion of their family and friends, another reason for regarding it with attachment, but the emotional tie to a religion learned at an impressionable age is probably even stronger.

Religion is a language of a special kind. It is a form of communication, expressed in the form of gestural or verbal symbols that register their meaning emotionally as well as consciously. If this special language changes and splits in much the same pattern as the ordinary kind of language, as is argued above, then it should be possible in principle to construct a tree of all the world's religions, comparable to the tree one could in principle draw up for all the world's languages.

A major recent branching of the tree is evident enough in the derivation from Judaism of Christianity, Islam and Mormonism. Judaism itself, as discussed below, developed from the religion of the ancient Canaanites, whose rites were centered around agricultural festivals. The specific names of religions that existed before then have been lost, but the general nature of the tree's growth can be reconstructed. The tree would start with the religion of the ancestral modern human population that lived in northeast Africa prior to 50,000 years ago. Its trunk would be the hunter gatherer religions that endured until the first settled societies of 15,000 years ago and the institution of religious officialdom.

With the development of agriculture, beginning some 10,000 years ago in the Old World, the new hierarchical religions seem to have been focused on agricultural festivals, such as those of spring planting and fall harvest. Through the festivals, religion helped coordinate people's activities and entrain them to the rhythm of the seasons, reducing the risk that crops would be planted or harvested at the wrong time. Early peoples developed a deep knowledge of astronomy and from Stonehenge to Mesoamerica oriented their temples on axes that marked significant events such as the sun's position at the spring equinox.

These early agricultural religions would still have emphasized ritual over belief, but dancing and ecstatic trances were suppressed as priesthoods worked to make themselves the sole intermediaries between the real and the supernatural worlds.

With the advent of literacy some 5,000 years ago, the character of religion changed yet again. With the help of written texts, beliefs could be shaped to more specific purposes, like nation building. The sacred texts further increased the distance between believers and the supernatural. Direct experience of the interface with the supernatural world, as experienced by hunter gatherers in their trance dances, was long gone. The evidence of the supernatural world increasingly came from sacred texts recording revelations held to have occurred in the distant past.

Hunter gatherer religion sprang from a few behaviors, presumably genetically prompted, such as a belief in supernatural agencies which set rules of social behavior, fear of divine punishment for breaking these rules, and confidence that the supernatural powers could be manipulated through ritual and sacrifice. This relatively simple set of evolutionary behaviors proved capable, as settled societies grew larger and more sophisticated, of supporting the cultural development of more elaborate religions, such as the three Judaic-related monotheisms. The emergence of these religions is worth exploring in some detail because they demonstrate the power of cultural innovation to improvise systems of belief that transformed the dance and trance rituals of hunter gatherer religions into creeds that could bind not a tribe but a state or empire.

## Origins of Judaism

Judaism is a religion whose formation from roots in the agricultural past is now understood in some detail. The language, religion and culture of the ancient Israelites were derived from those of the Canaanites, the West Semitic peoples who inhabited the southern Levant, now Syria, Jordan and Israel. Hebrew is a dialect of Canaanite. The earliest known Hebrew inscriptions are written in the Old Canaanite script of the Late Bronze Age (1500–1200 B.C.). Several festivals of the Israelite and Jewish liturgical calendar are adaptations of Canaanite agricultural festivals. Rosh Ha-Shanah marks the onset of the fall rains, heralded in Canaanite mythology by the resurrection of the storm god Ba'al. Sukkot is the Canaanite fall harvest festival, adapted in Judaism to commemorate the wandering in the desert after the exodus from Egypt. Pesach was a Canaanite spring feast at which young lambs, born the previous fall, were sacrificed; in Judaism Pesach has become Passover and historicized to mark the exodus from Egypt, with the lambs' blood translated for the Israelites into a rite commemorating the sparing of their first-born children from the tenth plague sent against the pharaoh. Shavu'ot, 50 days after Passover, is a late spring festival that marks the conclusion of the wheat harvest.[159]

Canaanite texts of the fourteenth to thirteenth centuries B.C. from Ugarit in Syria describe the Canaanite religion in some detail, including its gods El and Ba'al and the tradition of animal sacrifice. The Israelites adopted animal sacrifice and their early name for the deity is *elohim,* the plural of El. The opening words of Genesis are customarily translated "In the beginning God created the heaven and the earth," but the Hebrew text says *elohim*—the gods created heaven and earth—and in verse 26 of the first chapter of Genesis it is the *elohim,* the gods, who say "Let us make man in our image, after our likeness." Though *elohim* can also be singular in Hebrew, its plural form may reflect the polytheism that preceded the monotheism associated with Yahweh, according to the biblical archaeologist William Dever.[160]

Early Israelite religion seems to have been polytheistic just as was its Canaanite predecessor. Monotheism was imposed much later by the priestly caste in Jerusalem and during the Babylonian captivity, but the priests then devised an ancient pedigree for their new religion which back-projected its origins into the distant past. "Virtually all mainstream scholars (and even a few conservatives) acknowledge that true monotheism emerged only in the period of the exile in Babylon in the sixth century B.C., as the canon of the Hebrew Bible, or Old Testament, was taking shape," writes Dever.[161] The Hebrew Bible's frequent imprecations against the worship of Ba'al, golden calves and other idols were required because that was indeed the prevailing religion among the general population.

Much is now known about the development of the Hebrew Bible, from textual analysis, from archaeology and from the independent records of other contemporary civilizations, such as those of Egypt and Assyria. Textual analysis by the nineteenth-century German scholar Wilhelm de Wette showed that of the first five books of the Bible, known as the

Pentateuch, Deuteronomy had been written much later than the others. He identified it with the book of law said in the Bible to have been discovered during a renovation of the temple in the eighteenth year of the reign of King Josiah of Judah, namely in 622 B.C.[162]

Another German scholar, Julius Wellhausen, laid out evidence for supposing that the Pentateuch seemed not to be the work of a single author—traditionally held to have been Moses—but was based on four different sources, each with a specific perspective, and some using different names for God (Yahweh or *elohim*).

More than a century of study by textual scholars and archaeologists has established that the Bible is indeed a composite document. Some of its sources are drawn from legends of the great Babylonian civilization on Israel's eastern borders. Some are historical accounts. Some are folklore explanations of how a certain place or people got its name. The complex of materials has been skillfully shaped, probably to forge a political and religious identity for a small nation buffeted between two powerful neighboring states.

The story of Noah illustrates the composite nature of the biblical narrative. In the late nineteenth century archaeologists began to recover Mesopotamian versions of a very similar story. A man, called Utnapishtim in the Sumerian Epic of Gilgamesh, was advised by the gods to load his family, possessions, and living creatures onto a boat to escape a great flood. The Mesopotamian versions of the story are much older, and the Bible's version is clearly derived from them, not vice versa. Besides, the hilly countryside of Israel is not a plausible place for everything to be washed away in a flood, unlike the flat plains of Mesopotamia.

The biblical scholar James L. Kugel notes that both the Sumerian and Hebrew versions of the story contain the same curious anthropomorphic vignette of the deities savoring the smell of the sacrifice made to thank them at the end of the voyage.[163] After Utnapishtim's sacrifice, the Epic of Gilgamesh reports, "The gods smelled the savor, the gods smelled the sweet savor, the gods crowded round the sacrificer like flies." After Noah's, "the Lord smelled a sweet savour; and the Lord said in his heart, I will not again curse the ground any more for man's sake . . . neither will I again smite any more everything living, as I have done."[164]

The borrowed nature of the Noah story is underlined by the fact that it seems itself to be composed of two different versions of the Mesopotamian myth. In one version, Kugel notes, Noah is directed by the deity in person to load seven pairs of every clean species of animal on the ark, presumably needing the extra six for sacrifice: "And the Lord said unto Noah . . . Of every clean beast thou shalt take to thee by sevens, the male and his female: and of beasts that are not clean, by two, the male and his female."[165] But the second version of the story reports specifically that Noah embarked with only one pair of each clean species: "And they went in unto Noah into the ark, two and two of all flesh, wherein is the breath of life. And they that went in, went in male and female of all flesh, as God had commanded him: and the Lord shut him in."[166]

The Hebrew words for the deity also differ between the two versions. The passage calling for seven pairs of animals cites Yahweh, but El/elohim, the usual word for god, is used in the second version. "Scholars have little doubt that the biblical narrative was ultimately based on one or another version of this Mesopotamian legend," Kugel concludes.

The Bible's version of the Noah story seems clearly the work of an editor who pasted together two versions of a Mesopotamian myth, and there are many other parts of the Pentateuch where the narrative contains two or even three traces of the same story.

While literary scholars were sorting out problems in the Bible's text, archaeologists were trying, with increasing frustration, to match its assertions to the evidence on the ground. The Bible offers a long historical narrative in which many of the events that occurred after 622 B.C. can be corroborated by documents from ancient Egypt and Assyria. But earlier episodes in the Bible, such as the deeds of the patriarchs, the exodus from Egypt, the conquering of the promised land of Canaan by Joshua, the glorious reign of King David, the magnificent palace of Solomon, have left almost none of the traces that archaeologists had expected to find.

Some details even conflict with the evidence outright. From dates given in the Bible, principally that the exodus from Egypt took place 480 years before the start of construction of Solomon's temple, the period of the patriarchs can be placed between 1000 and 2000 B.C. A well-known episode in that period is when Joseph's jealous brothers, about to kill him, decided instead to sell him to passing Ishmaelites riding camels in a spice caravan headed for Egypt. But camels were not domesticated until shortly before 1000 B.C. and did not become common until well after that time. Trade with Arabia in balm and myrrh flourished between 900 and 600 B.C. These telling details would have been familiar to someone writing around 622 B.C., say, but are an anachronism when set in events alleged to have occurred some 1,400 years earlier.[167]

The most substantive evidence contradicting the story of the promised land comes from archaeology. Joshua's conquest of Canaan and sacking of its cities should have left telltale ruins datable to around 1200 B.C. Some 40 cities that the Bible says were conquered by Joshua have now been identified and excavated. Only at three have archaeologists found possible evidence of pillage at the right date. Jericho at that time had no walls to fall at the blast of Joshua's trumpet. "There was simply no Israelite conquest of most of Canaan," says Dever.[168]

But if there was no conquest of Canaan, there was no exodus from Egypt. Perhaps a small group of people escaped, and their story became extended to apply to everyone, but the Israelites as a people did not escape from captivity in Egypt. They did not spend 40 years traversing the Sinai desert nor did their army conquer Canaan. There is no need for a Moses, and the fact that his name is not mentioned in the earliest reference to the exodus, Miriam's song of the sea (Exodus 15), could suggest he is a later construct. The same may be true of Joshua, given that his feat of conquering the promised land seems to belong to legend, not history.[169]

So if the Israelites never invaded Canaan, how did they come to occupy it? Because they were Canaanites and always had been. That is the conclusion at which archaeologists have finally arrived after many decades of bafflement. "The recent archaeological evidence for indigenous origins of some sort is overwhelming," says Dever.[170] According to Kugel, "As contemporary scholars have wrestled with earlier theories, as well as with new archaeological data, most of them have come to agree on one point: at least a good part of what was to become the future nation of Israel had probably always been there—or, to put it somewhat sharply, 'We have met the Canaanites and they are us.' "[171]

The central theme of the Hebrew Bible is that Yahweh intervened in history in order to free the Israelites from captivity in Egypt, lead them across the desert and deliver the promised land into their hands. But this uplifting theme is not supported by the available historical and archaeological evidence.

What is going on here? What were those who put the Bible together trying to accomplish? A recent interpretation that combines new archaeological data with the scholars' textual analysis has been offered by two archaeologists, Israel Finkelstein and Neil Asher Silberman. Their thesis may not persuade all of the experts in the field, but it makes sense of many of the known facts.

First, they believe it was not just Deuteronomy that was "found" during the temple renovation in 622 B.C. but rather the whole first half of the Hebrew Bible comprising both the Pentateuch (Genesis, Exodus, Leviticus, Numbers and Deuteronomy) and the group of books known as the Deuteronomic History (Joshua, Judges, 1 and 2 Samuel, 1 and 2 Kings).

This collection of works appeared at a special moment in history. During the Iron Age (1150–586 B.C.), the Israelites lived in two small kingdoms, those of Israel and Judah, set in the region's central hill country. The two kingdoms led a precarious existence because they lay in a buffer zone and battleground between the two regional superpowers of the time, ancient Egypt to the west and Assyria to the east.

In or around 722 B.C., the kingdom of Israel was destroyed after Hoshea, the last king, defied the Assyrians. The Assyrian king Sargon II records how he resettled 27,000 Israelites in Assyria and repopulated

Samaria, the capital of Israel, with people from elsewhere in his empire. Many other Israelites migrated to the southern kingdom, Judah, and the population of its capital, Jerusalem, then a modest highland town, increased fifteenfold.

A century later a major shift in the balance of power in the region led Assyria, between 640 and 630 B.C., to withdraw from Palestine. Seeking to take advantage of the new situation, Jerusalem planned to regain the territory of the northern kingdom and unite it with Judah's. The Bible was its political and religious strategy for doing so.

On the political front, the Bible presented a stirring nationalist theme, that the Israelites had left Egypt in the exodus, conquered Canaan, and established a glorious unified kingdom under kings Saul, David and Solomon. It would be legitimate for the current king of Judah, Josiah, to take over the remnants of Israel, ran the Bible's message, because he would be reestablishing the united kingdom of David.

On the theological side, the Bible argued for centralizing Yahweh-worship in Jerusalem, for national observance of Passover and other festivals, and for suppression of local cults, which the Bible's authors saw as symbolic of chaotic social diversity.

The Bible's message of political and theological unification was reinforced with a thorough rewriting of history. The Israelites had been defeated by the Assyrians whenever their kings had affronted Yahweh by worshipping other gods, the Bible stated. They had enjoyed political success, and would do so again in the future, as long as they worshipped Yahweh correctly, as specified in the book of Deuteronomy. "In what can only be called an extraordinary outpouring of retrospective theology," write Finkelstein and Silberman, "the new, centralized kingdom of Judah and the Jerusalem-centered worship of YHWH was read back into Israelite history as the way things should always have been."[172]

History, unfortunately, did not take the course the Bible's authors had hoped for. Before Josiah could unite the two kingdoms, he was killed in battle in 610 B.C. by the Egyptian pharaoh Necho II. A few years later the Assyrian empire itself was shattered by the Babylonians. The new

Babylonian king, Nebuchadnezzar, set out to reconquer the territory the Assyrians had held. He captured Jerusalem in 597 B.C. Following a rebellion he destroyed both the city and its temple in 587 B.C. and deported much of the population of Judah, with many prominent citizens, to Babylon.

These unexpected events required an explanation of why, if Josiah was as righteous as the Bible had said, he and his people suffered such a harsh fate. The Pentateuch and Deuteronomistic History were revised during or after the exile, and the new edition supplied an explanation. The turn of events was blamed on Manasseh, who had been king of Judah from 698 to 642 B.C. Because Manasseh had resisted religious reforms and reintroduced pagan worship into the temple, Jerusalem and Judah were to be destroyed, said a prophecy inserted into the first edition's text.

Wasn't this a little harsh on Josiah, who was hardly responsible for his predecessor's transgressions? Another insert to the revised edition explained the bleak reward for Josiah's piety. The prophetess Huldah conveyed to him this message from the Lord God of Israel: "Behold therefore, I will gather thee unto thy fathers, and thou shalt be gathered into thy grave in peace; and thine eyes shall not see all the evil which I will bring upon this place."[173]

Though the Bible failed in its political goal of uniting the two kingdoms, it succeeded beyond measure in creating a sacred text that bound believers together in a common purpose. The Israelites would surely have disappeared as a distinct people, along with the Midianites and Amonites and Moabites, had they not grown into a cohesive community through allegiance to their new sacred text.

The text elicited in the strongest possible way the innate propensity for religious behavior. It satisfied the desire for contact with the supernatural by providing, in place of trance dances, a more intellectually satisfying alternative in the form of prophets who had communed with the deity. It furnished a theological explanation for the historical disasters that continued to rain down on a small people caught between warring superpowers. It wove the deeds of the deity into a historical narrative, embedding a supernatural presence into ordinary human affairs. An elaborate system of rituals and sacrifices allowed the faithful to believe they could manipulate Yahweh's behavior to their advantage. And Judaism required a set of demanding rituals and behaviors, in particular circumcision and a ban on marrying foreigners, that kept the community confined to committed believers.

The binding force of the new religion was almost too strong. Jews resisted Roman rule and the requirement for adherence, or at least lip service, to the Roman state religion. They were drawn into a succession of disastrous revolts against Roman rule, which led to the destruction of Jerusalem and the second temple by the Roman general Titus in A.D. 70. But Judaism also preserved Jews as a people during the diaspora around the Mediterranean world, a process already in train but accelerated by the loss of the temple. And remarkably, Judaism inspired two major sects, Christianity and Islam, as well as more recent offshoots such as Mormonism, all of which have claimed access to their own special revelations that update and improve on that of the Old Testament.

## The Rise of Christianity

Judaism, both before and for some time after the Babylonian exile, was not just a religion but a system of belief constructed around a specific political goal, the restoration of a Davidic kingdom centered on the temple at Jerusalem. In general form it resembled most other religions of settled societies of the period, which were essentially tribal religions shaped so as to reinforce the authority of the ruler.

These tribal religions had been successfully adapted to the social cohesion problems faced by archaic states. They were less suitable for large, polyglot polities such as the Roman empire. Roman emperors were well aware of the cohesive properties of religion and insisted that subject peoples acknowledge Roman gods and engage in emperor worship, though they were free to have whatever other religion they wished.

But Roman religion was largely one of outward observance and was not a compelling faith for many people. Many competing sects, originating from the Romans' subject peoples, spread into this creedal void. The worship of the goddess Isis spread from Egypt to all corners of the Roman empire. The wild priests of Cybele, with their public self-castrations, amazed and shocked the Roman public. Gnosticism was popular among sophisticated urban elites of the first century A.D. The strange mystery cult of Mithras took hold among Roman soldiers but quickly disappeared after a peak of popularity in the third century A.D. "The Darwinian image is appropriate: the central and eastern Mediterranean in the first and second centuries AD swarmed with an infinite multitude of religious ideas, struggling to propagate themselves," writes the historian Paul Johnson.[174]

The most successful of these competing sects was a new version of Judaism. Well before the destruction of the temple in A.D. 70, Jews had set up thriving communities in the major cities of the Roman empire. In Antioch, Tarsus, Ephesus, Alexandria and Rome, Jews had synagogues, and freedom of association, and were accorded considerable privileges. They were exempted from the official emperor worship and allowed to make sacrifices instead.

These expatriate Jewish communities were influenced not only by Judaism but also by the powerful ideas of ancient Greek literature and philosophy. They spoke Greek, which had become the lingua franca of the eastern Mediterranean in the fourth century B.C., and were so Hellenized that many no longer spoke Hebrew. They used a special translation into Greek of the Old Testament, known as the Septuagint, which differed frequently from its original.

These Hellenized Jews of the first century B.C. were unlike their counterparts in Judaea in several ways. They were a sophisticated urban elite, whereas the Jews in Judaea were a more rural population, centered on the Jerusalem temple's main activity, that of serving as a vast sacred abattoir for sacrificial cattle. The Jews of the Septuagint were more interested in spreading their religion than were the Jews of the Hebrew Bible. And the population of expatriate Jews seems to have been around 4 million, far outnumbering the 1 million Jews in Judaea.

This vibrant network of urbanized, Hellenized Jewish communities probably provided the fertile ground in which Christianity spread so widely within the Roman empire. Several special factors then eased the transmission of Christianity from the expatriate Jewish community to Roman citizens at large. The Hellenized Jews were well integrated into Roman society, in which they enjoyed special status. Jewish ethics and commitment to charity were noticed and well regarded in the Roman world. "Jews were admired for their stable family life, for their attachment to chastity while avoiding the excesses of celibacy, for the peculiar value they attached to human life, for their abhorrence of theft and their scrupulosity in business," writes Johnson.[175] Because of the attractions of the Jewish faith, an important class of non-Jews had sought and received membership in synagogues. Known as God-fearers, they did not have to be circumcised but were affiliated in various degrees with Jewish worship.

The Hellenized Jews and the God-fearers would have been the most receptive audience for Christianity, a creed that claimed continuity with Judaism. The sociologist Rodney Stark, after doing fieldwork with modern religious movements such as the Moonies and the Mormons, noted that missionary efforts are most likely to yield results when pursued within existing social networks. People often convert if approached by or through close friends or family members. Cold calls seldom succeed. This is much as would be expected on the evolutionary assumption that religious behavior evolved as a means of group cohesion: there is good reason to follow the same rituals as one's friends and families, none to adhere to that of strangers unless one is seeking to assimilate with them.

Stark considers that Christianity too must have spread through already existing social networks. These would naturally have been the networks between the Jews of Judaea and those elsewhere in the Roman empire. The expatriate Jewish communities were used to visiting teachers from Jerusalem. Even though the apostle Paul declared that his mission was to the gentiles, it would have been the Hellenized Jews and God-fearers who were most receptive to his message.

It is clear from Acts of the Apostles and Paul's epistles that there was a tussle in the early church between those who wished to remain in the Jewish fold and those, like Paul, who sought to broaden the appeal of the new sect beyond ethnic Jews by dropping barriers to entry such as strict observance of Jewish laws including circumcision.

At first Paul's opponents, based in Jerusalem, seemed likely to prevail. They set in motion the train of events that led to Paul's transfer in custody to Rome, where he is believed to have been executed in or shortly after A.D. 64 during the emperor Nero's crackdown on Christians. The little sect, numbering at most a few thousand, would in the normal course of events have doubtless been reined in by the authorities in Jerusalem. But in the disaster of A.D. 70, many of the Jerusalem-based members of the early church perished. The central focus of Christian activity passed from Jerusalem to the large group at Rome. They and the Jewish communities in Antioch, Alexandria and other Roman cities now had a free hand to shape the new faith as they thought best.

Evidence that the early missionaries focused their efforts on expatriate Jewish communities comes from the following facts, Stark argues. Many of the converts mentioned in the New Testament can be identified as Hellenized Jews. Many of the New Testament's quotations come not from the Hebrew Bible but from the Septuagint. And archaeological evidence shows that the first Christian churches outside Judaea tended to be in the Jewish quarter of Roman cities.[176]

Jews of the diaspora "provided the initial basis for church growth during the first and early second centuries," Stark estimates. They were a significant source of Christian converts until about A.D. 400, and Jewish Christianity remained significant for another century. How could the diaspora community, with a population of just 4 to 5 million people, have had such an impact on the rise of Christianity? The number of Christians was very small for 250 years. But if there were 1,000 Christians in A.D. 40, and if the community grew by 40 percent per decade, which is close to the

43 percent growth rate per decade achieved by the Mormon church over the last century, then the population growth would have been as follows, Stark calculates[177]:

A.D. 40: 1,000
50: 1,400
100: 7,530
150: 40,496
200: 217,795
250: 1,171,356
300: 6,299,832
350: 33,882,008

Two factors that may well have spurred such a striking growth of early Christianity were its social cohesion and the high birthrate induced by its doctrines. The cohesion of the Christians was evident even to their enemies. Celsus, an anti-Christian writer of the second century A.D., commented on their close-knit structure, even though he attributed it to their fear of persecution. The Christians' willingness to help one another was particularly noticeable in a society like that of the Roman empire which was severely lacking in social services. Living conditions in Roman cities were appalling, since most people lacked proper sanitation or heating systems. Buildings frequently collapsed. Major disasters like fire, earthquake, famine or epidemics ravaged the major city of Antioch once every 15 years during the 600 years of Roman rule.[178]

The numbers of Christians started to increase because of the ethical attraction of the new creed and its provision of a mutual assistance network that provided better social services than those on offer from the Roman authorities. But there was a more decisive factor that drove the Christians' swelling population: they achieved a far higher fertility rate.

The population of the Roman empire was failing to reproduce itself. As early as 59 B.C., Julius Caesar had passed a law awarding land to the fathers of three or more children. The falling birthrate was of increasing concern to Roman emperors, who had to rely on mercenaries to fill the army's ranks. The reasons for declining fertility were not obscure. Female infanticide was common. Husbands could order their wives to have abortions, which often ended in the mother's death or infertility. Homosexuality was common; Roman and Greek cities maintained large numbers of male prostitutes. Many different methods of contraception were practiced. "It is notable too," observes the historian Sarah Pomeroy, "that the woman with a small rump was not considered desirable, owing, no doubt, to the practice of anal intercourse which was also a useful method of contraception."[179]

All these practices, with the possible exception of contraception, were forbidden by the new creed. Fertility among Christians presumably rose as a result although its exact contribution to demographic increase cannot be estimated. "All that can be claimed," says Stark, "is that a nontrivial portion of Christian growth probably was due to superior fertility."[180] The role of religion as a significant demographic force is discussed in a later chapter.

Roman emperors frowned on the threat to social order posed by the Christians' growing numbers and by their refusal to sacrifice to Roman gods. But even as the emperors sporadically persecuted the Christians, they came to perceive the need for an improved state religion and cast about for deities more compelling than the Roman pantheon. Astrology was one of the swirl of new beliefs competing for the Roman public's allegiance. Aurelian, a successful general who restored the empire's territorial integrity in the late third century, made Sol, the sun god, the principal divinity of the Roman pantheon, with the intent of giving citizens throughout the empire a single god to worship in addition to their local gods.

Diocletian, one of Aurelian's successors a few decades later, also favored unity of religion, but under the traditional Roman pantheon. He first suppressed the Manichaeans and then, in 303, launched against the Christians the severest persecution to which they had yet been subjected.

But the campaign did not last long. Diocletian was eventually succeeded by Constantine, who reversed the policy. In his Edict of Milan of 313, Constantine granted tolerance for all religions. He showed many favors to Christianity and was the first emperor to become a convert. In pursuit of his interest in having Christianity serve as a unifying imperial creed, he convened the Council of Nicaea in 325 to deal with the heresy of Arianism and to settle unresolved issues such as the date of Easter.

Constantine's support of Christianity may have been as much a political decision as a matter of personal faith. Though he built two churches in his new capital city of Constantinople, he also placed a statue of the Sun god, bearing his own features, in the forum, as well as a statue of the cult goddess Cybele.[181] Nor did he make Christianity the official religion of the empire, though he paved the way for his successor to do so; in 380 Theodosius made Christianity and belief in the Trinity, as defined by the Nicene Creed, the religion of the Roman state. The emperors' interest in a cohesive religion was probably a decisive factor in the eventual success of Christianity. "It is possible, therefore, to speculate that Christianity achieved its success in the empire in part because it answered best to the empire's need for a universal religion with which it could identify itself," writes the church historian Henry Chadwick.[182]

In just 300 years, a tiny cult from a population that regularly defied Roman rule had grown to become the dominant religion of the empire. What made the new religion so attractive to so many?

## The Shaping of Christianity

Early Christianity has two distinctive features that greatly influenced its later development. The first is that its founding prophet of record seems to have had little or no intention of founding a new religion. The second is that, whereas Jesus' language was Aramaic, Hebrew in his time being no longer a spoken language, the founding language of Christianity was Greek. Somehow, in the transition zone between these two strong cultures, a powerful new religion took shape.

Despite the occasional sparring with Pharisees depicted in the gospels, Jesus seems to have been a conventional Jew, observant of the Jewish law. "Think not that I am come to destroy the law, or the prophets: I am not come to destroy, but to fulfil," he says in Matthew.[183] E. P. Sanders, an authority on the New Testament, concludes: "In view of the indisputable fact that Jesus thought that the Jewish scripture contained the revealed word of God, and that Moses had issued commandments that should be followed, we should be very hesitant to accept the common view of New Testament scholars that he had actually opposed the Jewish law."[184]

Jesus urged people to repent before an imminent catastrophe heralding the kingdom of God but seems to have had little interest in spreading his views beyond the world of Judaism. He instructed his apostles, "Go not into the way of the Gentiles, and into any city of the Samaritans enter ye not. But go rather to the lost sheep of the house of Israel."[185] Later, a command to "teach all nations" is attributed to him but only after the resurrection.[186]

In Sanders's view, Jesus' interest in gentiles was secondary to his interest in Jews, being perhaps related to the idea that if Israel was to regain its former greatness, it would help if gentiles worshipped the same god. The writers of the four gospels believed in the mission to the gentiles, yet do not cite much support for it. "What is striking is that the evangelists had so few passages that pointed towards success in winning Gentiles to faith," Sanders notes.[187]

After his death the leadership of Jesus' movement passed into the hands of his brother James and the apostle Peter. Many scholars have pointed to deep differences between the beliefs of the Jesus movement and those of what might be called the Christ movement, which after 300 years eventually became the dominant form of Christianity in the Roman empire. The Jesus movement remained restricted to Jews who followed the Torah's rules. They believed Jesus was a human prophet, not a god, born of human parents; they had no use for the concept of the virgin birth. Their sacred text was a version of Matthew's gospel translated into Aramaic but without the passages on the virgin birth.

Adherents of the Jesus cult became known as Ebionites. A closely related sect known as the Nazarenes survived until at least the fourth century. The idea of Jesus as a human prophet, sent by a single god, is strongly reminiscent of Islam. Indeed, the Qur'an refers to Christians as al-Nasrani, an archaic term used by East Syrian churches. The Ebionites were condemned as heretical by the victorious Christ movement and slowly faded from the historical record. "We do not know when they ceased to exist," writes the religious historian Barrie Wilson. "Perhaps, some speculate, they were absorbed into Islam, which shares some of their views of Jesus—as human, teacher, and prophet." [188]

The Christ movement, in contrast, saw Jesus as a divine being whose death and resurrection, as in the mystery cults prevalent in the Roman empire, was celebrated by symbolic consumption of the god's sacrificial body. Jews expected the prophesied messiah of the Hebrew bible to be a human prophet with the temporal role of evicting the Roman occupiers. But in translating the word *messiah* into Greek—both *mashiah* and *christos* mean "anointed"—the framer of the Christ movement made Jesus into a god who was heir to a heavenly kingdom, not an earthly one.

The framer was presumably Paul, from the internal evidence of the New Testament documents. Unlike the Jesus movement, which was directed to Jews, required strict observance of Jewish laws and operated in Aramaic, Paul addressed his Christ movement to the Greek-speaking gentiles of the Roman world. He dropped the requirements of circumcision and observance of Jewish law. Paul in his letters refers very little to Jesus' life or teachings. His most important statements, such as those concerning the eucharist and resurrection, are based on his personal revelations and not from information about Jesus from those who had known him. "But I certify to you, brethren," Paul tells the Galatians, "that the gospel which was preached of me is not after man. For I neither received it of man, neither was I taught it, but by the revelation of Jesus Christ." [189]

During the first three centuries A.D., many different religions and brands of Christianity competed with one another. Christianity slowly displaced the mystery cults that were its rivals, helped by the fact that the

Christ movement had adopted the cults' central idea of a sacrificial god and grafted it onto the ancient religious heritage of Judaism. The Christ movement prevailed over the Jesus movement, many of whose members perished in the siege of Jerusalem in A.D. 70, and all the other early brands of Christianity, until it was chosen as the state religion of the Roman empire by Constantine and Theodosius.

Just as the victors usually write the history books, it was the inheritors of Paul's Christ movement who shaped the New Testament to support their version of Christianity. Many documents about Jesus and his followers were in circulation during the first three centuries of the Christian era. The Gospel of Peter seems to have been one of the most popular, to judge by the number of surviving fragments.[190] But like many other documents, it was rejected by the compilers of the official record.

Their selection of books apparently did not become final until the mid-fourth century A.D. when the list of books now in the New Testament was first mentioned by Athanasius, the patriarch of Alexandria, in a letter of A.D. 367. If these books had been arranged in order of their date of composition, the letters of Paul would have come first, given that all the authentic ones were written before A.D. 70, and the four gospels, all of which were written after A.D. 70, would follow. But that would have given the impression, which the compilers of the New Testament presumably sought to avoid, that Paul shaped Christianity as a religion for gentiles and loosely tied it to the person of Jesus, an orthodox Jew interested only in making a minor adjustment to Judaism. By placing the lives of Jesus first, the compilers lent support to the official story, that Jesus was the founder of Christianity who sent his disciples and apostles to preach the gospel to Jew and gentile around the world.

The New Testament's book of Acts records the disagreement between the leaders of the Jerusalem church, who wanted recruits to obey Jewish law in all respects, and proselytizers such as Paul who understood the new cult's great potential in the world outside Judaea if it could only break free from the ethnic barriers, such as circumcision and the rigorous Jewish dietary laws, that restricted it to Jews. The author of Acts also implied that the differences between the two movements were patched up, which seems not to have been the case given the very different directions taken by Paul and the Jesus movement. But by implying a resolution, the book of Acts helps to graft Pauline Christianity onto the Judaic rootstock of the Jesus movement.

Because the writers of the New Testament took such care to integrate their work with Judaic belief, it is hard at this remove to appreciate the Greekness of Christianity. All the books of the New Testament were originally written in Greek. Jesus (Iēsous) is the Greek form of Yeshua or Yeshu, his name in Aramaic. Because Greek was the lingua franca of the eastern Roman empire, all early church services outside Judaea took place in Greek, even in Rome. Followers of Jesus were first called Christians in the Hellenistic city of Antioch. The Hebrew Bible was read and referred to in its Greek translation, the Septuagint. Only around A.D. 200 did Roman congregations start holding services in Latin, retaining even then such Greek phrases as *kyrie eleison*—"Lord have mercy."

Not only was the culture of early Christianity Greek but several of its central beliefs have little or no counterpart in Jewish thought. They were, however, perfectly familiar in the Greco-Roman world of the first two centuries A.D. One is the worship of a mother and child, as in the ancient cult of the Egyptian goddess Isis. She is often shown as suckling her infant son Horus, who was conceived by a virgin birth. The Isis cult was popular throughout the empire, particularly in Rome during the first century B.C. The church in Egypt co-opted the cult, plagiarizing its iconography to depict mother and child in the now familiar image of the virgin and Jesus.

In the world of early Christianity, the Egyptian church—now known as the Coptic church—was very large and its patriarchs in Alexandria rivaled those of Constantinople and Rome for influence. It was they who pressed for a stronger role for the virgin in Christian worship and theology. "The Egyptian patriarchs, Theophilus and Cyril, led the Greek world," writes the historian Peter Brown. "The Council of Ephesus in 431, in declaring that Mary was the *Theotokos*—'She Who gave birth to God'—

ratified the fervour of the Copts, who had worshipped her as such, suckling the new-born Jesus. This prototype of the most tender scene in
medieval art was a Coptic adaptation of Isis suckling the infant Horus."[191]
The figure of Isis and Horus "is so like that of the Madonna and child that
it has sometimes received the adoration of ignorant Christians," noted
the anthropologist James Frazer.[192]

A prominent feature of several popular mystery cults of the time was
the theme of a god who dies and is later resurrected, as in the cults of
Dionysus or of Attis and Cybele. The common idea, presumably inherited from the dawn of agriculture, was of a vegetation god who dies in
autumn and must be resurrected in the spring with appropriate ritual.
Followers of Dionysus, the god of wine, would tear apart a live bull—
or occasionally a person—and eat the flesh raw, in commemoration
of the killing and resurrection of the god. As for Attis, he was born of
a virgin—his mother Nana conceived by placing a ripe pomegranate in
her bosom—and his death and resurrection were celebrated at a spring
festival at which his followers shed copious amounts of blood through
self-mutilation.[193]

Mithraism, a religion with a large following among Roman army
officers, included among its rites "sacred meals not unlike the Christian
eucharist and offers souls a way through the seven planetary spirits which
bar the ascent to the Milky Way after death," writes Chadwick.[194]

A follower of any of these mystery cults, whether of Adonis, Isis, Mithras, Dionysus or Attis, would have recognized many familiar elements in
Christianity, such as the virgin birth, the death of the god, the springtime
resurrection festival, and the symbolism of the eucharist in which celebrants consumed bread and wine that were taken as representing the
body and blood of the sacrificial god.

Given that Jews are strictly forbidden to taste blood, which must be
drained away before an animal can be eaten, it would have been strange
indeed for Jesus, an observant Jew, to recommend that his disciples should
drink his blood, even symbolically.[195] Indeed in a very early description of
the eucharist, that of the Didache, also known as "The Teaching of the

Twelve Apostles," no such symbolism is indicated nor is any connection made with Passover or the resurrection. Celebrants are told simply to give thanks "for the holy vine of thy servant David which thou has made known to us through thy servant Jesus" and similarly for the broken bread.[196] The Didache, known to the early church fathers but excluded from the New Testament canon, was lost for many centuries and rediscovered only in 1873. It is so unlike other Christian literature that scholars have not known how to date it. But its strangeness may arise from its early date: it seems to come from or reflect a period before Christianity had taken its final form.

What then is the origin of the communion rite or eucharist? The earliest description in the New Testament appears in the apostle Paul's first letter to the Corinthians. Paul, a Jew born around A.D. 5 in Tarsus in present-day Turkey, was doubtless familiar with the several mystery cults then popular in the Roman world. He was a forceful advocate of spreading Jesus' message to non-Jews in the world outside Judaea, as the Roman province was then known.

His seven authentic letters in the New Testament were probably composed between A.D. 49 and 55, and several decades before the four gospels which scholars generally agree were all written after the destruction of the Jerusalem temple in A.D. 70.[197] Paul had met in Jerusalem with members of the Jerusalem church who knew Jesus, including the apostle Peter, and might be expected to have heard from them of the eucharist service. But he attributes his knowledge of it directly to Jesus: "For I have received of the Lord that which also I delivered unto you," he writes in introducing his account of how the eucharist should be conducted.[198] Since Paul never met Jesus, he implies the information was imparted in a personal vision, perhaps similar to the one on the road to Damascus in which Jesus instructed him to cease his persecution of Christians.

Some scholars suggest Paul's phrase means that he was handing on his account through the authorization of the church, or that he meant just to emphasize its authenticity. But the simplest construction is that he means he received the account through direct revelation. If so, the rite was an idea of his own which the gospel writers later followed. They did not, however, use Paul's unfortunate name for the rite—*kuriakon deipnon* or "lordly meal"—which was apparently the same phrase as used for sacred meals in the mystery cults.[199] They called it instead the eucharist, a Greek word meaning thanksgiving.

At the very least, the early church had two versions of the eucharist. In one, there was a simple benediction for food and wine, similar to Jewish blessings, and an invocation of Jesus. In the other, the mystery cults' central idea of a sacrificial and resurrected god is elegantly fused with the conventional benediction, generating a powerful rite attractive to both cultists and Christians.

It is perhaps possible to catch a glimpse of another element under construction in the case of the resurrection. The Didache might be expected to mention the redemptive resurrection of Jesus but does not do so. The earliest document in the New Testament to describe the resurrection is again a Pauline epistle, his first letter to the Corinthians. He says that Jesus, after his resurrection, "was seen of Cephas [the apostle Peter], then of the twelve: After that, he was seen of above five hundred brethren at once; of whom the greater part remain unto this present, but some are fallen asleep. After that, he was seen of James; then of all the apostles. And last of all he was seen of me also, as of one born out of due time."[200] The letter was probably written in A.D. 49 or 52.

Paul, certainly on his own behalf, is describing a vision of a spiritual resurrection, and he makes no distinction between the form of his own experience and those he attributes to others. But by the time of the gospels, two decades or more later, the spiritual resurrection described by Paul had been solidified into a bodily resurrection, possibly to quench objections from Jews who criticized the idea. The treatments of the resurrection in the gospels bear some indications of being later additions to the main texts.

Mark, the earliest gospel, seems to have been written after the fall of Jerusalem in A.D. 70. Mark and an inferred lost document, known as Q, are the principal sources for Matthew and Luke, both of which were probably written between 70 and 100. Mark is therefore the second earliest source after Paul for the events of Jesus' life. Most scholars are agreed, however, that the last 12 verses of Mark, which describe Jesus' appearance to his disciples after his death, are a later addition. Of its 163 Greek words, 19 do not occur elsewhere in the gospel, suggesting it is by a different author.

The status of the last 12 verses, Mark 16:9–20, also worried Eusebius, the first historian of the early church and a critic who influenced the selection of books that were to be accepted into the New Testament. The authentic text of Mark seems to end after the first 8 verses of chapter 16, which relate how Mary Magdalene and others visited Jesus' tomb, only to find it empty except for a young man who told them Jesus had risen and would be seen in Galilee. Eusebius, writing at some time between 290 and 340, was aware that some versions of Mark contained the extra 12 verses and some did not. The latter, he said, were the more accurate. "The accurate copies, at least, fix the end of Mark's account at the conversation with the young man. . . . It is in effect at this place that the end has been marked in almost all the copies of Mark's gospel; the things which follow, which are transmitted by some rare copies, and not by all, could be super-fluous. . . ."[201] The tradition of the early church held that Matthew was the earliest gospel, which is why it is placed first in the canon. Eusebius, who would presumably have considered Matthew to be the prime source, may therefore not have realized the significance of Mark's testimony to the resurrection. For if so striking an event goes unmentioned by the ear-liest gospel, it has perhaps less credibility in later ones.

Christianity is a complex set of beliefs and practices. There is little reason to think that all are necessarily drawn from a single religious tra-dition. The date of Easter coincides with Passover, itself adapted from a spring agricultural festival. The birth of Jesus is celebrated at the winter solstice, the date when devotees of the Roman sun god, Sol Invictus, cel-ebrated the sun's rebirth.[202] Sunday is a day of rest in Christian countries because in 321 the emperor Constantine himself declared it should be so—in honor of Sol Invictus. It seems likely that the early church, with the aim of attracting new followers, may have appropriated some of the beliefs as well as the symbols and ceremonial dates of other religions. The Christian Holy Week and Easter resembled the Attis cult's Day of Blood and the Hilaria, days marking the death and the resurrection of Attis. Both festivals had an all-night vigil with lights and were so similar that pagan critics of the fourth century accused the church of plagiarism.[203]

Judaism is a religion that generates an extraordinary degree of cohesion. But it was and is confined by its practices to a single ethnic group. The framers of Christianity saw how a mystery cult adaptation of the Jewish religious tradition could be made to transcend Judaism's tribal boundaries. They succeeded so well that they captured an empire and defined a civilization.

## Origins of Islam

Two centuries of scholarship have uncovered much of the historical background of Judaism and Christianity. As described above, the steps by which Judaism was molded from a Canaanite agricultural cult into a state religion are reasonably clear. So too is how Paul fused Judaism with elements of the mystery cults to create a powerful new faith, one so attractive that Roman emperors eventually embraced it as a unifying imperial creed.

Islam, the third great monotheism, has long resisted such analysis. The Qur'an is presented as a revelation that is not to be doubted. Islamic history includes an explanation of why the Qur'an has no history—the caliph who compiled the canonical version is said to have ordered all earlier manuscripts to be destroyed. Most scholars believe that the corpus of Islamic historical writings, though of varying reliability, holds the essential facts of Islam. Only recently have a few researchers started from the position that all Islamic writings are suspect as historical accounts and that the historical origins of Islam first must be sought in non-Islamic sources.

The documentary evidence for the origins of Islam consists of the Qur'an; the interpretations of it, known as Tafsir; the Sirah, or lives of Muhammad that also record the development of the Islamic state; and the Sunna, statements that justify points of Islamic law, together with the Hadith, or sayings attributed to Muhammad. Textual analysis of these documents has lagged behind that of the Old and New Testaments, and Western scholars have differing views on the degree of historical weight that should be accorded to the corpus of Islamic writings.

Traditionalists believe that the collection of Islamic documents, although full of internal inconsistencies, contains essential historical truths, which can be extracted by diligent study. A small number of revisionists, also known as rejectionists, view the documents as "salvation history," or nonhistorical literature designed to wrap a theological message in historical trappings; they see non-Islamic sources and archaeology as more reliable evidence of the period. "It is not generally appreciated," writes the Islamic historian Patricia Crone, "how much of our information on the rise of Islam, including that on Meccan trade, is derived from exegesis of the Qur'an, nor is it generally admitted that such information is of dubious historical value."[204] According to another historian of the Islamic world, Jonathan Berkey, "The reader should at least understand that the usual accounts of the origins of Islam are based on sources of dubious historical value."[205]

Here, for instance, is a recent account, based on the traditionalist method, of the battle of Yarmuk of A.D. 636. Islamic sources hold the battle to have been a turning point in the Arab conquest of the Byzantine empire's holdings in the Near East. "The battle of Yarmuk is, along with the battle of Qadisiya in Iraq, one of the major conflicts that has come to symbolize the Muslim victories in the Fertile Crescent," writes the historian Hugh Kennedy. "As with Qadisiya, the Arab accounts are extensive and confused and it is difficult to be clear about exactly what happened. There is no contemporary or reliable account from the Byzantine point of view."[206]

The revisionist view of the event is this: there is confusion among the

Arab accounts of this allegedly crucial battle, and no Byzantine account, for a simple reason—there was no battle of Yarmuk, nor indeed an Arab conquest.

The revisionist view of early Islamic history is described in more detail below because, if true, it furnishes a case study of how a religion can be adapted with great success to a state's purposes. The conclusions of this minority view may not yet be widely accepted, but its methodology of giving serious weight to archaeology, and to non-Islamic texts, seems a reasonable approach.

According to traditional Islamic history, Muhammad converted his followers to Islam before his death in 632. The first caliph Abu Bakr, ruling from Mecca in the Hijaz, the western region of the Arabian peninsula, directed Muslim armies northward to conquer the Near Eastern provinces of the Byzantine empire in the name of Islam. Many have noticed the parallel between this account and that of the Hebrew Bible; Muhammad, like Moses, died in the desert without seeing the Promised Land, and Abu Bakr, like Joshua, was the trusted general who implemented the prophet's design.

The revisionist view is different. Arabs didn't invade Syria and Palestine because they were already there, say Yehuda Nevo, an archaeologist at the Negev Archaeological Project, and his colleague Judith Koren of the University of Haifa. And the Arabs could not have been Muslims at that time; the word *Islam* does not appear in history until inscriptions on the Dome of the Rock in Jerusalem, built in 692, and its meaning even there is disputed.[207]

The policy of the Byzantine empire was to settle Arab tribes in border areas of Syria and Palestine, both to prevent them from raiding and to rely on them for defense. Eventually the Byzantines decided to withdraw altogether from their Near Eastern provinces, establishing their line of defense just south of Antioch in northern Syria. In 632 they even stopped payments to their Arab allies. Syria and Palestine were on their own.

The Arabs who had been settled in those provinces found that they had only to push and one territory after another fell into their hands.

There was a struggle for dominance between rival Arab tribes until one ruler, Mu'awiyah, defeated all the others. Coins suggest he was the first Arab ruler, reigning from Damascus from 661 to 680. No caliph's name before Mu'awiyah is mentioned in non-Islamic manuscripts, meaning that there is no independent evidence of their existence. And if there was a great invasion "it would seem that, at the time, nobody noticed," Nevo and Koren assert.

A similar conclusion has been reached by Peter Pentz, an archaeologist at the National Museum of Denmark, who describes the Arab takeover as "the invisible conquest" because of the lack of historical or archaeological evidence to support the Muslim accounts of invasion.[208]

The proposal that the Arab takeover came about through an uprising in place, not an invasion from Mecca, would ease several geographical problems in the traditional account. Archaeological and literary evidence shows that some early mosques in Iraq and Egypt were oriented to an unknown sanctuary in northwest Arabia, not toward Mecca.[209] The Hijaz was very sparsely populated during the period. Though the traditional account portrays Mecca as a thriving trade center, the historian Patricia Crone has shown it did not lie on the trade routes from Yemen and is not mentioned by the classical geographers.

The Qur'an itself has several details that point to its composition in a setting farther north. Muhammad's opponents are said to have grown grain, olives, grapes and dates, but Mecca is unsuitable for any kind of agriculture. The pagans are invited to reflect on the destroyed cities of Lot's people, given that "you pass by them in the morning and in the evening," suggesting a location near the Dead Sea.[210]

A broader point is that the Qur'an assumes its readers are familiar with the Pentateuch and the Psalms. It contains many polemical passages, which give the impression of having been developed within a rich environment of Christian-Jewish theological discourse. The Hijazi desert seems less likely as the locale for this development than somewhere in the more populous regions of Palestine, Syria or Iraq. "Islam is obviously part of the Semitic monotheistic tradition and must have arisen within its matrix, and it is not futile to attempt to define rather more precisely how that happened," writes G. R. Hawting, a historian at the London School of Oriental and African studies.[211]

The canons of both the Old and New Testaments took shape over several centuries before being frozen in their present forms. It would be no surprise if the same were to be true of the Qur'an. But the traditional account allows little leeway for such a process. In traditional belief, the Qur'an was dictated by an angel to Muhammad, preserved on palm leaves, flat stones and in people's memories, and assembled from these disparate sources within a few decades of Muhammad's death in 632; whereupon the Caliph 'Uthman, who had directed that a standard text be prepared, "gave orders to burn every leaf or codex which differed from it."[212] In the revisionist view, the process took much longer, and at least in part in the setting of sectarian religious communities somewhere in Palestine, Syria or Iraq.

The founder of the revisionist school was John Wansbrough, a historian at the London School of Oriental and African Studies whose principal works were published in the late 1970s. After a textual analysis of the Qur'an, Islamic interpretations of the Qur'an, and the Sirah, he concluded that all belong to the genre of "salvation history," meaning that the writing is a literary description of religious events, not a historical account. Without independent corroboration, a historian simply could not assess how much of the Islamic corpus corresponded to fact. "With neither artifact nor archive, the student of Islamic origins could quite easily become victim of a literary and linguistic conspiracy," Wansbrough wrote.[213]

Wansbrough concluded that the Qur'an was assembled over a long period of time and probably did not take final form until around 800, more than 150 years after Muhammad's death. The interpretations of the Qur'an, called Tafsir, and other Islamic documents were shaped with a specific purpose, in his view: "*Tafsir* traditions, like traditions in every other field, reflect a single impulse: to demonstrate the Hijazi origins of Islam."[214] The insistence that Islam originated in the Hijaz, in Wansbrough's view, suggested there had been an internal debate, now lost, as to whether or not that was the case.

Why should the Qur'an and Muhammad's life have been located in the Hijaz if in fact the origin of both was elsewhere? The revisionists' proposal is that the shapers of the Qur'anic canon, who were perhaps scholars working under the caliphs, believed the prophet of the new religion would fittingly have had an Arabian identity and needed to have lived in a place that clearly distanced Islam from both Judaism and Christianity.

Wansbrough's work is not widely known, in part because of the obscurity with which he wrote. One scholar has accused him of "relentless opacity," a charge against which even his admirers may be reluctant to defend him.[215] His ideas are known mostly through the writings of his students and others. Following up on his work, the historians Patricia Crone and Michael Cook reviewed all the non-Islamic sources they could find and tried on that evidence to reconstruct early Islamic history.

Accounts from the 640s in Syriac, the version of Aramaic spoken in Syria, refer to the Arabs as *Mahgraye*, which can be rendered as Hagarenes—descendants of Hagar—in English, and the equivalent word *Magaritai* appears in Greek sources. Crone and Cook suggested the roots of Islam lay in Hagarism, a Jewish-Arab movement to repossess Jerusalem from the Byzantines, whom both peoples had reason to resent. But after Jerusalem was captured, the Arabs broke with their Jewish allies and entertained an alliance with Christianity instead. The rapprochement was temporary but is vividly captured in the surprisingly pro-Christian inscriptions on the Dome of the Rock in Jerusalem. The rulers of the new Arab empire then decided they needed to develop a faith of their own, independent of both Judaism and Christianity.

Nevo and Koren have developed a different perspective on Islamic origins. From study of coins and inscriptions on rocks and buildings, they have defined a period of Arab monotheism during which writings often included the *tawhid*, the assertion that Allah is the one god, which was intended to contradict the Christian belief in the Trinity. Strangely, the earliest *tawhid* inscriptions make no reference to Muhammad. The first known historical reference to Muhammad may occur on an Arab-Sassanian coin minted in Damascus in 690/691, depending on how the coin's legend—*muhammad rasul allah*—is translated. "Muhammad is the messenger of Allah" is the obvious translation but another, to be considered later, is "The messenger of God is to be praised."

Even if the coin does refer to Muhammad, its date is 70 years after the Islamic era began, according to the traditional account, with the migration or hegira of Muhammad and his followers to Medina in 622. "Before 71 A.H. [After the Hegira] he is not mentioned; after 72 A.H. he is an obligatory part of every official proclamation," Nevo and Koren write, using the Islamic dating system.[216]

Mu'awiyah, the first Arab ruler recorded by non-Islamic sources, and his eventual successor, 'Abd al-Malik, had created a large state, most of whose subjects were Monophysite or Nestorian Christians. Now they needed a unifying religion. All early documents about the formation of the Qur'an have disappeared. One very interesting text that reflects the emergence of Islam survives. It is made not of paper but of stone, and was completed probably in 692, many decades before the earliest known copy of the Qur'an. Constructed by 'Abd al-Malik on the site of the Jewish temple in Jerusalem, the Dome of the Rock, like other early Islamic buildings, does not face toward Mecca. It has eight equal sides, which point if anywhere to itself as the center of worship.

The octagon's outer inscription contains statements that are mostly in the Qur'an and a few that are not, such as "There is no God but Allah alone, he has no associate (*lā ilāha ilā llāh wahdah, lā sharīk lahu*)." These phrases suggest that the text of the Qur'an had not yet been finalized. The inner inscription addresses the interminable Christian disputes as to whether Jesus' nature was human, divine or some admixture of the two. 'Abd al-Malik takes what Nevo and Koren characterize as the Judeo-Christian position, that Jesus was a true prophet but merely human. His inscription expresses, in another non-Qur'anic statement, the highest respect for Jesus: "Allah, incline unto your messenger and servant Jesus son of Mary and let peace be upon him the day he was born and the day he dies and the day he shall be raised alive." The inscription continues, in mostly Qur'anic language, "The following is the truth about Jesus son of Mary, about whom you dispute: why should Allah acquire a son?"

The Dome of the Rock inscription had several purposes, Nevo and Koren write. "It called for an end to dissension, and for the population to unite into one community under their caliph, now firmly in control after several years of civil war. As the reason and justification—and framework—for this communal consensus, it presented an official religion: a form of Judaeo-Christianity, with particular emphases. To this end it took issue with, and rejected, the tenets of Trinitarian Christianity. And finally, it set within this framework an element which became the focal point of that religion—the Arab prophet."[217]

Nevo and Koren raise the possibility that the Arab prophet did not in fact exist, based on their speculation that the word *muhammad*—which is used only 4 times in the Qur'an, compared with 79 mentions of Abraham, 136 of Moses and 24 of Jesus—could have meant "the chosen one" and was not in this context a proper name. Their inference is that the corpus of Islamic literature consists of layer upon layer of stories each of which builds further detail about the life and sayings of the chosen one, developing a personality, biography and whole salvation history from a single word.

There is indeed an accretionary process evident in Islamic writings, whereby a later writer is somehow able to supply the interesting historical details which an earlier writer had neglected to include. "If one storyteller should happen to mention a raid, the next storyteller would know the date of this raid, while the third would know everything that an audience might wish to hear about it," writes Crone. Thus the Islamic historian Al-Waqidi, born in 748, relates far more copious information about Muhammad's life than does the earlier historian Ibn Ishaq, born in 704. "No wonder that scholars are fond of al-Waqidi," Crone writes: "Where else does one find such wonderfully precise information about everything one wishes to know? But given that this information was all unknown to Ibn Ishaq, its value is doubtful in the extreme. And if spurious information accumulated at this rate in the two generations between Ibn Ishaq and al-Waqidi, it is hard to avoid the conclusion that even more must have accumulated in the three generations between the Prophet and Ibn Ishaq."[218]

Crone, however, rejects Nevo and Koren's suggestion that the entire life of Muhammad has sprouted from a mere title, saying Muhammad's existence is well attested by several early texts, including an Armenian chronicle written in 660 and ascribed to a Bishop Sebeos. "Most importantly," she adds, "we can be reasonably sure that the Qur'an is a collection of utterances that he made in the belief that they had been revealed to him by God."[219] Nevo and Koren, on the other hand, say the reference to Muhammad in Sebeos's history is probably "a later explanation added by a copyist who saw that Sebeos did not know what he was talking about."[220]

Estelle Whelan, a critic of Wansbrough and the rejectionist school, argues that the Dome of the Rock's inscriptions that appear to be non-Qur'anic are abbreviations of the canonical text, made to fit the limited architectural space. Nevo's failure to find any mention of Muhammad in early Arabic inscriptions in the Negev simply reflects the fact that Islam was developing far away in the Hijaz, Whelan argues.[221]

The Arab prophet may have lived, as Hawting suggests, somewhere within the matrix of Judeo-Christian monotheism, but if so the locale of his ministry, at some stage during the development of the Qur'an, was transferred from Palestine or Syria or Iraq to the purely Arab background of the Hijaz.

## An Alternative Hypothesis About Islam

The Islamic era began in 622, a date held to mark Muhammad's flight from Mecca to Medina. But why is this era dated to a mere shift of residence rather than to the prophet's date of birth, for instance? The year 622 was indeed of the greatest significance in the Arab world, but for a reason that has been allowed to recede from historians' sight: it was the date on which Arab independence began.

For a century beforehand the Byzantine empire had been locked in a generally losing struggle with the Sassanid rulers of Iran. The Arab populations of Syria, Mesopotamia and Iran were caught in the middle of these rival power centers, both of which set up and manipulated vassal Arab buffer states. The Byzantines controlled the Ghassanids in Syria while the Sassanids were allied with the Lakhmid dynasty based in southern Iraq. In terms of the complicated Christian politics at the time, the Ghassanids were Monophysite Christians (Christ has only one nature—divine) whereas their Byzantine patrons were Chalcedonian (Christ has two natures, one divine, one human). The Lakhmids, on the other hand, were Nestorian Christians (Christ has not two natures in one person but two persons, one human, one divine).

What happened in 622 was that the Byzantine emperor Heraclius, a superb commander, decisively defeated the Sassanid army under its great general Shahrvaraz, who seven years earlier had captured and sacked Jerusalem. The defeat was so devastating that the Sassanid empire collapsed a few years later. But the Byzantine empire also had systemic weaknesses and Heraclius, rather than taking possession of the captured buffer states, simply withdrew from them. For the first time, the Arab peoples in the region were on their own. Their first ruler, who was naturally a Christian like his people, certainly recognized the importance of 622: he measured his reign from this foundational date, and a Greek inscription in his name at Gadara (in present-day Jordan) records the year in terms of *kata Arabas*—Greek for "according to the Arabians."

All this is by way of historical background to a new statement of the revisionists' thesis which takes their position much farther than before and directly contradicts traditional accounts of the first century of Islamic history.

The revisionists, it should be noted, constitute a small minority of the scholars in this field, and their arguments have not yet been seriously addressed or subjected to the academic cut and thrust through which new ideas are tested. If extraordinary claims require extraordinary proof, the revisionists have so far provided more of the first than the second. Their position should probably at this stage be regarded as no more than a hypothesis. But their approach of testing Islamic literature against independent historical evidence is perfectly reasonable and justifies a hearing for their views from both Muslim and Western scholars.

In a new book, *The Hidden Origins of Islam*, a collection of essays edited by Karl-Heinz Ohlig, a historian of religion, and Gerd Puin, an expert on Qur'anic paleography, the revisionists substantially extend the position described in the previous section. The Umayyad dynasty, in their view, were the first Arab rulers, there being no non-Islamic historical evidence for the existence of earlier ones. And the Umayyads, the revisionists say, were Arab Christian rulers who asserted, as against the Byzantines' doctrine of the Trinity, that there was only one God and that Jesus, a mere human, was his messenger.

The first Arab leader who began to seize the reins of power in the void between the two exhausted regional superpowers was Mu'awiyah, the founder of the Umayyad dynasty. The sign of the cross appears on one of his inscriptions and on his coins, according to the Oriental numismatist Volker Popp.[222] He based his capital at Damascus in order to proclaim himself protector of the shrine of John the Baptist, said to be buried there. Given that in the traditional Islamic account Mu'awiyah is the fifth caliph, the difference between the revisionist and Islamic positions is evident.

The remarkable quiescence with which the populations of Syria, Palestine and Egypt yielded to Arab rule, and the strange absence of evidence for an Arab conquest, become much easier to account for under the premise that Mu'awiyah and his eventual successor 'Abd al-Malik were Christians. These peoples would have been yielding to Christian Arab rule, not to Muslim Arab conquest, and had no particular reason to fear that Christian Arabs would be worse masters than the widely resented Byzantines.

Mu'awiyah was a vigorous leader who launched a sustained though ultimately unsuccessful attack on Constantinople, which was beaten back with the first use of the Byzantine naval weapon known as Greek fire. Internally, the principal political problem that faced him and his successor, 'Abd al-Malik, was that of how to unite the Arab populations under their rule. As noted, those in the eastern parts of their domains were Nestorian Christians, and those in the west were either Monophysites or Melkites (adherents of the Byzantines' Chalcedonian rite).

Looking for a unifying creed that all could subscribe to, 'Abd al-Malik chose a generic phrase that in essence meant no more than "Praise Jesus!" The exact wording of this phrase in Arabic is of great significance but the theological context in which 'Abd al-Malik placed it needs first to be outlined.

Since around 1000 B.C., the lingua franca of the eastern Mediterranean had been the Semitic language known as Aramaic and later as Syriac. Displacing Hebrew, Aramaic became the language of Jesus and of the Jews. Aramaic/Syriac was also the language of the early church in Syria. It long remained the liturgical language of the region and was so used by the Arabs under 'Abd al-Malik's rule, even though in daily life they spoke Arabic.

Because the early Christians of Syria spoke the same language as the Jews, they were particularly open to Jewish influence and to the belief of some Jews that Jesus was no god but just another in the honored line of Jewish prophets. Syriac-speaking Christians thus had little sympathy for the trend being developed in Hellenistic Christianity to endow Jesus with divine as well as human aspects. They had no enthusiasm for the concept of the Trinity, first made official by the Council of Nicaea in A.D. 325, or for the interminable debates about the nature of Christ that followed from this strange, unbiblical doctrine.

In defining a unitary creed for Arab Christianity, 'Abd al-Malik seems to have reached back to this early Syriac tradition of Jesus as a plain human prophet and used it to oppose the Trinitarian approach of Hellenistic Christianity. In the "Praise Jesus" motto he put on his coins and in his great building, the Dome of the Rock at Jerusalem, he referred to Jesus, the revisionists say, as the "messenger of God."

Thus in Arabic, 'Abd al-Malik's unifying motto about Jesus was rendered as *muhammadun rasūl allāh*—"The messenger of God is to be praised." *Muhammadun* is a gerundive, meaning "one who should be praised," *rasūl* is "messenger" and *allāh* is "God."

To anyone with a passing knowledge of Islam, this is a central phrase of the faith and has an entirely different meaning—"Muhammad is the messenger of God."

What proof is there that 'Abd al-Malik meant *rasūl allāh* to refer to Jesus? The proof, say the revisionists, is unambiguous and is provided by the inscriptions that 'Abd al-Malik had written inside the Dome of the Rock. "*Allāhum sallī alā rasūlika wa 'abdika īsā ibn maryam*—God bless your messenger and servant, Jesus son of Mary" states the text on the inner northwest-north face of the octagonal arcade. The inner, east-southeast face includes the words, "*Inma l-masīh 'īsā ibn maryam rasūlu llāh*—For the Messiah Jesus, son of Mary, is the messenger of God."

The next sentence conveys 'Abd al-Malik's anti-Trinitarian message: "So believe in God and his messengers, and do not say 'three.' Stop that—better for you. For God is one, unique—may he be praised! How could he then have had a child?"

The Dome of the Rock's inscriptions include the phrase *muhammadun 'abdu llāhi wa-rasūluhū*, traditionally translated as "Muhammad is the servant of God and his messenger." But in the view of the revisionist who writes under the pseudonym of Christoph Luxenberg, the intended meaning is "The servant of God, his messenger, is to be praised," the subject being Jesus.[223]

The inscriptions also contain the first known use of the word *Islam*, traditionally understood to mean submission to God. But in Luxenberg's view it means simply conformity or agreement, in this case to the "book" mentioned in the inscription. This book is traditionally taken to be the Qur'an but, given what Luxenberg sees as the entirely Christian context of the inscriptions, it must in his view refer to the Gospel.

The revisionists thus assert a radical and, if true, astonishing recon-struction of the genesis of Islam. The religion, in their view, began as the faith of an Arab Christian empire, rooted in the Syriac Christian tradi-tion. At least the first two rulers of the new empire, and maybe others, were Christians, and its principal edifice, the Dome of the Rock, was a Christian place of worship, asserting the Syriac Christian view that God is one against the Byzantine concept of the Trinity. In place of the Byz-antine empire's system of dating years from the birth of Christ, the new Arab rulers constructed their own, starting from the year of their inde-pendence from their Byzantine and Sassanid overlords. "Long before the idea of a Hijra," writes Karl-Heinz Ohlig, "there was an Arabian-Christian reckoning of time which began with the year 622 and which was only later 'converted' to a Muslim meaning. Until approximately the end of the eighth century, so it seems, Arabian-Christian tribal leaders governed the regions of the Near East and of North Africa; indeed, the Umayyad leaders and even the early Abbasids were Christians."[224]

How then did Islam begin? Its genesis, in the revisionists' view, lay in a change of dynasty. The Umayyad dynasty to which Mu'awiyah and 'Abd al-Malik belonged was overthrown around 750 by the Abbasids, who had little respect for their predecessors' accomplishments, including their religion. The Abbasids desecrated the Umayyads' tombs and made Mecca the holy city in preference to Jerusalem or Damascus. God remained one but at some time under the Abbasids, perhaps during the rule of the caliph Al-Ma'mun (813–833), even the Umayyads' prophet was Arabized: Jesus and the gospels receded and in their place an Arabian prophet and his own revelation were emphasized.

The framers of Islam, in the revisionists' reconstruction, simply appropriated the early history of Arab Christianity to their own purposes. They, just like the editors of the Pentateuch, "retrojected their religion into a 'canonical' time of beginnings, in which they then grounded and legitimated it," writes Ohlig. Mu'awiyah's era of the Arabs was switched to years after the Hegira, which had to start at the same time, the year 622. 'Abd al-Malik's unifying formula "Praise the messenger of God" was reinterpreted as "Muhammad is the messenger of God." The Dome of the Rock was declared to be an Islamic building, and the Abbasid caliph Al-Ma'mun substituted his name as the builder in place of 'Abd al-Malik's.

The architecture of the Dome of the Rock and many other mosques is drawn from a kind of Byzantine church called a martyrium, designed for the display of sacred relics. "If you take a Middle Byzantine martyrium, and take out the icons and images—which is roughly what the iconoclasts did during the eighth century—what you are left with looks uncannily like a mosque," writes the historian Philip Jenkins. [225]

The origin of the Qur'an, in the revisionists' view, is obscure, but it is probably derived from a Syriac Christian liturgical work. "Qur'an" itself is in origin a Syriac word (*qeryān*) meaning lectionary, a selection of holy texts. According to Luxenberg, some of the many obscure passages in the Qur'an become clear if the Arabic text is transliterated back into Syriac with correction of likely copying errors. The original version of the Qur'an "was put together entirely in the Syriac script," he declares.[226]

Most of the Qur'an's statements about Jesus and Mary seem to be derived from gospels that were popular in the Near East but were excluded from the New Testament, such as the story found in the Infancy Gospel of Thomas about the infant Jesus breathing life into a clay bird.

The assertion of a Syriac Christian background for the Qur'an would, if verified, provide a historical context for the emergence of Islam, more plausible to some than the traditional Islamic view that the sacred text was dictated by an angel. But a weakness in the revisionists' case is that they lack evidence about the wholesale appropriation process they allege. In their defense they cite the traditional Islamic account that the caliph 'Uthman, in producing a standard edition of the Qur'an, ordered all earlier manuscripts to be destroyed; this destruction, they suggest, would have included the Syriac antecedents of the Qur'an and all available evidence of Umayyad Christianity. The Dome of the Rock and its inscriptions survived only because they were misunderstood, Luxenberg writes.

If the Umayyad inscriptions refer to Jesus, as the revisionists contend, then what is the historical basis for the life of Muhammad? In Luxenberg's view, scholars must in future distinguish between two Muhammads, the first of whom is Jesus. He writes: "The inscription on the Dome of the Rock cannot be used to defend the position that 'Muhammad II' lived from 570–632 CE, as the 'Muhammad' named there was entirely referring to Jesus, the son of Mary, that is, 'Muhammad I.' It is the task of historians to discover whether 'Muhammad II,' about whom the 'Sira' has so much to report, actually lived shortly before the appearance of the biography of the prophet (ca. mid-eighth century), or whether he should be seen merely as a symbolic figure."[227]

Whatever the eventual outcome of the differences between the revisionist and traditional historians as to the origins of Islam, the new Arab religion served its purpose with striking success. It provided the emerging Arab rulers with an effective religious identity to uphold against that of the Byzantines. The new religion inspired fervent loyalty. It was evidently well suited to the needs of the early Arab empire, enabling the Umayyads and then the Abbasids to unite many different peoples in an empire that stretched from Spain to the borders of India.

## Religion and Borders

Religious behavior evolved to knit a tribe together. As such it reinforced other affiliative behaviors, such as those based on kinship, ethnicity or language. There is perhaps a natural tendency for each of these binding behaviors to maximize its overlap with the others, producing the most cohesive possible society.

In language, for instance, dialects form very fast because people in each region or village tend to develop their own special variations on a parent tongue. Before travel became common, these minor variants would have served instantly to identify strangers who might be spies. Kinship was also adjustable, at least among hunter gatherers and primitive farmers. When groups grew larger than 150 or so people, quarrels tended to break out and the group would split, usually along kinship lines, with the result that the average degree of relatedness in the two new groups was higher than before. "There appears to be an upper limit to the size of a group that can be cooperatively organized by the principles of kinship, descent and marriage, the integrating mechanisms characteristically at the disposal of primitive peoples," writes Napoleon Chagnon, a social anthropologist who has worked for many years with the Yanomamo of South America.[228]

Until the advent of archaic states and empires, religions too may have been mostly congruent with tribal and linguistic boundaries. Within larger empires, however, a single religion may split along political lines into rival sects if it proves too weak to unite the empire's many regional interests and cultural differences. The Roman empire imposed an undemanding state religion on all its subject peoples, while generally allowing them to practice their own religions as well. But the old Greek and Roman rituals had been shaped for smaller societies. They were challenged by ecstatic religions from the eastern provinces before yielding to Christianity. But even the new faith could not bind the vast empire that now circled the shores of its private sea, the Mediterranean.

Fissures erupted in Christianity, along the fault lines that separated people by language, ethnicity and politics. The Bishop of Rome and the Patriarch of Constantinople had different binding problems, not least of which were the political forces that divided their congregations. The doctrinal dispute over the word *filioque*—an addition to the Trinitarian Nicene Creed implying that Jesus enjoyed the same level of divinity as God— was perhaps a convenient excuse for the western and eastern branches of Christianity to shape versions of their common faith that would define their mutual antagonism. A second major schism, Protestantism, also took place along fault lines of language and ethnicity, dividing the Germanic language countries (Germany, Holland, Scandinavia, England and Scotland) from Romance language powers (Italy, France and Spain).

The Islamic empire faced similar issues. Iran, a major part of its eastern conquests, was an ancient nation that had vied with the Greeks, the Romans and the Byzantines. Its people were not Arab and spoke an Indo-European language. After the Sunni-Shi'a split developed in Islam, Iran in 1501

adopted a Shi'a identity that differentiated it from the mostly Sunni populations to its east and west. Its religion, ethnicity and language were thus
brought into congruence, probably a necessary step for a large polity with
many different ethnic minorities to maintain its overall cohesion.

Though new religions are derived from old ones and seek, as it were,
to steal their clothes, the promoters of a new religion are often at pains to
differentiate it from its predecessor. An obvious instance is that Christianity and Islam, both derived from Judaism, have separated themselves from
it liturgically. Both religions accept the week (borrowed by Judaism from
the Babylonians) as the unit of religious time but choose Sunday and Friday
respectively as their principal holy days, in distinction to the Jews' Saturday.
Since the Last Supper before the crucifixion was a Passover meal, the date of
Easter should be linked to that of Passover, but the early Christians severed
the link, at least in part to distance themselves from Jewish practice.

LOOKING BACK AT THE emergence of the three monotheisms, a striking process is evident: throughout history, religion has been repeatedly
reshaped to serve new needs as the nature of society changed. And this
reshaping, brought about by daring cultural innovations, has taken place
within a superbly flexible genetic framework, a set of propensities for religious behavior.

Hunter gatherer religion is based on implicit negotiation with supernatural agents whose requirements make members of a community
behave in socially cohesive ways. The principal form of interaction with
the supernatural world was sustained communal dances and the trances
through which the agents of the other world could be encountered.

Then came settled societies, grappling with the uncertainties of early
agriculture. They recentered their religions on the cycle of the seasons
and the demands of planting and harvesting. The dances were entrained
into agricultural festivals like the early Canaanite predecessors of Passover and Rosh Ha-Shanah.

As human populations expanded in the Neolithic age that began

10,000 years ago, social hierarchies replaced the egalitarianism of the hunter gatherer bands. Priests took over the organization of religious activities and enhanced their power by monopolizing access to the supernatural. Much larger numbers of people could now be brought under the sway of the sacred.

With the invention of writing 5,000 years ago, ideas about the supernatural were put into written form and a sacred text became a standard component of urban religions. In around the seventh century B.C., Judaism, an amalgam of ritual, history and an irredentist political agenda, became the first modern religion, replacing the usual miscellany of special purpose deities with a single divine being, and making direct interactions with the supernatural a matter of past history, not present experience.

This new religion was just as effective as its hunter gatherer predecessors in binding a community together, even though the community in this case was not a hunting band but a small nation. Inspired by their religion, Jews rebelled repeatedly against their Roman occupiers. Thereafter, during 19 centuries without a homeland, Jewish communities depended for survival on the cohesion provided by their faith.

For all its strengths, Judaism had a severe limitation. It was a religion of the tribe, tied to a single ethnicity by circumcision and its dietary laws. With Christianity and later Islam, religious behavior proved adaptable to a much larger role, that of uniting people who had few other bonds.

The Hellenistic Jews who shaped a more permissive version of their faith created in Christianity the first universal religion, one that came to bind the many different nations of the Roman empire and its Christian successors.

Islam achieved a similar success. Mu'awiyah and 'Abd al-Malik needed a universal religion to bind together all the disputatious Christian sects within the new Arab empire and to hold its own against the faith of their adversary, the Byzantines.

With the emergence of the three monotheisms, the tree of religion took what has been close to its final shape, at least in the West, for the last, 1500 years. The powerful civilizations of Christianity and Islam

dominated the Mediterranean world and the Near East, tolerating Judaism but allowing no new rival to appear. The tree's principal new growth
has been in sects emerging within Christianity and Islam including, most
recently, the exotic flower of Mormonism. But human societies have
changed vastly in the last 1,500 years. Because religion has not changed as
fast, it has found itself in increasing conflict with modernity. Early peoples
used religion as an explanatory framework for understanding physical
and biological phenomena, like weather or disease, that are now better
explained by science. Religions have not always ceded this ground grace-
fully. New religions that might have been more compatible with the rise
of scientific knowledge have not been allowed to emerge because established faiths have blocked the process of religious innovation in which
they themselves were created.

Historians and political scientists tend to see religions as simply one
component of culture. But they are much more than that. They knit societies together, and with particular power when they overlap with other
integrative forces such as ethnicity and language. Religions may in fact be
essential for social cohesion. No society yet known has lasted long without a religion. The Soviet Union endured a mere 70 years. To be sure, it had
other problems, but the fact remains that it tried to extirpate religion, it
failed to do so, and the Orthodox rite is once again Russia's official faith.

Religion plays a vital role in societies old and new because, as discussed in the three chapters ahead, it shapes morality and trust and the
institutions that depend on them, such as trade and commerce; it strongly
influences reproductive behavior and demographic growth rates; and it
is intimately involved in many aspects of a society's severest test, that of
warfare.

# 8

---

# MORALITY, TRUST
# AND TRADE

*Thus religious or magical behavior or thinking must not*
*be set apart from the range of everyday purposive conduct,*
*particularly since even the ends of the religious and magical*
*actions are predominantly economic.*

MAX WEBER[229]

*Lastly, those are not at all to be tolerated who deny the being*
*of a God. Promises, covenants, and oaths, which are the bonds*
*of human society, can have no hold upon an atheist. The*
*taking away of God, though but even in thought, dissolves all;*
*besides also, those that by their atheism undermine and destroy*
*all religion, can have no pretence of religion whereupon to*
*challenge the privilege of a toleration.*

JOHN LOCKE, *A Letter Concerning Toleration*, 1689

The philosopher John Locke, in common with many of his day, believed religion was integral to the working of society. Society might allow different Christian sects to exist but atheists, he wrote in his *Letter Concerning Toleration*, could not be tolerated: their oaths and promises were worthless because without fear of divine punishment they had no reason to keep them.

Locke's conception of the social fabric—that people trust one another because they know others will keep their promises from fear of divine punishment—has been held throughout history and is still widely believed today. The idea is not without basis. The extent to which people observe moral constraints is heavily influenced by religion. So too is the level of trust in a society, which in turn affects the costs of transactions and the operation of an economy. Because religion shapes the quality of the social fabric, it may have a greater influence than commonly acknowledged on modern economies.

In ancient and medieval societies, religion pervaded almost every action, in particular the exchange of goods and services. In modern states, secular institutions have taken over many of religion's roles, masking the central place it held in social life until recent times. Yet religion retains, even in modern economies, an essential role in establishing the trust on which all economic transactions ultimately depend.

## Religion and Trade in Early Societies

In the economies of primitive societies, which lacked modern institutions for regulation and enforcement, religion played a central part in supporting trade and commerce. One of the most remarkable instances of religion undergirding an economy was the Kula exchange system of the Trobriands, part of the Melanesian islands that lie off the east coast of Papua New Guinea.

The Kula consisted of two parallel transactions, one ceremonial and the other commercial. The first was based on gifts of immense prestige but no commercial value or utility, exchanged between partners in far distant islands who were bound in a lifetime bond of giving and receiving ceremonial gifts. The meetings in which the gifts were exchanged also served as the occasion for bartering commercial goods between the

islands. Presumably the high standards of honor and obligation in ceremonial exchange also governed the commercial exchange since the same
partners were involved in both.

The Kula, a remarkably elaborate institution for a primitive society,
involved thousands of individuals and fleets of up to 80 sailing canoes
which traversed islands hundreds of miles apart and separated by dangerous seas.[230]

The ceremonial gifts of the Kula were of two kinds. One was armbands made from a species of large shellfish; the other was necklaces,
crafted from disks of red shell. The gifts were traded in opposite directions around the ring of participating islands, with the necklaces going
clockwise and the armbands counterclockwise.

The armbands and necklaces were so precious and unique that
each had its own name. Possession of one conferred enormous prestige
on the owner. But the gifts could not be kept. The recipient of a famous
armband had to regift it after a few weeks or months to his exchange
partner in the next island counterclockwise in the ring. In return, he
would in due course receive a necklace, judged by his partner to be of
equal value.

A gift might take 2 to 10 years to make the full circuit of islands in
the Kula ring. Though the same gift reappeared several times in a person's lifetime, the participants on each island had little notion of how the
whole system worked. "Not even the most intelligent native has any clear
idea of the Kula as a big, organized, social construction, still less of its sociological function and implications," writes Malinowski, the anthropologist who has provided the most detailed account of the Kula.[231] (It could
of course be the case that many intelligent Americans and Europeans
have no clear idea of the complex institutions that underpin their own
economies.)

The Kula armbands and necklaces were gifts, so no haggling was
allowed. Everyone was on his honor to give in due course a gift of equal
value for one received. The bartering channel was kept entirely separate
in people's minds, even though the fleets that brought the ceremonial

gifts also carried items of trade. These included such essentials of Melanesian life as cassowary and parrot feathers, obsidian, fine sand for polishing
ax blades, red ochre, boars' tusks, wooden dishes, combs, pots, mussel
shells and ebony spatulas.

All these items were traded by barter. A comb that might be exchanged
for 4 coconuts in the Trobriand Islands, in the northwestern sector of the
Kula trading ring, would fetch 4 coconuts and a bunch of betel leaves in
Dobu, an island some 50 miles to the south.

The Kula exchange was a prominent part of the islanders' lives.
The arrival of a fleet from a neighboring island was a big event. Months
would be spent each year in building new canoes and patching up
old ones. The whole system was deeply embedded in religious concepts.
Magic incantations were required to keep the canoes safe, make them
light when heavily laden, and avert the many dangers of sailing. The
inhabitants of Kitava Island, to the east of the main Trobriand island,
wielded special magic that controlled the southeasterly wind, while those
in the Lousançay Islands on the other side were masters of the northwestern winds.

Magical protection was doubtless a comfort because the Kula fleets
faced many dangers. The shallow seas between the islands are full of reefs
and sandbanks. The crews of canoes shipwrecked on strange shores were
liable to be killed by the inhabitants. Canoes forced into the open ocean
by wind or currents were unlikely ever to return.

There were other dangers, perhaps less tangible but just as much
feared. The *kwita*, a giant octopus the size of a village, lay in wait beneath
certain waters. If it attacked a canoe it could be assuaged only by sacrificing any young boy who might be aboard. There were *yoyova,* flying witches,
and vast jumping stones that leapt out of the ocean. For those who might
drift north of the Trobriands, there was the much dreaded land of Kaytalugi, inhabited by women whose lust was so intense that no man could
survive their favors.[232]

The islanders of the Kula ring braved all these hazards for the sake of
their trading system, a seamless blend of religion and economics.

In the view of the sociologist Marcel Mauss, the Kula system of the Trobriands, like the potlatch ceremonies of Indian tribes of the Pacific Northwest, demonstrated the power of gifts to drive large-scale systems of exchange in primitive societies. Goods of all kinds—dried fish, canoes, or slaves—could be included in the potlatches, which were in essence large-scale regional exchange systems between various tribes such as the Kwakiutl and the Haida.

The gifts had thick strings attached, compelling the recipient to return an item of the same or greater value at an appropriate interval, or else suffer serious loss of social status. "An obligation to give is the essence of the potlatch," Mauss wrote. A chief could only preserve his authority by proving he was so favored by good fortune that he had a bounty of gifts to give away. Since every receiver had to reciprocate at a later date, the net result was a large exchange of goods. "It is therefore a system of law and economics in which considerable wealth is constantly being expended and transferred," Mauss noted.[233]

The exchange systems among the Trobrianders and the peoples of the Pacific Northwest enabled goods to be traded but on a nonmonetary basis. The exchanges were driven not by profit but by honor, meaning the maintenance or accumulation of social prestige. They were regulated, in essence, by the gods whose retribution was feared for any failure to recip- rocate. "Where does the system get its energy? In each case from individu- als who are due to lose from default heaping obloquy on defaulters and from beliefs that the spirits would punish them," writes the anthropolo- gist Mary Douglas.[234]

The roots of this honor-based trading system may be very ancient. The first settled societies may have generated agricultural surpluses not for nutrition but to exchange in return for honor and power, advantages of greater interest to them than extra food. Religious behavior too may have had an ancient role in securing the regimen of trust under which such exchanges could take place.

In the view of the anthropologist Roy Rappaport, religious behavior may have evolved in step with language as a way of offsetting language's power to deceive. The greatest internal threat to early societies would have been freeloaders and cheaters, people who took from others while giving less in return. As language evolved, freeloaders' ability to take advantage of others would have increased, threatening the stability of society. Religion, in Rappaport's view, offered a truth-testing function to offset the freeloaders' lies. In primitive societies without any central authority, "the sanctification of norms goes far to insure that they are honored," Rappaport writes. "Sanctity, thus, is a functional equivalent of political power among some of the world's peoples."[235]

The idea of the sacred is of central importance to the working of society because it helps certify the symbolic statements made in certain ritual contexts. Any secular statement may be a lie, but a statement made in a ritual context is presumptively true, and supernatural sanctions will follow should it prove otherwise.

Expectations of sacredness are usually induced by holding rites in a special place, such as a cave, grotto, temple or cathedral, decorated with symbols that mark it as hallowed ground. The words of a liturgy are recited not because they convey new information—to the contrary, they are deeply familiar to everyone—but because they reevoke the congregants' feelings of awe at communing with higher powers and their sense of communion with one another and society.

"We are inclined to think that sacred texts, canonical texts, have in themselves an intrinsic meaning and are by nature qualitatively different from other texts, but this is an error," writes the sociologist of religion Robert Bellah. "In fact, sacred texts must be read or listened to in the context of a community for which they are sacred: it is in the ritual practices of a living community that they become sacred. Ritual is the place where meaning occurs. . . . The ritual of reciting the Lord's Prayer reiterates the meaning of our worship of God."[236]

Besides their function in ritual, the sacred texts or narratives may include a cosmology that explains people's place in the world, sets out a framework for the moral code, and justifies the punishments inflicted for transgressing it. A set of beliefs common among Australian Aborigines holds that the landscape and its features were created by men who lived in the Dreamtime. This, in the Aborigines' view, is a long-ago epoch that continues in parallel with the present. By performing the appropriate rituals, living men can become the heroes for a brief time and participate in the Dreamtime. The actions of the Dreamtime heroes are full of moral examples, including their punishment for misdeeds such as incest. Among literate peoples religion performs the same role except that moral codes are made explicit in written texts such as the Ten Commandments or the Sermon on the Mount.

Belief in omniscient and punitive supernatural powers is a feature of most religions and, as discussed in chapter 3, seems likely to be an innate part of the mind's furniture. The belief helps enforce compliance with a society's prevailing codes of behavior. Each religion provides its own version of these supernatural deities and a list of the offenses that may be expected to trigger their wrath. Rites like confession help refresh congregants' sense of guilt and reliance on priests for intercession with angry deities.

Primitive religions held that the gods inflicted disease and disaster as punishment for flouting their rules. The religions of advanced societies extended the roster of punishments from this world to the afterlife as well. The dramatic escalation of penalties, from temporal to eternal, was perhaps necessary because in large settled societies crime and religious skepticism were more frequent.

The worlds of the sacred and of the profane may seem direct opposites but in fact are intimately linked. It is the social bonds created by worship that have long made trade and commerce possible.


## Religion and Trust

In modern societies goods are exchanged largely for profit, not honor, transactions are regulated by law, and compliance is ensured by courts. Religion is no longer required to underwrite commercial transactions and secular institutions seem to have taken over its role in maintaining the social fabric. But this is not really the case. The law, police and courts are invoked only as a last resort and their use imposes heavy transaction costs. The basis of all normal transactions, social or commercial, remains that of morality and trust.

Economists generally assume that the only human behavior relevant to their subject is self-interest. Their mantra has been Adam Smith's well-known saying that "it is not from the benevolence of the butcher, the brewer, or the baker, that we can expect our dinner, but from their regard to their own interest." But some economists and other social scientists have begun to take an interest in the moral underpinnings of economics, arguing that market exchanges only work because people tend to act virtuously. "In fact, our open, self-organizing economic system, which some of us describe in shorthand as 'free enterprise,' is effective only because most of the time most of its participants abide by internally motivated 'positive' values, such as trustworthiness, fairness, and honesty," write Oliver Goodenough and Monika Gruter Cheney.[237]

Trust is of particular importance for large modern societies in which people deal frequently with strangers, not their kin or neighbors, and must routinely place themselves or their assets in unknown hands, hoping they will not be taken advantage of. When trust is high, social and economic transactions proceed easily and efficiently.

A major role of religion is to create trust between coreligionists. In primitive societies trust is based on observance of a common moral code which is specified and enforced by the gods themselves. "God is regarded as the guardian of the social order and his intervention as a possible sanction for any rule of conduct," the anthropologist E. E. Evans-Pritchard wrote of the Nuer.[238]

The Nuer are "an unruly and quarrelsome people," in Evans-Pritchard's view, yet their religion makes them fearful of doing wrong and quick to apologize. "The Nuer," he wrote, "have the idea that if a man keeps in the right—does not break divinely sanctioned interdictions, does not wrong others, and fulfils his obligations to spiritual beings and the ghosts and to his kith and kin—he will avoid, not all misfortunes, for some misfortunes come to one and all alike, but those extra and special misfortunes which come from *dueri*, faults, and are to be regarded as castigations. . . . Any failure to conform to the accepted norms of behaviour towards a member of one's family, kin, age-set, a guest, and so forth is a fault which may bring about evil consequences. . . . Therefore, also, a man who is at fault goes to the person he has offended, admits the fault, saying to him '*ca dwir*—I was at fault,' and he may also offer a gift to wipe out the offence."

Reconciliation must then follow, further repairing the social fabric: "The wronged man then blesses him by spitting or blowing water on him and says that it is nothing and may the man be at peace. He thereby removes any resentment he may have in his heart. Nuer say that God sees these acts and frees the man from the consequences of his fault."[239]

In modern societies, religions are not the only component of trust—civic associations, custom, law and many other aspects of culture also contribute—but religious faith has surely not shed its role as the guardian of morality. Leaders from Washington onward have seen religion as an essential part of the social fabric. In his farewell address of 1796, George Washington said:

> Of all the dispositions and habits which lead to political prosperity, religion and morality are indispensable supports. In vain would that man claim the tribute of patriotism, who should labor to subvert these great pillars of human happiness, these firmest props of the duties of men and citizens. The mere politician, equally with the pious man, ought to respect and to cherish them. A volume could not trace all their connections with private and public felicity. Let it simply be asked: Where is the security for property, for reputation, for life, if the sense of religious obligation desert the oaths which are the instruments of investigation in courts of justice? And let us with caution indulge the supposition that morality can be maintained without religion. Whatever

may be conceded to the influence of refined education on minds of peculiar structure, reason and experience both forbid us to expect that national morality can prevail in exclusion of religious principle.[240]

Dwight Eisenhower, who seems to have had no great personal interest in religion, came to much the same conclusion. "Our government makes no sense unless it is founded in a deeply felt religious faith—and I don't care what it is," he is reported to have said.[241] Though he had not attended church in his adult lifetime, on becoming president he joined the National Presbyterian Church in Washington and announced he would attend services there on his inauguration day and every Sunday thereafter, so as to set an example for others.[242]

The quality of the social fabric is hard to measure, and for that among other reasons is often ignored by economists. In their view, society is a collection of self-interested individuals who seek only to maximize their profit, subject only to a few laws safeguarding property rights and contracts. In his book *Trust*, the political scientist Francis Fukuyama argues that, to the contrary, economic life is deeply embedded in social life, and depends integrally on the network of norms, rules and moral obligations that knit a society together. The denser this network, the higher the level of trust, which he defines as "the expectation that arises within a community of regular, honest and cooperative behavior, based on commonly shared norms, on the part of other members of that community."

Trust may rarely figure in neoclassical economists' accounts of society, but in Fukuyama's view trust is what enables people to build social capital, the network of associations that bind a society together. Where trust is highest, as in communities of shared ethical values, organizations are most effective. "A nation's well-being, as well as its ability to compete, is conditioned by a single, pervasive cultural characteristic: the level of trust inherent in a society," he writes.[243]

Of the many cultural factors that contribute to trust, few are more significant than moral values and the religions that shape them. In

Fukuyama's view, "Traditional religions or ethical systems (e.g., Confucianism) constitute the major institutionalized sources of culturally determined behavior."

Social capital is easier to destroy than rebuild, and there is some evidence its level in the United States has decreased in recent decades. Asked if "most people" could be trusted, 58 percent of Americans said yes in 1960, but the percentage had declined to 37 percent by 1993. A diminution in social capital, as measured by membership in organizations like bowling leagues, has also been recorded by the political scientist Robert Putnam in his book *Bowling Alone*.

Fukuyama traces the drop in social capital to a loosening of Protestant values. In the mid-twentieth century, the American corporate world was much more homogeneous than the population as a whole. Almost all the managers and directors were Anglo-Saxon Protestants who "knew each other through their interlocking directorates, country clubs, schools, churches, and social activities, and they enforced on their managers and employees codes of behavior that reflected the values of their WASP backgrounds. They tried to instill in others their own work ethic and discipline, while ostracizing divorce, adultery, mental illness, alcoholism, not to mention homosexuality and other kinds of unconventional behavior."

As other ethnic groups went through the WASP school system, they assimilated the same values, particularly the Protestant art of forming associations of all kinds. But the balance between individualism and community-building has shifted dramatically toward the former in the last 50 years, Fukuyama says. A profusion of lobbyists and special interest organizations have put private concerns ahead of community. Groups demanding rights for specific sections of the population have also undermined community in unintended ways. The upshot is that "communities of shared values, whose members are willing to subordinate their private interests for the sake of larger goals of the community as such, have become rarer. And it is these moral communities alone that can generate the kind of social trust that is critical to organizational efficiency."

Fukuyama's conclusion is that the role of religion in generating social capital has been undervalued. "Given the close relationship between religion and community in American history, Americans need to be more tolerant of religion and aware of its potential social benefits," he writes. "Many educated people have a distaste for certain forms of religion, particularly that of Christian fundamentalists, and believe themselves above such dogmas. But they need to look to religion's social consequences in terms of promoting the American art of association."[244]

Contemporary societies have developed many ingenious ways of establishing the trust that religious bonds once provided. Merchants on Amazon or eBay seek customers' ratings as evidence of their trustworthiness. Credit rating agencies provide assessments of people's finances and likely ability to repay loans. The sophistication of these procedures and their narrow goals contrast with the simplicity and effectiveness of the religious system—any observant coreligionist, at least in a demanding faith, is naturally trustworthy.

## Religion and Economics

Beyond its general role in creating the conditions for morality and trust, religion affects economics directly in several aspects, some positive, some otherwise.

One of the best-known links between religion and economics is that posited by the German sociologist Max Weber in his book *The Protestant Ethic and the Spirit of Capitalism,* published in article form in 1904 and 1905. Weber asked why Germany's managerial class—"business leaders and owners of capital, as well as the higher grades of skilled labour, and even more the higher technically and commercially trained personnel of modern enterprises"—were overwhelmingly Protestant, not Catholic. His treatment bore on the wider question, in which he was also interested, of why capitalism first arose in the West and not elsewhere in the world.

Calvinism, Weber suggested, worried the faithful no end with its doctrine of predetermination, which held that some people were selected for salvation, others for damnation. In the Catholic view, salvation could be obtained simply by confession of sins and acceptance of the church's authority, but how was a Calvinist to know to which fate he had been allotted? The idea developed that worldly success was a sign of divine favor. Calvinists and their Puritan descendants developed an ethic that combined hard work and asceticism—the accumulation of more and more wealth along with an asceticism that forbade spending it. Nothing could have been more conducive to amassing capital. The emphasis on success in a worldly calling as proof of faith "must have been the most powerful conceivable lever for the expansion of that attitude toward life which we have here called the spirit of capitalism," Weber wrote.[245]

Why did Western culture alone produce rational science out of alchemy and astrology and summon rational economics, meaning capitalism, out of the business of everyday life? In subsequent works Weber argued that in China, despite many factors favoring capitalism, Confucianist mandarins opposed new technology and other necessary institutions, while in India the Hindu caste system was inimical to the rise of a business class.

As a founder of sociology, Weber's widely known thesis on the Calvinist ethic and capitalism has had broad influence, even though he provided almost no data to support it. Economists, however, have had little use for his ideas. Since people the world over are utility-maximizing individuals, in their view, the answer to questions about the rise of capitalism and why the Industrial Revolution started in England in 1790 must be sought in institutions, like education or the availability of capital, which differ from country to country, and not in the clonelike populations of identical human units that inhabit them.

Strange to say, the attempt by economic historians to find an institutional explanation for the Industrial Revolution has not yet produced any generally satisfactory answer. Could it be that Weber was right after all, at least to the extent that the answer to the origin of capitalism lies not in institutions but in people and their beliefs, attitudes and behavior?

Whatever the relationship between Protestantism and capitalism, religion in general performs an essential role even in modern economies, that of creating circles of trust, whether in society in general or among particular religious groups. Jews and Parsees have built businesses based on the ties between coreligionists in distant cities. Islam is said to have spread through Africa as a vehicle of trade and trust. Its high price of entry—the Ramadan fast, no alcohol, going on pilgrimage to Mecca—encouraged trust among its members.

"Today, as in the past, handshakes, Yiddish, and trust still close the multimillion dollar deals," writes Renee Rose Shield of the diamond selling trade in New York.[246] Centered on New York's Forty-seventh Street, the business is run by a close-knit community, mostly Ultra-Orthodox Jews, among whom one's word is one's bond. A shared religion is a major component of establishing the trust that is necessary to let another dealer have a consignment of stones worth several million dollars and be confident he will not abscond with them.

The strength of religion-based trust is nowhere more evident than in schemes that exploit that trust. Fraudsters have learned that an effective way to part people from their money is to pretend to belong to the same group, and specifically the same religious group, as do their marks, an approach known as affinity fraud. "Affinity frauds can target any group of people who take pride in their shared characteristics, whether they are religious, ethnic, or professional," warns the Securities and Exchange Commission. Its Web site describes schemes that targeted Jehovah's Witnesses, members of African American churches, Baptists and born again Christians.[247]

The most spectacular recent case of affinity fraud was the $50 billion Ponzi scheme run by Bernard Madoff. Jewish himself, Madoff targeted many of his coreligionists, as well as Jewish charities and educational institutions. His marks were educated and sophisticated people, yet they ignored salient red flags such as an opaque investment scheme and returns that seemed too good to be true. Religion induces so powerful an urge to trust members of the same faith that rational calculation can be swept aside. "He really undermined the fabric of the Jewish community, because it's based on trust," said Rabbi Burton L. Visotsky of the Jewish Theological Seminary. The rabbi went on to explain that "There is a wonderful rabbinic saying—often misapplied—that all Jews are sureties for one another, which means, for instance, that if a Jew takes a loan out, in some ways the whole Jewish community guarantees it."[248]

There are many other instances of coreligionists doing business together, particularly in long-distance trade networks before the advent of modern banking. By establishing a separate community, whether defined by dress, diet, or onerous duties, small religious groups can cheaply and effectively monitor the behavior of all their members, notes the anthropologist Richard Sosis. Anyone who cheats another member pays no end of penalties. "Because ruined reputations affect not only business opportunities but also one's social life, including diminishing the marriage prospects of one's children and siblings, these threats help to maintain cooperative exchanges," he notes. The sanctions are so severe, in his view, that it is inexact to speak of trust as the force that holds these business links together. This is not the open-ended trust between people who are powerless if a deal goes wrong, but rather behavior controlled by a heavy threat of ostracism and social ruin, reinforced by supernatural sanction.[249]

Religious behavior is a way of committing members of a community to a common goal. But these goals, set essentially by the wisdom of society in preceding or current generations, sometimes have adverse effects. Offsetting the positive economic role of raising levels of morality and trust in a society, the three monotheisms probably retarded economic growth for centuries by their prohibitions on charging interest. Judaism barred internal interest rates: Deuteronomy, after banning prostitution and sodomy, stipulates that "Unto a stranger thou mayest lend upon usury; but unto thy brother thou shalt not lend upon usury." Christians interpreted a ban on interest to arise from Luke: "But love ye your enemies, and do good, and lend, hoping for nothing again." The first Council of Nicaea in A.D. 325 barred clergy from lending money on interest. A thousand years later the charging of interest was no better regarded: Dante put usurers in the seventh circle of hell.

Muslims, similarly, were admonished that "Allah permitteth trade and forbiddeth usury."[250] But both religions gradually found ways of evading the ban on charging interest. Usury came to be defined as excessive interest. Islamic lawyers developed a series of legal maneuvers to give tacit acceptance to charging interest.

With its communal ideas—"Sell all ye have and give to the poor"— and its strong ascetic strain, early Christianity was not a sound basis for capitalism, and its prediction of an imminent wrap-up of all worldly affairs doubtless did little to encourage long-term investment. Nonetheless, after many centuries and false starts, Christian countries, whether because of their religion or despite it, did stumble upon a set of social attitudes particularly conducive to capitalism.

## Morality Without Religion

With the rise of capitalism, many civil institutions came into being and took over roles long performed by religious bodies, from education to welfare. States became increasingly secular and, since the Second World War, church attendance in all European countries has decreased. Growing numbers of people express no interest in religion, describing themselves as agnostics or atheists.

Was Locke correct that atheists cannot be trusted? Atheists and others insist this is not the case. "Though equating morality with religion is commonplace," writes the biologist Marc Hauser, "it is wrong in at least two ways: It falsely assumes that people without religious faith lack an understanding of moral rights and wrongs, and that people of religious faith are more virtuous than atheists and agnostics."[251]

Richard Dawkins, the evolutionary biologist, endorses Hauser's arguments that religion is unnecessary for generating moral judgments. "We do not need God in order to be good—or evil," he writes. He ridicules the idea that people are good through fear of divine punishment. A believer who would commit murder if he thought he was no longer under divine surveillance is surely not a very moral person, Dawkins argues. "It seems to me to require quite a low self-regard to think that, should belief in God suddenly vanish from the world, we would all become callous and selfish hedonists, with no kindness, no charity, no generosity, nothing that would deserve the name of goodness," he writes.[252]

Neither argument is fully convincing. The issue is not whether atheists understand moral rights and wrongs but whether or not they will act on this understanding if they harbor no fear of divine punishment. As the Roman poet Ovid confessed: "*Video meliora proboque, deteriora sequor*—I see the better course and know it's right, but I take the worse one."

Hauser and Dawkins are in principle correct that atheists are just as moral as other people. But the reason is presumably that atheists take at least as good care as everyone else to abide by their community's moral standards. And religion surely plays a leading role in shaping and enforcing the community standards that both atheists and believers observe.

Hence the fact that atheists are as moral as anyone else does not means that religion is unnecessary, as some atheists contend. In most European countries less than half the population attends church regularly. But people seem to treat one another with much the same level of concern as when churchgoing was de rigueur. It may be that it requires only a small number of people to establish what moral standards should prevail. The opinion leaders certainly include religious believers, though need not be confined to them. In this way communities achieve consensus on how members should behave toward one another; morality is not an area where diversity within a society is particularly welcome. Just as a vaccine may achieve what immunologists call herd immunity, by immunizing merely enough people to break a pathogen's chain of transmission, religion can help create a moral community if enough people either are believers or behave as if they were.

An interesting question is whether a society composed entirely of atheists could generate ties of morality and trust strong enough for the community to operate effectively. The test of such a society would be whether it could maintain order and civility not just during times of peace and prosperity but also under stressful conditions, such as war and depression. But a large society composed only of atheists may not be available for observation any time soon. Given that religious behavior is part of human nature, such a society is no more likely to emerge than one in which no one plays or appreciates music.

Some neoatheists have tried to turn the argument on religion, saying religion is a source of immorality. By citing bloodcurdling passages from the Old Testament, they accuse Judaism and Christianity of promoting immoral doctrines. If your brother or son or daughter should entice you to worship other gods, advises an author of Deuteronomy, "Thou shalt not consent unto him, nor hearken unto him; neither shall thine eye pity him, neither shalt thou spare, neither shalt thou conceal him: But thou shalt surely kill him; thine hand shall be first upon him to put him to death, and afterwards the hand of all the people. And thou shalt stone him with stones, that he die. . . ."[253]

In his book _The End of Faith_ Sam Harris cites this passage in the course of an argument that "we have been slow to recognize the degree to which religious faith perpetuates man's inhumanity to man."[254] Christopher Hitchens cites a similar exhortation in Numbers as "certainly not the worst of the genocidal incitements that occur in the Old Testament."[255]

But the morality of religions cannot be reduced to texts, especially ancient anecdotes that play no role in daily practice. Religions are based on rituals that generate emotional commitment to behave in certain ways. These behaviors for the most part reflect and enforce the current social consensus on what moral standards should be. Religions sometimes get out of step with the consensus—as Mormonism did with polygamy and Catholicism does with birth control—but by and large there is an interactive process between each religion and its society in establishing standards of morality and of trust.

RELIGION HAS LONG BEEN the essential guarantor of a cohesive society. Its role is less evident in modern societies that have divided the world into sacred and secular. Still, whether religious or not, people everywhere tend to abide by their society's moral standards, and religion plays a strong role in shaping expectations of what those standards should be. These standards are the basis of trust, on which economic activity and much else depend.

Adam Smith described the marketplace as an invisible hand that induced each individual, by following his self-interest, to serve the common interest. But hands come in pairs. An efficient marketplace can operate only on the basis of trust. The counterpart of the invisible hand that works on self-interest is the one that induces moral self-restraint. In most, if not all, societies moral standards have been secured by religion and the fear of divine retribution.

But the influence of religion is not confined to shaping just a society's public life. The most intimate aspects of private life, starting with reproduction, are subject to religious regulation, for reasons discussed in the next chapter.

# 9

---

# THE ECOLOGY
# OF RELIGION

*And God blessed them, and God said unto them, Be fruitful,
and multiply, and replenish the earth, and subdue it: and have
dominion over the fish of the sea, and over the fowl of the air,
and over every living thing that moveth upon the earth.*

GENESIS 1:28

*Your wives are your field: go in, therefore, to your field as ye
will; but do first some act for your souls' good: and fear ye God,
and know that ye must meet Him; and bear these good tidings
to the faithful.*

QUR'AN 2:223

Religion is based on an implicit negotiation with supernatural powers as a result of which they decree the rules that a society's leaders consider to be in its best interests. If so, then religions should
include many prescriptions that bear on activities critical for a society's
survival, such as its rate of reproduction and the management of natural
resources. This is indeed the case. Religions, both ancient and modern, have

a lot to say about marriage and sexual activity. Older religions also show evidence of elaborate concern with agriculture and ecological management, matters that in modern states have been taken over by secular institutions.

Because people will follow rules that they believe include divine penalties for disobedience, compliance is high and the society works intensely to accomplish whatever common goals the gods have set. Such an arrangement greatly improves the chances of survival compared with a society that lacks cohesion or common purpose. But survival is by no means assured. The wisdom of the gods, as Durkheim might have noted, can be no better than the collective wisdom of the society and of its past and present leaders. From time to time societies fall under the control of irrational leaders, and when such people impute destructive commands to the gods, the result can be disastrous.

## Controlling Fertility

The rate of reproduction is a critical parameter of existence, especially among primitive societies, and religions are a potent means of regulating fertility. Religious practice is usually set so as to increase fertility. Having too few people makes a group vulnerable to attack from more populous neighbors, whereas maintaining a high birth rate is the surest path to survival and dominance, and presents an acute demographic threat to neighbors with a lower fertility rate. But religions can also be used to ratchet down fertility if population numbers exceed the natural resources required for their support.

There are few aspects of human reproduction to which the gods' interest does not extend. According to the Babylonian Talmud, "The times for conjugal duty prescribed in the Torah are: for men of independence, every day; for labourers, twice a week; for ass-drivers, once a week; for camel-drivers, once in thirty days; for sailors, once in six months. These are the rulings of Rabbi Eliezer."[256]

Many societies have religious rules on the timing of intercourse, some of which capture the time of peak fertility quite well, even though the underlying physiology was unknown to the rule-makers. In Jewish law and custom, intercourse is regarded as ritually impure from the start of menstruation until 7 days after its end. The woman then goes to a ritual cleansing bath and it is her husband's religious duty to make love to her when she returns home. The requirement ensures that the first intercourse occurs within the 3 day period of greatest fertility.

Religious bans on contraception, like that of the Catholic church, presumably increase fertility. Mormons, among whom contraception was banned until the mid-twentieth century, have always had a much higher than usual birthrate.

So too have many Muslim communities. Muhammad is said to have ruled polygyny legal after the battle of Badr in 624, when many of his men were killed. Polygyny probably does increase the birthrate in societies with a surplus of women. In balanced societies it seems to reduce fertility, because the richer men who can afford multiple wives are older and less fertile. The surplus of unmarried young men, however, can be helpful for military purposes.

Bans on abortion, instituted by Islam and the Catholic church, may increase fertility. So too may arrangements that allow an infertile wife or husband to be divorced, and place no bar on the remarriage of widows. Homosexuality has traditionally been condemned in Judaism, Christianity and Islam. These prohibitions presumably reflect the belief that homosexuality will reduce a society's overall fertility.

While some religious rules increase fertility, others have the effect of reducing it. Some Christian churches forbade intercourse on ritual occasions, such as on Sundays or during Lent. In the Middle Ages, marital intercourse was forbidden for three 40-day periods each year, on major feast days and for three days before taking communion. Given all these restrictions, intercourse among the devout could occur on only 160 days out of 365, which must surely have reduced birthrates.[257]

The venerable Shaker community of the United States carried sexual abstinence to an extreme. Shakers separated the sexes and forbade procreation. Those who wanted children had to adopt them. The sect could therefore grow only by conversion, but turnover was high. Despite their many distinctive cultural contributions, Shakers could not flourish and their last community is now nearly extinct.

Religious practices can also reduce fertility by raising the age of marriage, permitting abortion, increasing the spacing between children, forcing widows to immolate themselves on the husband's pyre (the Hindu practice known as suttee), and forbidding divorce between couples who cannot have children.

Some religions countenance the killing of unwanted infants. In India and other countries where sons are more prized than daughters, female babies are allowed to die in various ways. Archaeologists have recovered evidence of child sacrifice from the Inca and Moche civilizations of Peru, from the Aztecs of Mexico, and from Minoan Crete. The most egregious example of the practice is reported from ancient Carthage, where members of the nobility and others were expected to sacrifice their firstborn children to the god Ba'al Hammon. The children seem to have been placed in the arms of a bronze statue which, when the statue was heated, opened and dropped the victims into flames. According to the historian Philo, the children were sacrificed to secure favors from the god, such as safe arrival of a shipment to a foreign port.

So compelling are religious beliefs that people throughout history have accepted the dictates of the gods as governing the most intimate aspects of their private lives. Even when the gods require actions deeply repellent to human nature, such as the sacrifice of a child, their decrees are obeyed. It was presumably in order to control population numbers that societies chose to extend the iron discipline of religion into reproductive behavior.

## Religious Adjustment of Population Size

Religious rules like those above may thus affect almost every point in people's reproductive lives. To any historian of religion it may seem strange that the gods, in their distant supernatural realm, are so intensely interested in the minutiae of human reproductive activities. But from an evolutionary perspective, the gods' preoccupation with sex makes perfect sense. The rules they decree serve as a powerful method of adjusting a community's population size to prevailing circumstances.

Whether or not societies throughout history have in fact used religious rules to control population size cannot at present be proved. The adjustments do not seem to have been made explicitly. But the fact that these powerful methods were available strongly suggests they were put to use, even if for the most part implicitly.

Most if not all religions regulate marriage, usually decreeing monogamy or polygyny. Marriage confers several obvious survival advantages. One, probably the origin of the institution, is that a woman has a much better chance of raising infants to adulthood if she has a man to protect her and her family. A man too has a better chance of getting his genes into the next generation if he is committed to the welfare of his children and their mother. Another highly significant benefit of marriage from a society's perspective is that wedlock, at least in principle, settles a principal cause of strife among men, that of access to women. Marriage finalizes and sanctifies the distribution of women and is thus a central pillar of social stability in monogamous societies. In polygynous societies, a state of generally lesser stability is achieved because many young men cannot find wives and a common solution is to let them risk their lives in military exploits.

Marriage is the most necessary institution for a society keen on reproducing itself. This and other religious rules that increase fertility confer the obvious benefit that greater numbers lead to greater military strength. But larger populations are sometimes at a disadvantage; they may leave everyone living at the edge of starvation, and indeed have done so for much of the agrarian past.

Religious rules are formulated in tacit negotiation with the gods and include many arbitrary elements. Nor is the negotiation process necessarily conscious; religious officials are guided by tradition and what has worked in the past. So it is hard to establish cause and effect between a religious rule and its demographic impact.

Still, religious policies affecting fertility seem too often aligned with a community's requirements for the association to be mere chance. After a survey of religions around the world, the social scientists Vernon Reynolds and Ralph Tanner concluded there was a clear pattern between religious rules and a society's environment. In conditions of poverty, frequent natural disasters, disease, infant mortality and low expectation of life, religions fostered the view that people should have many children. "We found this kind of religious attitude to be prevalent in many Moslem countries, in Hindu India, and in rural African societies," they report. But where affluence prevailed, and disease and natural disasters were rare, "then religious attitudes to childbearing were anti-natalist . . . This attitude we found to be characteristic of modern Westernized countries, whose primary religion is Christianity."[258]

Maintaining a high birthrate is a powerful demographic strategy, especially for small beleaguered sects threatened by larger populations. The Mormon church, for instance, achieved a growth rate of about 40 percent per decade for the first century of its existence, with a temporary spurt of 70 percent per decade in the 1980s, though its growth seems now to be leveling off. The remarkable increase, attained through both a high birthrate and a vigorous missionary program, has secured the church's continued existence. This was in doubt during its early years when its prophet, Joseph Smith, was killed and its followers driven into exile in the frontier wildernesses of Utah. They doubtless understood that there was safety in numbers and worked to gain them.

Pro-natalist doctrines or practices are evident in other small sects, such as the Amish, Doukhobors and certain Jewish populations, that strive to survive within larger host populations. Demographic growth and fertility can be influenced by many factors, from the spacing of children to the timing of intercourse to the issue of whether widows are allowed to remarry.

Islam was shaped as the state religion of an expansionary Arab state.

Whether or not high fertility is a continuing legacy from that period, Muslim populations in many places have a higher fertility rate than their non-Muslim neighbors. This demography has potent political consequences, as for instance in Palestine and Israel where the Muslim birthrate far exceeds that of Jews. Even in the United States Muslim population growth exceeds that of all other religious groups except Mormons, as measured by family size. In the population at large 9 percent of families report 3 or more children living at home, but 21 percent of Mormon families do, and 15 percent of Muslims.[259]

The various conflicts between Muslim countries and their neighbors have been accompanied by a high birthrate in many Islamic countries and this, in the view of some observers, has had unsettling consequences. "The demographic explosion in Muslim societies and the availability of large numbers of often unemployed males between the ages of fifteen and thirty is a natural source of instability and violence both within Islam and against non-Muslims," writes Samuel Huntington. "Whatever other causes may be at work, this factor alone would go a long way to explaining Muslim violence in the 1980s and 1990s."[260]

Demographers generally see economic factors such as affluence and education, not religion, as being the prime influences on birthrate. But religious rules may be one of the mechanisms through which these factors operate. As already noted, the early Christian church adopted strongly pro-natalist rules by elevating the status of women, promoting marriage, prohibiting promiscuity, and classifying abortion and infanticide as murder. The outlawing of abortion gave Christian women in the Roman empire a better survival rate than pagan women, many of whom died while undergoing the frequent abortions demanded by their husbands. The extra Christian women available to marry pagan men often converted their spouses. All these factors improved fertility, writes the sociologist Rodney Stark, who concludes that "superior fertility contributed to the rise of Christianity."[261]

Once Constantine legalized Christianity in the Roman empire, however, the imperative to be fruitful and multiply became less pressing. Christian hermits had begun to live in the Egyptian deserts in the third century A.D. to escape unrest and the persecution of the emperor Diocletian. Their numbers continued to grow after Constantine's Edict of Milan in 313, in which he ended the persecution of Christians throughout the western half of the Roman empire. Monasteries were soon established throughout the eastern half of the Roman empire, and later in the West.

By the eighth to ninth centuries, 100,000 monks were said to be living under the rule that had been established by Basil, bishop of Caesarea, around 360. Eastern monasticism was "essentially parasitic," writes Paul Johnson. The monks "had no economic purpose. Indeed, they were one of the spiritual luxuries a rich society could, or at any rate did, afford."[262]

Monasticism grew more slowly in the West but eventually a large fraction of the arable land of Europe had fallen into the possession of monastic estates. The European monks, however, became efficient administrators of their extensive holdings and made a more positive contribution to society.

Nonetheless, monasteries and nunneries of any kind curtail fertility. From a biological perspective, do they represent a pathological use of religion, in a similar category to that of cultic mass suicides, or something more conducive to survival?

An obvious possibility is that monasticism, along with abortion and the other methods of reducing fertility, could in fact have served a practical purpose, whether or not it was consciously exercised. That purpose has to do with the nature of agrarian societies, which perhaps from near the beginning of agriculture 10,000 years ago operated under much the same conditions as those described by the Reverend Thomas Malthus in his gloomy treatise on population growth. Any increase in agricultural productivity raised living standards for a few years but induced people to have more children. Within a generation the surplus was eaten up by the extra mouths and the standard of living reverted to normal, which for most of the population was essentially a notch or two above starvation.

Modern economies escape Malthus's trap through their high rates of productivity, but agrarian economies were caught at the edge of misery, for the reasons Malthus defined, except while recovering from harsh population declines.

The only prolonged improvement in living conditions in European economies seems to have occurred after terrible plagues. "The explanation for the very high living standards of Europeans in the years 1350–1600 was undoubtedly the arrival of the Black Death in 1347," writes the economic historian Gregory Clark. "Its first onslaught in the years 1347–49 carried away 30–50 percent of the population of Europe. . . . After its initial onset the plague offered Europeans a greatly enhanced material lifestyle at small cost in terms of the average length of life. In the Malthusian world gifts from God took surprising forms!"[263]

Clearly agrarian societies could have attained better living standards by constraining their fertility, and religious practices such as monasticism and abortion, whether or not consciously shaped to this end, would have been a means to do so.

Throughout history religious beliefs have proved strong enough to govern people's sexual behavior, overriding even the strongest biological imperatives. A modern-day example is provided by a renegade Mormon sect, the Fundamentalist Church of Jesus Christ of Latter-Day Saints, whose polygynous prophet, Warren Jeffs, shared out women with his associates, giving each man a right to three wives. But this required some social engineering to adjust the sect's sex ratio accordingly. Jeffs's solution was to force parents to expel teenage boys from the community, using any minor infraction of the sect's strict rules as an excuse. Fathers who failed to oust a young boy designated as a rule breaker would have their wives taken away.[264] Few human bonds are stronger than those of family, but the prophet's dictates induced parents to abandon and exile their teenage children. Once the innate susceptibility to fear supernatural justice is triggered, people will go to almost any lengths to obey what priests or rulers tell them is the gods' will.

## When Religions Go Wrong

Religion is conducive to survival because ideally its doctrine embodies each society's collective wisdom and gives leaders authority for certain actions. The system works well in general, but not in every instance. When a single leader or group monopolizes interpretation of the gods' wishes, and promulgates irrational doctrine, disaster may follow. Though religious behavior has conferred a significant survival advantage in general, it has undoubtedly brought many societies to ruin.

Among the most striking examples of religious pathology is the cattle-killing movement that took place among the Xhosa people in the late 1850s. The Xhosa, who live in southeast Africa, had fought eight losing wars with the British colonial administration and were under the further stress of an epidemic of lung sickness among their cattle. In April 1856 a 16-year-old girl, Nongqawuse (the *q* represents a click sound), had the first of a striking series of visions.

She said that the Xhosa should cease all witchcraft, kill all their cattle and destroy their corn because new people would arise from the sea and river mouths. The new people would cause fresh cattle, free of the devastating lung sickness, to appear from a huge cavern hidden beneath the earth. At the same time the granaries would be miraculously filled with new grain. As for the British, the sea would part and open a road for them to retreat to the place of creation from which they came.

The biblical overtones in Nongqawuse's prophecy she may have picked up from her uncle Mhlakaza, who had been the first Xhosa baptized into the Anglican church. Other elements were standard parts of Xhosa traditional beliefs, particularly the idea that the sacrifice of cattle was the only effective way of communicating with the spirit world.

Nongqawuse would doubtless have been ignored had not she and her uncle been visited by Sarhili, the Xhosa king. Sarhili somehow became convinced that her visions were real and issued orders that people were to kill their cattle. He began by slaughtering his favorite ox, an animal renowned throughout his kingdom.

Nongqawuse's message offered hope to people who did not have much. Many had to kill their cattle anyway because of the epidemic. The Xhosa began to sacrifice cattle, destroy the corn in their granaries, and build new cattle pens to hold the fresh herds they anticipated. Hundreds of cattle were killed every day, and those not eaten were left to rot.

The resurrection of the new people was expected to occur on the full moon of June 1856. When nothing happened, Mhlakaza explained that the real date would be the full moon of mid-August. The day after the night of the full moon, he said, there would be a great storm, and the righteous dead and the new cattle would arise out of the earth at the mouths of four local rivers.

"No believer slept that night. The young people danced and reveled, while the older men sat about in silent groups or nervously paced about the huge cattle folds, which had been prepared for the new cattle," writes the historian J. B. Peires in his account of the cattle killing. "But nothing happened. If anything, the promised day of darkness was particularly bright."[265]

Many Xhosa had believed Nongqawuse's prophecies but many had not. Even among the believers, a common strategy had been to kill a few cattle and hold the rest back while waiting to see what happened. If Nongqawuse's prophecies had been ignored after the second disappointment in August 1856, no one would have been much worse off.

But the unfolding of the tragedy could not be halted. The reason the new people did not show, Mhlakaza explained, was because many Xhosa had failed to sacrifice all of their cattle, as directed. King Sarhili ordered the killing of cattle to continue. Believers assaulted those who tried to protect their animals. People wandered through their uncultivated fields or sat in the shade of their empty cattle pens, talking of the better world that lay ahead. The Xhosa were told to adorn themselves in celebration of the approaching event. Xhosa working for the British on public works "cheerfully mocked their white overseers and frequently burst into song until they abandoned their labor altogether to prepare for the great day," Peires reports.[266]

But the cheerfulness was one of desperation. By August people had already started to go hungry. With their grain pits empty, their fields unplanted and their cattle dead, the best way to get food was by visiting those who still had cattle to sacrifice. Others turned to digging up roots and eating the bark of mimosa trees. In late September the first deaths from starvation began. Children and the elderly passed out from lack of food. The dogs were too weak to bark.

Yet the believers even then did not abandon their belief in Nong-qawuse's beguiling prophecies. Before each new moon, orders went out for every last animal to be sacrificed, even goats and chickens. King Sar-hili continued to cull his once immense herds. By mid-January 1857 he had none left.

Meeting with his advisers, he decided one final effort should be made to meet the prophetess's demands. The final cattle were slaughtered. The last stocks of corn were burned. Widows who had remarried returned to their former homes, ready to greet their first husbands reawakening from the dead. Despite their hunger, the Xhosa cheerfully expected the new cattle to burst forth from the ground at any moment. Some stood on their roofs or climbed hills to catch a first glimpse of the resurrected people.

On the appointed day, the 16th–17th of February 1857, the dead once again failed to appear. The new cattle remained beneath the earth in their concealed underground cavern. The emptied granaries were not magically refilled. King Sarhili at last admitted his error. "I have been a great fool in listening to lies," he said. "I am no longer a chief. I was a great chief, being as I am the son of Hintza, who left me rich in cattle and people, but I have been deluded into the folly of destroying my cattle and ordering my people to do the same; and now I shall be left alone, as my people must scatter in search of food; thus I am no longer a chief. It is all my own fault; I have no one to blame but myself."[267]

His regrets were too late. With their cattle sacrificed and their fields untilled, his people died by the thousands of starvation. The British colonial administration of South Africa, interested in breaking the power of Xhosa chiefs and inducting their people into the labor force, did almost nothing to help. The Xhosa population of British Kaffraria, as the province was then known, plummeted from 105,000 in January 1857 to 25,916 by the end of 1858. Some of the loss was through emigration, but at least 40,000 people died from hunger. An estimated 400,000 cattle had been sacrificed in vain.

The Xhosa, of course, were neither the first nor the last people to commit themselves to a disastrous course because of their religious beliefs. Some 909 people belonging to the Peoples Temple Agricultural Project, a cult founded by Jim Jones, died in 1978 in Jonestown, Guyana, after drinking cyanide. The cult practiced "apostolic socialism," a path which eventually led its members from California to a guarded commune in Guyana which no one was allowed to leave. After the murder of a visiting congressman, Leo Ryan, Jones ordered his followers to commit suicide by drinking cyanide. Almost the entire membership of the cult perished. It seems some did so voluntarily, but the community operated under severe coercion from its leader.

Stranger still were the mass suicides and murders conducted in 1994 at two villages in Switzerland, and in Morin Heights, Quebec, by members of the Order of the Solar Temple. The cult believed it was a descendant of the Knights Templar, a crusading order. About 50 people died in each country.

Members of another strange sect, the Heaven's Gate cult, believed the earth was about to be wiped clean of life and rejuvenated. In preparation for this event, they lived such an ascetic life that six of their male devotees underwent castration. Their leader, Marshall Applewhite, believed that he and the woman who nursed him after a near-fatal heart attack were the two witnesses mentioned in the New Testament's book of Revelation.[268] He persuaded 38 of the cult's members to escape the impending purification of the earth by committing suicide, which they did on March 26,

1997, in a rented villa in Santa Fe, an upscale community of San Diego, California.

The cult members took their own lives in shifts, with surviving members cleaning up after each group's death. They were found dressed in identical black shirts and sweatpants, new Nike athletic shoes and armband patches reading "Heaven's Gate Away Team." All carried in their pockets a $5 bill and three quarters. Their bodies were each covered with a square, purple cloth. Their deaths coincided with the reappearance of the comet Hale-Bopp.[269]

At first glance, the Xhosas' disastrous religious beliefs and the suicide pacts of modern cults pose something of a challenge to the view that religious behavior evolved because it promoted survival. But what these episodes more directly demonstrate is the extraordinary hold that religion can exert on people's minds, compelling them to override the strongest human emotions, including those of self-preservation and the protection of family.

Such committed group behavior is clearly invaluable when harnessed to rational goals, as it is for the most part. Most leaders are keenly interested in their own and their society's well-being, and the will of the gods is usually interpreted by a consensus of some kind, whether of priests or rulers. But evolved behaviors are often vulnerable to malfunctions, which are tolerated if they do not make too much of a difference overall. The subversion of religious belief systems by irrational leaders shows only how potent a force they can be in the hands of those interested in their societies' survival.

## Managing Natural Resources

Just as religion provides an agreed set of rules for managing fertility, it can also be pressed into use in other forms of management, such as coordinating a group of people in the control and distribution of natural resources. Resource management often requires agreement among affected parties to subordinate their particular interests to the common good, and religion was the means used by early societies to accomplish this goal.

Hunters and gatherers may live off nature's bounty but when people first settled down and started to practice agriculture, they discovered that farming requires hard, cooperative labor of a kind quite novel in human experience. The Natufians of the Near East devised a religious solution for the problem of getting people to work for others: as mentioned earlier, they acquired supernatural supervisors of the community's behavior. The supervisors were people's own ancestors. To make sure everyone knew the ancestors were watching, the skulls of the dead were decorated and set in commanding positions in the walls of the Natufians' houses.

In early societies ancestor worship seems to have been a household affair, with the people under each roof acknowledging through appropriate rituals their relationship to the dead ancestor and to one another. Some archaic states, such as those of the ancient Maya and the T'ang dynasty in China, conceived the idea of replicating ancestor worship outside the household. The rulers claimed especially close ties to the supernatural world through their descent from the founding ancestors. They required that offerings previously made to the household ancestors be diverted to, or at least shared with, themselves. They thus gained access to much of the society's surplus production which they could use for managing natural resources, as well as for their own purposes. Mayan rulers, for example, built reservoirs to collect water and distribute it in the dry season. A symbol of royalty throughout the Mayan lowlands was the water lily, a plant that grows only in clean, still water and affirmed by its presence that the rulers were keeping the stored water drinkable.[270]

Early agricultural societies used religion not just to make people work but also to coordinate their activities quite precisely with the rhythm of the seasons. Failure to do so led to crops being planted or harvested at the wrong time, with possibly serious consequences for the community. Religious festivals held at appropriate times proved to be an effective means of organizing early farming societies. These agricultural festivals, as noted earlier, were later adopted by organized religions and reassigned to commemorate critical events in the sacred text; Easter, Passover and Rosh Ha-Shanah are all co-opted from the farmers' calendar.

Modern states have many ways of coordinating people's activities, and the role of religion, probably once pervasive, is no longer so prominent. The organizing powers of religion are more visible in societies like that of Bali in Indonesia. A system of temple management there, led by a high priest, allocates water supplies throughout the island and sets farmers' planting schedules so as to minimize infestations of pests.

This remarkable system, long ignored by the Dutch, Bali's colonial rulers, came to Western knowledge through the eyes of Stephen Lansing, an anthropologist who was studying Balinese religion in the early 1980s. At the time, high-yielding strains of rice, part of the Green Revolution, were being introduced by agricultural officials unaware of the temples' role. The officials found yields were better at first, then rapidly diminished as pests overwhelmed the crops.

Delving into the matter, Lansing learned that Balinese farmers had for centuries controlled pests through an elaborate, religiously based system centered on the goddess Dewi Danu and her high priest.

The island of Bali is a long extinct volcano with a vast, deep lake occupying its central crater. The rivers that rush down the mountain gulleys would be useless for irrigation but for numerous weirs that divert water into tunnels and canals. Each canal is used by from 60 to 120 farmers to irrigate terraced fields built up around the mountain.

The principal crop is rice, but the paddies also produce eels, frogs, fish and ducks. The farmers' main problem is pest control, which is achieved by flooding fields, as well as burning them after harvest and by letting the ducks graze for insects. The flooding, to be effective, must take place over a very large area or the pests will simply migrate from one farmer's fields to another's.

To achieve large-scale flooding, and to manage the water supply, the farmers are organized into associations, called *subaks,* membership of which includes all who depend on a specific irrigation canal.

The basic unit of the system is the weir that supplies water to several canals. Each weir has a shrine beside it and, usually several kilometers below, a temple to which belong members of all the *subaks* served by the weir. These are large organizations. The Ulun Swi temple in central Bali has seven *subaks* with 1,775 members who farm 558 hectares of rice fields.

It is at the temples that the farmers meet and decide the irrigation and planting schedule for the area served by their weir. The *subaks* agree to stagger their planting times and to flood the fields where pests are worst.

The local temples are all subject to the Temple of the Crater Lake, the lake at the heart of Mount Batur in central Bali. The temple has 24 priests, chosen in childhood by a virgin priestess to be lifelong servants of the goddess of the lake, Dewi Danu. The high priest, known as the Jero Gde, was chosen by the priestess in a trance when he was a boy of 11. He wears his hair long and is always dressed in white, the color of purity. By day, he offers sacrifices to the goddess of the Crater Lake on behalf of all the *subaks* under his sway, and by night he may receive guidance from the goddess in his dreams, Lansing reports.[271]

It is the Jero Gde who decides water allocations over his vast domain in the name of the goddess. He also oversees disputes between temples and their member *subaks*. Even though he directly controls only central Bali, he is in effect the high priest of the water cult for the whole island, since all irrigation systems are believed to be connected to his lake.

The farmers acknowledge the Jero Gde's sway because they are linked to him through a hierarchy of shrines and an elaborate set of rituals. In each field a farmer owns, at the corner where it receives its irrigation water stands a shrine to the rice goddess. Holy water from the Crater Lake is used in ceremonies at local water temples. Frequent festivals and sacrifices knit the farmers together in a shared system of religious belief. It is from this that the Jero Gde derives his authority to manage the island's vital water resources.

The practical domain of the goddess of the Crater Lake extends across political boundaries. Her high priest regained at least informal control over the water distribution system after the Green Revolution's agricultural engineers came to understand the superior efficiency of the goddess's system.

## A Cycle of War

A striking instance of how religion can be applied to managing resources comes from the Maring, who live by farming in the Bismarck mountain range in east-central New Guinea. Their lives are governed by a multiyear religious cycle that serves in essence to readjust the human population, and that of its domestic pigs, to the carrying capacity of the land.

The Maring plant temporary gardens in forest clearings where they grow sweet potatoes and other crops. The sexes live somewhat separately: men reside in communal houses and the women live in individual houses with their children and pigs. Each pig has an individual stall entered from outside the house but can poke its nose through the inside to be petted or fed scraps.

The pigs do not breed very fast because all males are castrated as piglets, leaving the females to be inseminated by wild pigs. These are hard for them to encounter because the Maring live at a high altitude, above the usual range of wild pigs. But though the domestic herd grows slowly, after a while the pigs become very burdensome. A woman can grow enough sweet potatoes to feed only 5 or 6 animals and the pigs have to forage for the rest of their food. They soon take to raiding neighbors' gardens, causing fights between their and the gardens' owners. The women complain bitterly to their husbands. Tension in the community rises, and the men eventually agree it is time for a *kaiko*.

The *kaiko* is a series of dances that brings the Maring's ritual cycle to its culmination. At various points during the *kaiko*, most of the pigs are sacrificed to the red spirits that inhabit the upper forest, and war is declared on neighbors to avenge those whom the neighbors killed in the last cycle.

These wars can evolve into deadly affairs. The Maring number about 7,000 people, divided into some 20 groups. The anthropologist Roy

Rappaport studied the Tsembaga, one of these groups, which numbered about 200 people. In one battle the Tsembaga lost 18 people, 6 of whom were women or children.

The pigs fared even worse. Only 75 survived out of a herd of 169. The rest were sacrificed to the red spirits, with the Tsembaga consuming a third of the meat and the rest being given to allies who came to fight on their side.

After a series of battles, the warring parties declare a truce, which is marked by the ritual planting of a special species of tree known as a tanket, and the retirement of the sacred fighting stones which lie in a special hut during times of truce but are hung high on a pole when a battle has been agreed on.

The philosopher Giambattista Vico may have erred in saying that all history proceeds in a cycle, but his thesis applies perfectly to Maring history. After the fighting stones are retired and the tanket tree planted, the Maring cannot look forward to permanent peace, only to the renewal of the cycle. The populations of people and pigs start to grow again and after a period, which averages 10 years but ranges from 5 to 25 years, the carrying capacity of the land is eventually pushed toward its limit.

Once a surplus of pigs and people has built up, however, the Maring can afford to go to war again. They are now able to repay in pig sacrifices the debts they incur both to allies who come to their aid in the ax battle, and to the red spirits of the upper forest. The red spirits are the souls of those who die in battle.

Talk begins of renewing warfare. The Maring unwrap fighting stones from the fight ash house. The fighting stones come in pairs, which the Maring designate as male and female. Found occasionally in the ground of the Maring people's territory, these sacred relics are in fact the mortars and pestles of a long-vanished culture. They have a different significance for the Maring: hanging them on the hut's pole is in effect a declaration of war. "By hanging up the fighting stones, a group places itself in a position of debt to both allies and ancestors for their assistance in the forthcoming ax fight," Rappaport writes.[272]

The tanket tree is uprooted, preferably by the man who planted it many years before. The men then prepare for a *kaiko* dance by decking themselves out in plumes and shells. The dance serves several purposes. The people from other groups who come and dance at the *kaiko* thereby pledge to be allies in the impending round of ax warfare. Since the Maring have no leaders, the turnout on the dance floor is the best way the hosts have of assessing their likely numerical strength in battle. All the men of the district are on display on the dancing floor and the women, who take the initiative in courtship, can judge whom they fancy. And the assembly of so many groups is also an occasion for trading.

Before battle the men spend much of the night chanting while their shamans, enjoying a tobacco high, make contact with a powerful supernatural being known as the smoke woman. They ask her which of the enemy's men are likely to be most easily killed, and who of their own members are vulnerable. Some of the men may carry magical fight packages containing the skin or nail clippings of enemy men they hope to kill; these objects will have been sent by people in the enemy village who would like to see the owners eliminated, perhaps because they have bad personalities, or are too successful as gardeners.

The Maring fight with axes, bows and arrows, and enormous shields. They have set-piece battles, on a specially prepared fighting ground, and line up in formations several ranks deep. The opponents stand toe to toe, with no tactical maneuvering being attempted. These ritual combats may not seem too serious. Occasionally a man is felled by an arrow, and opponents rush to finish him off with axes. Casualties seem light, even after battle has been continued every day for weeks.

But this stability is deceiving. Each side depends on its allies turning up every day in order to maintain its battlefield strength. Sooner or later, the allies on one side or the other get tired of the fight and fail to show. As soon as the larger group realizes it has a numerical advantage, it charges, and the side that is routed will suffer many casualties.

The Tsembaga, Rappaport reports, do not necessarily understand the function of their ritual cycle. Presumably they see it as an essential interaction between the living and the dead. But in the anthropologist's analysis, the ritual cycle accomplishes many essential ecological tasks. It brings back into balance the relationship between pigs, people and their gardens. It allows fields to revert to fallow. It helps conserve wild fauna, many of which are placed under taboo during the cycle and cannot be eaten. It redistributes land among the various groups. And although the cycle culminates in a large battle, it reduces the overall severity of fighting by restricting it to a single period of a long cycle.[273]

If the Maring people do not understand the ecological implications of their religion, as Rappaport says is the case, they presumably did not design it for its observed functions. The design could have emerged because groups with religions that failed to bring their pig population and their own numbers into balance with the environment eventually perished, while the Maring, with a more effective ritual, survived.

The religion of the Maring may seem a long way from that of modern societies. But it is very relevant to understanding the role that religion played for thousands of years until the modern era. It is evident from the case of the Maring, and indeed of many other primitive societies, that the role of religion was pervasive. Almost every aspect of Maring life is governed by ritual, from which foods are taboo to when to go to war.

Durkheim argued that religion separates the sacred from the profane but it is only modern societies that may make such a distinction. Elsewhere Durkheim called religion "a system of ideas by means of which individuals imagine the society of which they are members," and this is the description that seems more appropriate to the Maring.

Their ritual practices may seem strange and arbitrary—pigs to be sacrificed to the red spirits of the upper forest must be cooked in ovens above ground but pigs for another category of spirits, the fertility spirits who dwell in the lower parts of the territory, must be cooked below ground. But the arbitrariness is irrelevant. So too, no doubt, is the existence or otherwise of the red spirits and the fertility spirits. What is relevant is that in performing these rituals participants maintain or strengthen their emotional commitment to each other and to the belief system invoked by the rituals. In so doing, they bind themselves to behave in the ways their religion requires.

With the Maring, as with other primitive societies, religion has become a comprehensive guide to life, presumably because all socially required actions have been integrated into ritual practice over the course of time. The Maring, who have no chiefs or other source of authority, have successfully devised a ritual that keeps everyone marching to the same drum and placing society's needs above their own interests.

In modern economies, the state now performs, with varying degrees of success, many social functions that used to be the province of the church, such as educating the young, ministering to the sick, and looking after the poor. Pigs are killed without sacrificial ceremony, and according to market demand, not the blood thirst of spirits. For the most part, people no longer look to supernatural explanations for earthquakes, hurricanes or epidemics, since all now have generally more consistent scientific explanations. Religion is no longer a comprehensive guide to daily life. People in modern societies make the distinction noted by Durkheim between the sacred and the secular. Time and place are now predominantly secular, with the sacred often pushed into a tiny corner of both.

Yet religion continues to play many of its former roles, even if less obtrusively than in the past. None is more important than in preparing people for an especially difficult behavior that is vital to survival, the waging of war.

# 10

---

# RELIGION AND WARFARE

*Then out spake brave Horatius, the Captain of the Gate:*
*"To every man upon this earth death cometh soon or late.*
*And how can man die better than facing fearful odds,*
*For the ashes of his fathers and the temples of his Gods?"*

THOMAS BABINGTON MACAULAY[274]

Ὦ παιδες Ἑλληνων ἰτε
Go, sons of Hellenes
ἐλευθερουτε πατριδ᾽, ἐλευθερουτε δε
Free your fatherland, free
παιδας, γυναικας, θεων τε πατρῳων ἑδη
Your families, the altars of ancestral gods
θηκας τε προγονων:
And the graves of your fathers
νυν ὑπερ παντων ἀγων.
Now is the fight for everything

*The paean sung by Greek warriors as they sailed to meet*
*the Persian fleet at the battle of Salamis in 480 B.C.*

R eligion evolved as a response to warfare. It enabled groups to
commit themselves to a common goal with such intensity that
men would unhesitatingly sacrifice their lives in the group's

defense. Because this remarkable behavior has become engraved in human nature, people throughout history have died in defense of their religion and their fellow believers, putting their own and their family's interests second to what they considered a higher cause.

But though religious behavior has been deeply shaped by warfare, it is not inseparably linked to it. Religion provides a social cohesion, militant if necessary, which a society or its leaders may use to support an aggressive or pacific policy. The adaptable nature of religion is evident from a consideration of how each of the three monotheisms has resorted to warfare over the centuries.

Consider Judaism, a religion first shaped as an aggressive advocacy of a promised land for a chosen people. "When thou goest out to battle against thine enemies, and seest horses, and chariots, and a people more than thou, be not afraid of them," advise the writers of the book of Deuteronomy, "for the Lord thy God is with thee, which brought thee up out of the land of Egypt. . . . But of the cities of these people, which the Lord thy God doth give to thee for an inheritance, thou shalt save alive nothing that breatheth: But thou shalt utterly destroy them; namely, the Hittites, and the Amorites, the Canaanites, and the Perizzites, the Hivites, and the Jebusites, as the Lord thy God hath commanded thee. . . ."[275]

The divine directive for a thorough ethnic cleansing could scarcely have been clearer. With a sacred text designed to support an expansionist political agenda of the seventh century B.C., the Israelite religion proved all too effective at mobilizing the population for war, which it did time and again despite one sanguinary defeat after another. The early Israelites fought unremitting battles with the large Egyptian and Assyrian empires that were their neighbors. Jews mounted at least three serious revolts against Roman rule—the Romans lost a whole legion during Bar Kokhba's revolt of A.D. 132–135—but the outcome was always disastrous for the Jews.

When the Jews' territorial ambitions were at last abandoned, Judaism turned inward and underwent a remarkable transformation, demonstrating how effectively a religion can be shaped to new circumstances.

The focus shifted away from sacrificing hecatombs of domestic animals at the Jerusalem temple and toward the reading of the Torah. Judaism proved as potent at generating internal cohesion as it had previously been at energizing people for offense. Far-flung communities of the Jewish diaspora, from Spain to India, preserved their ethnic and cultural identity for generations. Lacking a country of their own, Jews defined themselves by their religion, to which they clung tenaciously. Without their religion, the Jewish communities of the Mediterranean would surely have been absorbed into the general population of the Roman empire, and would have quietly disappeared from history like so many other peoples of the ancient world.

Jews' survival thus depended on the adaptability of Judaism, on its abrupt switch from aggressive defiance to the entirely pacific religion of defenseless populations who had to get along with unpredictable hosts. Judaism has remained a nonviolent religion, with the exception of its practice in the state of Israel, founded in 1948, which quickly developed and maintains one of the world's best professional armies.

Unlike Judaism, Christianity began as a religion of nonviolence, as befitted a small sect subject to intermittent persecution by Roman authorities. "All they that take the sword shall perish with the sword," Jesus had told a supporter who drew a weapon in his defense. Citing this directive, the early church at first forbade Christians to join the Roman army. But this prohibition changed after the emperor Constantine made Christianity a legal religion of the Roman empire, no longer subject to persecution. The night before the battle of the Milvian bridge in A.D. 312, Constantine is reported to have seen a cross in the sky with the Greek words "ἐν τούτῳ νίκα—In this [sign], conquer." Thereafter Byzantine soldiers carried on their shields the labarum, an emblem combining the Greek letters chi and rho, indicating an abbreviation for Christ.

Around 350 Athanasius, the Patriarch of Alexandria, decreed that though it was wrong to kill, it was lawful for a soldier to kill the enemy. As it began to share in the responsibilities of empire, the once peaceful church became habituated to the use of force in the state's interest.

The church long insisted that at least its bishops and priests should not shed blood, a prohibition that lasted until the Middle Ages when bishops, who ran many European cities, became military leaders as well. In the early sixteenth century, Pope Julius II twice led armies in attacks in northern Italy. Nonetheless, sects like the Anabaptists and the Quakers kept alive the ancient concept that Christians should not kill.

Even the official church did not entirely forget its early renunciation of force. The Lateran Council of 1139 condemned a deadly new weapon—the crossbow—as immoral, and forbade its use, at least against Christians. It could, however, be used against Saracens.

Before it foreswore pursuit of temporal power, the Catholic church was no stranger to the use of force in statecraft. It was a pope, Urban II, who launched the first crusade in 1095, and his successors continued the tradition. The fourth crusade, managed by the doge of Venice, was diverted into an attack on Constantinople and the Orthodox church.

With the crusades abandoned, Christian violence turned inward and a long series of wars within Europe took place between Catholic and Protestant powers. Christian states then gradually learned an important lesson, that wars fought in the name of absolute beliefs are hard to settle by negotiation. From this experience emerged the solution of separating the powers of church and state, beginning with the Peace of Augsburg of 1555; under the formula *cuius regio, eius religio,* each ruler was allowed to choose the religion for his region. With another treaty, the Peace of Westphalia of 1648, the European wars of religion came at last to an end.

Religious commands not being easily subject to debate, whoever got to speak in the religion's name wielded considerable influence in the decision to go to war. In a secular state the ruler had to make the case for war on more rational grounds. Separating religious and secular powers in a state was thus a significant stride toward loosening the potent union between religion and warfare.

Turning to the third monotheism, Islam has generally proved somewhat less adaptable than Christianity. Far from beginning as a persecuted sect, Islam was shaped as a religion of empire, with Muslim Arabs as the rulers and conquered peoples subjected to various forms of discrimination. Jews and Christians were allowed to practice their religions but accorded a second-rank "protected" status which, though it conferred certain rights, still left them subject to a poll tax and other burdens; many eventually converted to Islam.

Qur'anic discussions of fighting "made it clear that religious rewards, that is the joys of paradise, were more important than material success," writes the historian Hugh Kennedy. "In these ways, the Koran provided the ideological justification for the wars of the Muslim conquests."[276]

The ethnicity of Muslim rule changed when Seljuk Turks, then Mongols and later Ottoman Turks invaded the territories of the early Arab caliphate. But the invaders adopted their subjects' religion and the character of Islam did not greatly change.

Islamic countries have had difficulty in separating church and state. One reason, perhaps, is the nature of Islam. Unlike the case with Judaism or Christianity, its founding prophet was presented as a temporal ruler who commanded armies and set social policy. The religion specified only an Islamic state, not a separate church within it. "The idea that any group of persons, any kind of activities, any part of human life is in any sense outside the scope of religious law and jurisdiction is alien to Muslim thought," writes Bernard Lewis, a leading scholar of Islam.[277]

For over a millennium Islamic countries used the shari'a, regarded as divinely inspired, as their only source of law. It was only after the expansion of Islam had been firmly checked and reversed that reformers started to urge separating the state from religion, but they confronted deep resistance. "The general failure of liberal democracy to take hold in Muslim societies is a continuing and repeated phenomenon for an entire century beginning in the late 1800s. This failure has its source at least in part in the inhospitable nature of Islamic culture and society to Western liberal concepts," writes the political scientist Samuel Huntington.[278]

Mustafa Kemal succeeded in secularizing Turkey, after the fall of the Ottoman empire in 1918. More recently secular leaders have emerged in countries like Egypt and Syria, but they are far from being fully secure.

Radical fundamentalist movements agitated for a restoration of Islamic rule. Such movements have come to power in Iran and, for a time, in Afghanistan, and pose a serious threat to the stability of governments in Pakistan and Egypt.

Still, it's far from clear that Islam is the cause of Islamic countries' discontents. Although shari'a was presented as divine law, it was none-theless administered and interpreted by Islamic scholars, known as the ulema, who for centuries served as a check on the absolute authority of the caliph. The ulema did not have formal rights of judicial review, as in western countries, but they gave the ruler legitimacy and he required their support.

Ottoman reformers replaced the ulema with a Western-style legisla-ture, but Caliph Abdulhamid II abolished the legislature in 1878 and the caliphate itself was abolished in 1924. Islamic countries for most of the last century have been ruled by absolutist modern rulers, unchecked by either the ulema or a functioning legislature.

Calls to bring back the shari'a, with its medieval penal code of stonings and amputations, alarm Western observers but reflect the deep-seated desire of many Islamic populations for the rule of law and an institution for restraining the arbitrary power of unjust rulers. "The distinctive distortions of many Muslim states in this era were products of unchecked executive authority," writes the legal scholar Noah Feld-man. "The call for the restoration of the shari'a in contemporary Islamist politics may be seen in substantial part as a response to this constitutional defect." [279]

In two important exceptions, the voice of the scholars in polit-ical affairs has remained strong, but in neither case with entirely happy results. In Saudi Arabia, the royal family has a historic alliance with that of Ibn Abd al-Wahhab, a fundamentalist religious leader. In prin-ciple the scholars, on whom the Saudi rulers depend for their legitimacy, should hold them answerable to the people. In practice, the gushers of oil money have freed the rulers of many ordinary political constraints, and the Wahhabite ulema is under no compulsion to operate for the public benefit, Feldman argues.

In Iran the scholars are in control but too much so. When the shah was ousted, the Ayatollah Khomeini could have restored the ulema to its former role of advising and curbing a secular ruler. Instead, he instituted the unprecedented office of a scholar-jurist who was to be the supreme ruler. "The idea that the scholars as a class would rule directly was without precedent in Islamic history," writes Feldman.[280] Since the Iranian parliament is subject to review by the scholars' Council of Guardians, the system is close to being a dictatorship of the ulema, which is no better than any other kind.

A striking feature of all Islamic countries is the prominent place that Islam plays or is expected to play in national politics. Even in Turkey, the most secular of Islamic countries, a party with Islamist sympathies has gained power through its parliamentary majority. The point could not be clearer: in countries that have not had time to develop robust secular institutions, religion is often the only organizing principle, other than autocracy, to which people can turn.

All state religions are capable of supporting warfare, but Islamic countries, whether or not because of their apparently deep-seated unease with secularization, seem to some observers to have become embroiled in warfare with more than usual frequency. Along the fault lines between Islamic countries and the rest of the world, strife has been common. "Violence also occurs between Muslims, on the one hand, and Orthodox Serbs in the Balkans, Jews in Israel, Hindus in India, Buddhists in Burma and Catholics in the Philippines. Islam has bloody borders," Huntington observed in 1993.[281]

Though almost all Muslims are of course peaceful citizens, the recent terrorist activities by members of Muslim communities against their host European countries of Germany, England, Spain and Holland have added to the perception of Islam as a religion of violence. Religious behavior in itself prompts only social cohesion and purpose, but these can be shaped by leaders toward aggressive ends, as was the case with the Aztec religion. There are many Islams, just as there are many Christianities. Those who shape a sect's beliefs are probably responsible in some degree for what its followers do in the sect's name. Violence, in other words, is behavior more appropriately attributed to societies, not to the religion they may use to justify or incite it.

## Shaping Religion for Warfare

Looking back at the relationship between religion and warfare, each of the three monotheisms has followed a different course. Judaism started as an expansionary creed and transformed itself into a pacific one after defeat. Christianity began as nonviolent, became an aggressive religion of empire, and was then somewhat neutralized after the rise of secular states. Islam was created as a religion of empire but has generally not yet found an easy role in a secular state.

No consistent relationship emerges between religion and warfare, other than that religion is a potent instrument that can be wielded by rulers in many ways. This is as would be expected from the evolutionary perspective that religion emerged from the unremitting strife between early human societies. Religious behavior helped energize a society for war, induced people to endure privation and prepared men to sacrifice their lives in battle. But warfare is only one aspect of religion's cohesive powers. If a group needs to live peacefully with its neighbors, or within a more powerful host community, its religious behavior can be adapted to its needs.

Religious behavior is shaped in part by genetics and in part by culture. Both components may vary over time but the cultural component of religion can be changed more quickly. Through cultural shifts in the interpretation of a religion's requirements, a society can tailor its behavior, or a country its foreign policy, to whatever strategy fits the circumstances. Religions thus possess a considerable degree of flexibility, more than might be expected from their claims to reflect the unchanging commands of divine revelation. The malleability of religious doctrine is not so surprising, given that inflexible religions would soon have led their societies to destruction.

Still, religions have a certain inertia that may persist for generations. Doctrine derived from a divine founder cannot be changed too obviously or too fast. And in some societies leaders may not see the need for change or may fear to implement it. Reasons of this kind could explain the comparative stability of Islam over the centuries, in contrast to the continual turnover of Christian sects.

When states go to war, it is usually for a variety of generally secular causes. Religion may be quickly invoked, but only because it is such a potent instrument for energizing a society and motivating troops. It is usually no more a cause of war than are weapons; both are primarily means of war. Even when the formal cause of war is expressed in terms of religion, the underlying motives are usually secular.

The Bishops' Wars between England and Scotland, for instance, began when Charles I decided in 1637 to impose a version of the Anglican prayer book on the Scottish church. The Scottish nobles and Presbyterians found common cause in rejecting the bishops appointed by the king. In the course of these events Scotland declared itself a Presbyterian nation, sealing its difference with Anglican England, and declared that the appointment of bishops by the king was contrary to divine law. This blunt challenge to royal prerogatives and the divine right of kings to rule as absolute monarchs led to the second Bishops' War, to the English parliament's Grand Remonstrance against royal abuses of power, to the outbreak of civil war in England between the king and parliament and, in 1649, to the momentous event of the king's execution.

But these events can also be considered as a struggle between England and Scotland, followed by a civil war in England, in both of which the combatants used religion to energize their followers. The driving force of both Bishops' Wars was the desire, first of Scotland and then of the English Parliament, to reduce the power of the king; both found it useful to invoke religion against him.

## An Insatiable War Machine

A case in which religion seems much closer to being a prime cause of war is that of the sanguinary campaigns fought by the Aztec empire against its neighbors. The Aztec empire rose to power in the fourteenth century A.D. by shaping a horrific new religion for itself. Building on an ancient Mesoamerican tradition of human sacrifice, the Mexica, the principal members of the Aztec alliance, asserted the belief that their patron deity, the sun god Huitzilopochtli, required spilled human blood to replenish his life force.

"The imperial cosmology held that the Mexica must relentlessly take captives in warfare and sacrifice them," write the anthropologists Geoffrey Conrad and Arthur Demarest. "The spiritual strength of the sacrificed enemy warriors would strengthen the sun and stave off its inevitable destruction by the forces of darkness. Thus, it was specifically the Mexicas' sacred duty to preserve the universe from the daily threat of annihilation."[282]

Instead of the occasional human sacrifice at major festivals, the Aztecs now required routine slaughter of massive numbers of people. The whole society was given over to the mad objective of capturing as many victims as possible from neighboring states, while imposing demands for tribute.

With extraordinary cruelty, the Aztec priests would cut the heart out of living people, whose remains would then be eaten in a cannibal feast. According to a Spanish monk who accompanied Hernán Cortés's invading force in 1519, "The natives of this land had very large temples . . . with a house of worship at the top, and close to the entrance a low stone, about knee-high, where the men or women who were to be sacrificed to their gods were thrown on their backs and of their own accord remained perfectly still. A priest then came out with a stone knife like a lance-head but which barely cut anything, and with this knife he opened the part where the heart is and took out the heart, without the person who was being sacrificed uttering a word.

"Then the man or woman, having been killed in this fashion, was thrown down the steps, where the body was taken and most cruelly torn to pieces, then roasted in clay ovens and eaten as a very tender delicacy; and this is the way they made sacrifices to their gods."[283]

Aztec practice was for the warrior who had taken the captive to sponsor a feast at which a carefully prepared human stew was served.[284]

The scale of this macabre operation was enormous, given the resources of an archaic state. The Aztecs themselves claim to have sacrificed 80,400 prisoners during a 4-day festival in 1487, during the reign of the emperor Ahuitzotl. Historians consider the number exaggerated because the Aztecs could not have managed the logistics. Still, estimates are that at least 15,000 people a year were sacrificed in Central America, with hundreds or thousands of people being massacred in a single ceremony.

The new religion gave the Aztecs a pretext for continual campaigns against their neighbors for the purpose of taking captives and levying tribute. Both nobles and civilians were indoctrinated in the imperial cult and the gods' ceaseless thirst for blood. Their empire expanded rapidly. In the course of a century the Mexica and their allies came to dominate almost all of Central America.

Aztec soldiers fought fanatically because they gained wealth and prestige if they brought captives home, and were promised immortality if they died in battle. Priests accompanied the soldiers to the battlefield, bearing statues of the gods and murdering the first captive in a ritual sacrifice.

The speedy rise of the Aztec empire demonstrated the frightening power of a religious ideology to organize a society around a single goal, however irrational, and drive it to excel in warfare. The religion operated at every level of society, from guiding the state's military campaigns to motivating individual warriors. But the religious ideology the Aztecs created had a fatal flaw, which its designers and their successors failed to fix.

The empire's two goals were sacrificial blood for the gods and tribute for the state. But so much of the workforce of vassal states became depleted by the Aztecs' voracious demands for human blood that there were soon too few people to work the fields. Tribute revenues dropped, a serious threat for the Aztec polity where the noble and warrior classes had expanded in relation to the productive labor force.

In other societies religion has operated to manage natural resources or maintain an ecological balance. But religions are only as good as the thought put into their design and operation. The Aztec state was ultimately unsustainable because the two goals of its religious ideology—victims and tribute—were in effect contradictory.

Aztec armies had to campaign farther afield in search of victims, straining their logistics and leading to many defeats. The Aztec emperors seem to have believed in their sanguinary cult and feared the gods' wrath when the supply of captives started to dry up. Without assurance of the gods' support "the zeal and confidence of the imperial armies was greatly diminished," Conrad and Demarest observe.[285]

Cortés and his conquistadors arrived on the scene in 1519, at a time when the empire's war machine was failing and the Aztecs were hated by all the surrounding states on which they had preyed for so long. Under the assault of a few hundred Spanish troops, and tens of thousands of eager Indian allies, the Aztec empire disintegrated into Cortés's hands.

Though the Aztec wars were formally driven by their sun god's inordinate thirst for sacrificial blood, the question is why the Aztec society and its leaders embraced such a cruel and wasteful creed. Presumably Aztec rulers believed their religion's requirements to be in the state's interests, and indeed without the constant requirement for new victims it's possible that the Aztecs themselves could have ended up on a rival's altars.

"The Mexicas' sacrificial cosmology gave them the competitive edge needed for such victories: fanaticism," write Conrad and Demarest. "The unending hunger of the gods for mass sacrifices also generated the tireless dynamism of the Mexica armies, a persistence which allowed them to wear down some of the most obstinate of their opponents."

The Aztecs' error, from the perspective of their state's long-term survival, was less in adopting such a bloodthirsty creed as in failing to moderate it when circumstances required. Religion is a potent instrument for survival but it embodies only the collective wisdom of a society, and when that is insufficient religion is no salvation.

If religion plays a somewhat less prominent role in wars between modern states, the reason is in part the separation of church and state. The power to declare war rests with secular leaders, not a priest-king. But there is another reason for the detachment of religion from warfare: modern states are no longer dependent on religion for military training, because they have learned how to borrow and secularize religious techniques.

## Training for War

One of the most surprising achievements of the secular state, though it is generally taken for granted, is the ability to induce men to sacrifice their lives in battle without any explicit religious incentive.

In primitive societies and archaic states, religious indoctrination was a principal way of getting soldiers to fight. Boys were expected to endure painful initiation rites without showing pain, so as to toughen them as warriors. Their emotional endurance too was tested through long and frightening ordeals. They would often be trained with others of their age group to encourage solidarity. Among the Nilotic peoples of East Africa like the Nuer, the age-sets of initiated young men served as military companies who were always ready to go to war, and this organization enabled the Nuer to prevail over neighbors who were less well prepared.

In a cross-cultural survey of male initiation, the sociologist Richard Sosis and colleagues tallied the presence or absence of 19 ritual practices such as genital mutilation, teeth pulling, tattooing, scarification and piercing. They found that societies that went to war most often had the most painful initiation rites. Presumably the more militaristic the society, the more searing it made the initiation of its future warriors.

The pain and fear associated with these rituals stands in interest-ing contrast to the positive effects of religious rites involving dance and music, which leave participants emotionally uplifted. Sosis and col-leagues suggest that "through frightening and painful rites, religious symbols can acquire deep emotional significance that subsequently unites individuals who share the experience." Even though boys may not go to war until many years after their initiation, the emotional effect of initiation is enduring. Painful rituals "generate solidarity between men and serve as reliable indicators of group commitment, thus reducing the likelihood that men will defect when there is war," the researchers conclude.[286]

Besides the bonding of initiation rites, early societies seem to have depended heavily on ritual dancing before battle to spread a feeling of cohesion. Religious war dances were used by the Zulus, Swazis and many other peoples. The Aztecs required boys to live apart from their families and train with nightly dances to firelight. On the night before the battle at the Aztec capital of Tenochtitlán, the Spanish were alarmed by the sound of martial music. According to a Spanish survivor, "That night more than a thousand knights got together in the temple, the great loud sounds of drums, shrill trumpets, cornet and notched bones . . . They danced nude . . . in a circle, holding their hands, in rows and keeping time to the tune of the musicians and singers."[287]

Yielding one's life in war is, from the point of view of individual sur-vival, an irrational act. Yet untold millions of men have done so, prov-ing that to risk one's life in combat is a part of human nature. But this behavior cannot prevail unless the powerful biological instinct for self-preservation is overridden.

For men to become warriors, they must be imbued with several important attitudes. They must be trained to develop strong group cohe-sion, to lose their fear of the enemy, to believe victory is possible, to believe their valor will be rewarded, to believe right is on their side, and to sacri-fice their lives if necessary.

Religion, notes the evolutionary biologist Dominic Johnson, provides

an answer for all of these problems. Initiation rites inculcate group cohesion, belief in the god of one's tribe promotes confidence in victory,
religion-based morality defines the warrior's side as good and the enemy's
as evil, and religions may promise luxuriant rewards to those who fall in
battle, or punishment for those who desert the cause.

"Religion turns out to have many properties that make it an excellent adaptation for war," Johnson remarks. "Perhaps this is an accident.
Alternatively, perhaps it is so effective because it was designed for exactly
this purpose."[288]

How then do modern armies induce men to fight without the emotional goads of initiation rites, consulting oracles, war dances or the
promise of paradise?

First, modern armies are imbued with military rituals. As Johnson
observes, "Rituals dominate not only war itself but military organizations in their entirety: initiations, oaths of allegiance, ranks, duty training, drill, parades, indoctrination, standard operating procedures, combat
tactics, memorials to the dead, and offerings to the gods prior to battle or
after victory."[289] Religion no longer has a central role in warfare but it has
not been banished very far from the scene of action. Modern armies have
military chaplains in attendance.

Second, people in modern societies are probably easier to discipline
and mold into a cohesive fighting force than were people in early societies.

A third reason that modern societies have been able to train soldiers
without depending on the old religious methods is that they have in fact
borrowed and built on a central feature of religious training for war, that
of music and dance.

The historian William McNeill has traced how early armies, such as
that of the Spartans, practiced marching in unison to music and entered
battle to the sounds of flutes, executing precise maneuvers. The importance of moving in unison was rediscovered from ancient Roman sources
by Prince Maurice of Nassau, captain general of Holland from 1585 to
1625. His cousin Johann of Nassau had analyzed the motions necessary to
reload a matchlock and found there were 42 postures required. Maurice

trained his soldiers to move in unison through each of these actions and found, after endless practice, that a lot more lead could be delivered on the enemy through rhythmic coordination.

Training, drill and movement in unison proved very effective at making even the roughest classes into soldiers. "I don't know what effect these men will have on the enemy but, by God, they terrify me," the Duke of Wellington remarked on a draft of Irish troops sent to him during the Peninsula War in Spain in 1809.

Maurice made no secret of his methods, which were widely copied. Both in Europe and independently in China, McNeill writes, "prolonged drill created obedient, reliable and effective soldiers, with an *esprit de corps* that superseded previous identities and insulated them from outside attachments. Well-drilled new-model soldiers, whether Chinese or European, could therefore be counted on to obey their officers accurately and predictably, even when fighting hundreds or thousands of miles away from home."[290]

Acceptable as these modern armies were in fighting other European states, they were not nearly as good, in terms of martial valor, as the war machines of primitive societies that trained their warriors with purely religious methods. Despite their technological superiority, European armies did not always prevail. In 1879 the British army in South Africa was defeated by Zulus not once, but three times, at the battles of Isandlwana, Myer's Drift and Hlobane. Against the British artillery and Gatling guns the Zulus possessed only spears and ox-hide shields, although they enjoyed superior numbers.

In its wars with the Indians, the U.S. Army was usually defeated when caught in the open, such as by the Seminoles in 1834, and by the Lakota and Northern Cheyenne at the battle of Little Bighorn in 1876. The southern San or bushmen of the Sneeuberg Mountains in South Africa halted the advance of the armed and mounted Boers for 30 years.

Western armies won in the end, but because they had larger populations and more effective logistics, not because their soldiers were better warriors. It is remarkable that religion prepared primitive warriors for battle so well, and maybe equally remarkable that European countries succeeded in devising a secular alternative for inducing the strangest but most necessary of all human behaviors, the willingness to sacrifice one's life in warfare.

## Religion and the Causes of War

Critics sometimes point to religion as a source of war and strife. "Indeed, religion is as much a living spring of violence today as it was at any time in the past," writes the philosopher Sam Harris, listing the wars between religiously defined groups in Palestine, the Balkans, Northern Ireland, Kashmir, Sudan, Ethiopia and Eritrea, Sri Lanka, Indonesia and the Caucasus. "In these places religion has been the *explicit* cause of literally millions of deaths in the last ten years. . . . Add weapons of mass destruction to this diabolical clockwork, and you have found a recipe for the fall of civilization," he says.[291]

The vivid presence of religion in all these conflicts certainly raises the question of whether some of them might have been reduced or avoided did religion not exist. But the issue is not as straightforward as it seems.

Before the modern state was secularized, religion, politics and warfare were much more intimately intertwined and it was scarcely possible to separate them in many circumstances. The ritual wars of the Maring were governed by the build-up of the pig population; once the pigs were sacrificed and the sacred tanket tree was uprooted, the cycle of war inevitably resumed. But even with the Maring, although religion drove the cycle of warfare, the function of each war, whether the Maring realized it or not, was to readjust the populations of pigs and people to the carrying capacity of the land.

Religion appears to be the prime driver of the Aztec wars, given that the Aztecs' assaults on their neighbors were driven by the need for captives to sacrifice to their bloodthirsty god. But a deeper analysis is that the Aztec religion furnished the expansionary ethos through which the

Aztecs prevailed over their neighbors, rather than letting their neighbors conquer them. The Aztec empire was about survival, and religion merely provided the means.

"The peculiar Aztec merger of religion, politics, and war was, in fact, probably closer to the human norm than the separation between religions and politics to which we are accustomed," writes McNeill.[292]

The inextricable mixture of politics and religion is evident in the first crusade, launched with the apparently purely religious objective of recapturing Jerusalem from the Saracens. But there was another motive. The church was troubled by the outbursts of religious hysteria that were perturbing church authorities all across Europe. Led by their priests, crowds of flagellants marched from town to town, lashing themselves to a frenzy. Zeal leads inevitably to schism and is a constant threat to any established church. How better to cope with the masses of the ultra-faithful than to march them to the sunburned deserts of the Near East, at the end of an impossibly long supply train, in the expectation that few would return?

"It is, in fact, a misleading over-simplification to see the crusade simply as a confrontation between Christian Europe and the Moslem East," writes Paul Johnson. "The central problem of the institutional church was always how to control the manifestations of religious enthusiasm, and divert them into orthodox and constructive channels. The problem was enormously intensified when large numbers of people were involved. . . . Sometimes they attacked the Jews, regarded as devils like the Moslems, but more accessible. But if no Jews or Moslems were available, they nearly always, sooner or later, turned on the Christian clergy. Hence the anxiety to dispatch them to Jerusalem."[293]

Researchers at the University of Bradford in England assessed 73 major wars for the role played in them by religion and concluded that only in three did religion play an extremely intense role—the Arab conquests of 632–732, the crusades of 1091–1291 and the Protestant-Catholic wars of the Reformation. In 60 percent of wars, they found that religion played no role at all. Wars were scored according to a 6-point list including such factors as whether religion was used to mobilize nations for war, whether political leaders cited a religious motivation and whether one side's goal was to convert the other to its religion. "There have been few genuinely religious wars in the last 100 years," the researchers say.[294]

Religion may play a less central role in many modern wars, and secular powers conduct many wars without any official citation of a religious pretext. But religion, in addition to its offstage role even in modern countries in preparing soldiers for battle, is frequently evoked as a rallying cry. The struggle between Jews and Palestinian Arabs is primarily about land, but both sides seek to strengthen their claims and their populations' resolve by citing the imperatives of their respective religions.

In contexts like these, religion seems more a means of war than an end, and its contribution to causality is much like that of weapons. Weapons may provoke a war if one country's build-up of arms is deemed an intolerable threat by its adversary. But in general weapons are seldom considered a prime cause of war, and much the same is true of religion.

Religion, however, can be shaped to support aggressive or pacific policies. The implicit premise of those who criticize religion for fomenting warfare is that all wars are wrong. But this of course is not the case. Some wars are just—most Americans would say the majority of their wars have been so, particularly the War of Independence and the Second World War. Many wars are regarded as defensive, at least by the country that is attacked. Many are unavoidable, especially for neighbors of an expansionist power. Religion's contribution to just and defensive wars should surely be regarded as positive.

It may therefore be a wasted effort to draw up a scorecard for religion and its positive or negative contributions to warfare. As argued in an earlier chapter, religious behavior evolved to induce social cohesion and thereby to govern two essential human social behaviors, self-restraint within a society and aggression, if necessary, toward members of other societies. Religious behavior evolved in a dangerous world, amid hunter gatherer societies that did not hesitate to attack and sometimes exterminate their neighbors. The groups whose members developed the strongest emotional ties among one another were best able to prevail. These ties, forged in religious training and ritual, embedded in human nature its contradictory qualities of self-restraint and aggressiveness.

People today are the descendants not of those who lost out in these unremitting struggles but of the victors. We have inherited the capacities for extreme hostility, cruelty, even genocide, toward those who threaten us, along with the capacities for loyalty, love and trust toward members of our own community. That is why human nature is part angel and part brute. An individual may be either one or the other, but societies and nations are inextricably both.

# 11

---

# RELIGION AND NATION

*The importance of religion and war in the shaping of nations
should not even be debatable. Back in the sixteenth and
seventeenth centuries, they were the principal instruments of
world affairs. They were also principal instruments of English,
then British and American nationalism. From the birth of
Protestantism in the sixteenth century, no Western nation has
matched the English-speaking peoples in asserting their destiny
as God's kingdom. . . .*

KEVIN PHILLIPS, *The Cousins' Wars* [295]

*There is no country in the world where the Christian religion
retains a greater influence than in America: and there can be
no greater proof of its utility and of its conformity of human
nature than that its influence is powerfully felt over the most
enlightened and free nation of the earth.*

ALEXIS DE TOCQUEVILLE, *Democracy in America* [296]

As long as kings ruled by divine right, religion and politics were
essentially one and the same. The king's decrees had the sanction
of heaven, from which there was no dissent. With the separation
of church and state in modern societies, religion and politics started to

occupy distinct realms. Many European countries largely exclude religion from their domestic politics. As for international affairs, nations usually calculate their self-interest coldly, leaving no apparent role for religion in statecraft. In the index of Henry Kissinger's book *Diplomacy* there are 49 references to *Realpolitik*, none to Religion.

The steady growth of secularization in most Western countries has further eroded the political sway of religious authorities. At the beginning of the twentieth century sociologists predicted that religion would eventually disappear; at its end, *The Economist* magazine cheekily published God's obituary.[297] Secularization has indeed advanced in parallel with education, modernity and political security, particularly in Europe. Yet religion as a political force is far from spent. Religious behavior continues to be a primal glue of all human groupings, from tribal band to civilization. Religion remains central to the definition of culture, and it is culture that forms the fault lines between the world's major civilizations.

Religion is integral to the cohesion of groups, and hence to their power and to the competitive relationships between them. In hunter gatherer societies, religion was aligned with several other powerful social glues, notably those of kinship, ethnicity, language and culture. After people abandoned foraging and settled down, their communities became much larger. The degree of kinship was much diminished in these more populous societies but religion, in the form of ancestor cults, may have instilled the idea of common descent and a shared origin.

Religious behavior can be stronger than the other social glues because it creates bonds at an emotional level. Its reach is broader than that of language and ethnicity since it can draw together people of many different tongues and nationalities. The nation state—people of the same language, ethnicity and religion living in the same region—may be coming back into vogue in the wake of the Cold War: Czechoslovakia has fissioned into the Czech Republic and Slovakia; East and West Germany, despite different ideologies, have reunited. But for most of history many people have lived in large polyglot empires, whether of the Romans or the Holy Roman Empire or the Chinese imperium.

In these structures religion has played a central though double-edged role since it can both unite and divide. When Roman religion proved uncompelling as an imperial creed, Constantine and his successors chose Christianity to replace it as the empire's unifying force. The Holy Roman Empire, on the other hand, was hastened to its demise by the religious divisions ignited within it by Martin Luther and the Reformation.

In no country today does religion play a more intricate political role than in the United States. Europeans are continually astonished that this most materialistic of societies, as they see it, remains far more religious than theirs have become. But it is not adherence to a single church, like that of the Irish or Italians to Catholicism, that gives the United States its religiosity. A multitude of faiths are practiced, often in strong competition with one another. How does religion operate in American society? Why have Americans remained such assiduous church-goers when the populations of European countries have become increasingly secular?

## The Puritan Founding

Religious schisms are usually about far more than differences in religious doctrine. The advocates of a new doctrine may genuinely believe their cause is divine, but as adherents are gained, the doctrine becomes a source of influence, a rallying cry for all who are dissatisfied with the establishment for any of a multitude of reasons. Groups that hold many grievances against one another may then find that none is so potent a cause as the religious difference that is now at hand. Religion can polarize a struggle more forcefully than any other cause because it stirs emotional drives to unite with one's friends and oppose or kill one's adversaries.

The Reformation had just such an effect in Europe, setting off a century and a half of wars between Protestant and Catholic powers. One small eddy in this maelstrom enveloped Tudor England, a non-Catholic country menaced by the larger Catholic nations of Spain and France. One of the Tudors' successors, the Stuart king Charles I, polarized the country by ignoring parliament and flirting with Catholic authorities in France to keep himself in power. Religious schism became a focus for these political differences, and a particularly vehement sect within the English Protestant movement sought to purify the Anglican church of its Catholic-leaning tendencies.

These purifiers, otherwise known as Puritans, shared the core Protestant belief that the Bible, not Rome and its bishops, was the only impeccable source of religious authority. The Catholic church, not without good reason, had long sought to keep the Bible untranslated lest people develop their own ideas of how to interpret it and the text should become a source of schism. From their reading of the Bible, the English Puritans gleaned the idea that the English, and specifically themselves, were God's chosen people. These beliefs spurred them to emigrate in large numbers from East Anglia to the Promised Land which, naturally enough, they called New England.

"Belief that the English were a Chosen People was especially strong, and those who counted themselves among this elect body worried constantly about losing God's favor through some shortcoming, especially failure to promote moral reformation," says the political writer Kevin Phillips.[298]

The Puritans' religious views were not the only factor in their decision to emigrate. Bad harvests and epidemics were one stimulus for this unusual exodus. Hard times in the local cloth industry were another. A persecution of the Puritans was initiated by William Laud, a powerful cleric who became Archbishop of Canterbury in 1633. But it was religion that shaped all these factors into an unusual course of action: between 1620 and 1640 some 80,000 English people, amounting to 2 percent of the population, braved the risks of emigration to the American colonies, the Caribbean or Holland, with some 20,000 ending up in New England.

The Puritans' fervent faith continued to bind and motivate them in their new home. They were still the Chosen People, and the Promised Land turned out to be superbly extensible in a westward direction. When the Erie Canal was completed in 1825, linking the Hudson River to the

Great Lakes, their descendants spearheaded the settlement of the Mid-west. "From the earliest English settlement, Americans viewed them-selves within the great stream of salvation history: a New World people who were fully committed to completing the Protestant Reformation," writes the historian Frank Lambert. "One of Americans' most powerful and enduring myths is that of God's choosing the American wilderness as the site of a special outpouring of grace. . . . Massachusetts was noth-ing less than the New Israel, a chosen people with whom God had entered into a covenant that promised his blessings as long as the people obeyed his commandments." Proof of this belief was discerned in the British vic-tory over the French and their Indian allies in the war of 1754–1763, inter-preted as a Protestant triumph over Papists.[299]

The Puritan zeal gradually mellowed into the milder versions of Protestantism that followed it, such as Congregationalism and Presbyte-rianism. The Puritans did not help their own cause by excesses such as the Massachusetts witch trials and by persecuting other sects. But even though their movement lost momentum, many of their ideas passed into Americans' political and cultural outlook. Among these is the belief in American exceptionalism, that the nation has a providential destiny, and that it has a covenant that guarantees the deity's blessing in return for righteous behavior.

From an evolutionary perspective, the New England Puritans' views of their practical mission in the world were ideally suited to territorial expansion and survival. Their religion supplied a divine justification for developing new territories. By punishing heretics they maintained a strong internal cohesion. Pro-natalist religious policies, such as dis-solving marriages because of infertility, along with a favorable climate, spurred population growth, an essential engine of expansion. Though New England received fewer new immigrants after 1642, its population had already reached 120,000 by 1700 and continued to grow. Religion and politics were perfectly matched to the circumstances in which the Puri-tans found themselves, and enabled a once persecuted sect to expand vig-orously and ensure its long-term survival.

## The Religious Marketplace

As Puritan zeal faded into Congregationalism, other Protestant sects emerged in its wake. The Methodists rose to prominence, with a cadre of vigorous preachers who held revivalist meetings around the country. But then the Methodists became prosperous, their ministers developed a greater interest in theology than in stirring a crowd, and their meetings grew more sedate. "Their clergy were increasingly willing to condone the pleasures of this world and to deemphasize sin, hellfire and damnation. . . . This is, of course, the fundamental dynamic by which sects are transformed into churches, thereby losing the vigor and the high octane faith that caused them to succeed in the first place," note the sociologists Roger Finke and Rodney Stark.[300]

After steady gains from 1776 onward, Methodist numbers peaked around 1850. They were overtaken by the Baptists and by a new competitor in the religious marketplace, the Catholics. Not only were Catholic numbers enhanced by new immigrants, but the American Catholic church was much more aggressive than those of European countries. Indeed American bishops complained about the poor instructional work of their European counterparts. "It is a very delicate matter," wrote Bishop Thomas Becker of Wilmington, Delaware, in 1883, "to tell the Sovereign Pontiff how utterly faithless the specimens of his country coming here really are. Ignorance of their religion and a depth of vice little known to us yet, are the prominent characteristics."[301]

The Catholics in their turn have started to falter, a slide that may have been inevitable but which some critics say was hastened by ill-considered reforms initiated by the Second Vatican Council of 1962. Although 31 percent of Americans were raised in the Catholic faith, only 24 percent today describe themselves as Catholic, the greatest net loss of any religion.[302]

In countries with an established church, sects are suppressed and dissident prelates seldom become bishops. In the turbulent arena of American religious life, nothing seems fixed except a dynamic cycle whereby sects displace mainstream churches, lose their enthusiasm and become establishment themselves, and yield in turn to more vigorous new sects. In the period from 1940 to 2000, mainstream sects suffered heavy losses, as measured in their share of overall church membership, Methodists declining by 56 percent, Presbyterians by 60 percent, Episcopalians by 51 percent and Congregationalists by 66 percent. The winners in the religious marketplace were the evangelical churches, the Mormons and Jehovah's Witnesses.[303] These movements too, if the pattern continues, will eventually lose momentum and give up market share to insurrectionist sects.

The American religious scene is unlike that of any other country. It may owe much of its special quality to the absence of an official, government-backed religion, as specified in the First Amendment. This has allowed development of a "free market" for religion, to use an analogy invoked by a school of economists and sociologists. They believe the economic laws that govern the rise and fall of firms in the marketplace offer many insights into the equivalent process with religions.

In nations with established churches, the argument goes, the clergy's salaries are guaranteed and the official religion has a monopoly or at least unchallenged dominance. Hence priests have little incentive to push the brand or increase market share of their product. The upshot has been a steady decline in church attendance in Britain, Sweden and most other European countries.

In the United States, by contrast, religions must evangelize to survive, or competitors will lure away members of their flock. The overall size of the market for religious products is much greater than it otherwise would be because consumers' demand is stimulated by the incessant competition between different religious brands, argue the sociologists Finke and Stark. As a result the number of Americans who actually belong to a church—a better measure of belief than asking them for their religious affiliation—has steadily risen throughout American history. Just 17 percent of the population were church members in 1776, rising fairly steadily to a peak of 62 percent in 1980, a proportion that was the same in 2000, according to figures assembled by Finke and Stark.[304]

The religious marketplace thesis has been criticized on the grounds that it doesn't explain the extent of religious participation in other countries. Ireland, Italy, Poland, Colombia and Venezuela all have high levels of church attendance despite the fact that in each a religious monopoly— that of Catholicism—prevails. The political scientists Pippa Norris and Ronald Inglehart surveyed modern countries with several active religions and found "no support to the claim of a significant link between religious pluralism and participation."[305]

Norris and Inglehart propose an alternative explanation for the extent of religiosity in a country, suggesting it is related to people's feeling of insecurity during their formative years. The proposal owes something to Marx's idea that religion is an opiate to dull people's suffering. If people grow up in conditions that make them feel secure, both politically and economically, they will see less need to belong to a church, Norris and Inglehart suggest. Contrary to the religious market theory, they argue, the demand for religion should be highest in poor countries with high poverty and political unrest, and lowest in stable countries with a generous and dependable welfare system.

The Norris and Inglehart proposal explains quite plausibly the low level of church attendance in politically stable countries with a strong welfare system, like Sweden or England. But why is religiosity so high in a prosperous country like the United States? Norris and Inglehart argue that life is in fact quite insecure for the poor in America, given the inefficient nature of the welfare system, and that Americans turn to religion because they face higher economic uncertainty than do Europeans.

Their thesis may plausibly account for the extent of church-going in other countries. But for the United States, the religious marketplace theory seems a better explanation. Its central premise, that there is vigorous competition among religions for market share, is supported by a recent survey reporting that Americans switch religions with surprising frequency: no less than 44 percent of people profess a religious affiliation different from that in which they were raised. (This statistic includes switches among branches of the same denomination, i.e. from one kind of Protestantism to another.)[306]

The United States has made itself in some respects into a fine laboratory for the study of religion. Because of free competition without government interference, religious change seems to proceed at a much brisker rate than usual, with new sects rising to prominence in a matter of decades and declining almost as fast.

The rise of Mormonism has been particularly rapid, despite many apparent disadvantages. Judaism, Christianity and Islam all developed over many centuries, and were able to shape their founding myths and sacred texts in the relative obscurity of the distant past. But Joseph Smith lived in the nineteenth century, a well-documented historical period, and his claim to have transcribed sacred texts at the behest of a visiting angel, though little different from Muhammad's revelation, is not the most plausible of attestations. Nor is Mormonism as a creed well regarded by the Christians who are its most likely potential converts, given the seemingly strange elements it grafts onto conventional Judeo-Christian beliefs.

Nonetheless, Mormonism has been immensely successful in terms of its growth and cohesion. The persecution of the church in its early days doubtless strengthened the survivors' resolve and commitment. Its strictness is probably another ingredient of success. Unlike many liberal mainstream churches that require little of members, Mormonism requires members to donate not just a tenth of their incomes to their church but also a tenth of their time. According to the rational choice theory described earlier, a high entry price deters free riders who otherwise degrade a community's advantages for other members. And the heavy commitment of time leaves members little time to associate with outsiders.

The success of Mormonism shows how effectively a religion can promote a group's survival. Another example is that of the black churches formed after the Civil War. The churches were the one institution that

African Americans controlled. Their clergy, more willing to provide political leadership than those of most white churches, have worked to secure advantages for a particular ethnic group but have largely done so without raising the specter of separatism. Black ministers and their churches spearheaded the Civil Rights movement. Without the religious motivation, it is hard to see how the movement would have remained nonviolent, the key to its success.

## American Civil Religion

Given the acrid, religion-fueled wars in countries like Northern Ireland or Bosnia, how is it that the competing churches in the United States have kept their struggles so peaceful? The exceptions, on the whole, have been minor. Religious differences were evident between North and South in the Civil War, but were not a principal cause of war. Some religions, despite the freedom accorded to their own modes of worship, have tried to impose their doctrines on others. One flagrant abuse was Prohibition, a largely Protestant attempt to punish Catholic drinkers. Another, some would say, is the campaign to outlaw abortion, a largely Catholic and evangelical movement to force others to their own view.

Despite the occasional difference, the American religious polity has so far remained surprisingly united. The usual glues that hold nations together are a single dominant religion, language, ethnicity and culture. Until 1850 or so, the United States fitted this mold, being essentially an Anglo-Protestant culture. Many of its people originated from England, Scotland or Northern Ireland, and other Europeans became American by adopting at least the language of Anglo-Protestantism. De Tocqueville in the 1830s referred to the population as "Anglo-Americans."

The situation today is somewhat different. There are many different subcultures in the United States, no ethnicity prevails and even the universality of English is being challenged by large Spanish-speaking enclaves. As for religious affiliation, no denomination is dominant. Some 78 percent of adults describe themselves as Christian, according to a Pew Forum survey published in 2008, 5 percent belong to other religions (including almost 2 percent who are Jewish) and 16 percent claim no religion. Within the Christian grouping, 51 percent of Americans describe themselves as Protestant, 24 percent as Catholic and under 2 percent as Mormon. But the Protestants are divided into many different sects, with the major groupings being evangelical churches (26 percent of the U.S. population), mainstream churches (18 percent) and historically black churches (7 percent).[307]

If the evolutionary role of religious behavior is to provide social cohesion, to what extent, if any, does this plethora of different faiths bind Americans together? And if neither religion nor ethnicity provides common links, does anything?

Some observers believe there is in effect an overarching faith that unites Americans. It has no church or ministers, and no one claims it as their personal religion. Its presence in American public life is so ubiquitous and familiar that no one gives it a second thought. This mysterious higher creed was first given serious attention by the sociologist Robert Bellah in 1967. A principal ceremony of American Civil Religion, as he called it, is the inauguration of a president. Its sacred texts include certain presidential addresses, such as Kennedy's inaugural and Lincoln's Gettysburg Address. Its annual rituals include Memorial Day and Thanksgiving. The motto "In God We Trust" provides spiritual backing for the currency. The pledge of allegiance recited by schoolchildren describes the republic as "one nation under God." The chief officer of the American Civil Religion is the president. The art of his religious duty is to avoid sectarian references and stick to generic invocations of the deity.

A recurrent theme of the American Civil Religion, like that of other national religions, is that the United States has found special favor in the deity's eye or will do so if its acts are righteous. "With a good conscience

our only sure reward, with history the final judge of our deeds," said John
F. Kennedy in concluding his inaugural speech, "let us go forth to lead
the land we love, asking His blessing and His help, but knowing that here
on earth God's work must truly be our own."

This activist conception of religious duty, Bellah noted, has historically been associated with Protestant theology. That it should have been
articulated by the nation's first Catholic president "seems to underline
how deeply established it is in the American outlook."[308]

Others agree that American Civil Religion exists, despite the Constitution's prohibition of an established church. "Every nation has a faith of
sorts, a belief in itself, a civil religion—and in the United States this civil
religion is profoundly infused with a sense that God has provided Americans with special blessings," say the political scientist Robert Fowler and
colleagues.[309]

But there is disagreement as to the real nature of American Civil Religion. It is, say some scholars, simply the Protestant or Puritan creed, dis-
guised by the avoidance of any reference to Jesus. "The American Creed is
the unique creation of a dissenting Protestant culture," says the political
scientist Samuel Huntington. Its sources include various Enlightenment
themes and Anglo-Protestant culture with its long-standing English ideas
such as the rights of Englishmen and the limits of government authority.

American Civil Religion, in Huntington's view, has four major
elements. First is the assumption of a supreme being—as President
Eisenhower said, "Without God, there could be no American form of government, nor an American way of life." Second is the belief that America
is the new Israel and has a divinely decreed destiny. Third are the frequent references to God in public life, such as the phrase "So help me
God" which presidents traditionally add to their oath of office (the words
are not in the Constitution's version of the oath). Fourth are the national
holidays and certain sacred texts that have come to define the national
identity, including the Declaration of Independence and Martin Luther
King's "I have a dream" speech.

"The American Creed, in short, is Protestantism without God, the secular credo of the 'nation with the soul of a church,'" Huntington wrote.[310]

A similar conclusion has been reached by the historian George McKenna, who sees the creed as not only Protestant but as more specifically Puritan. "When the chips are down, when the stakes are high, American political leaders go back to the narrative and even the language of the Puritans; they do it then, especially, because that is when Americans especially want to hear it. They start talking about grace and consecration and sanctification, language found nowhere in the Constitution or even the Declaration of Independence. It is biblical, prophetic language, the language of sermons and jeremiads. It reappears each time the nation needs to gird its loins, concentrate its mind and throw itself against whatever threatens its life: a foreign foe, a domestic rebellion, a Great Depression, a conspiracy of terror."[311]

Equitable laws, a generally prosperous economy and a reasonably equitable distribution of wealth are all important ingredients of a cohesive society but probably do not fully account for the surprising social tranquillity of a nation as variegated as the United States. American Civil Religion, however, provides an emotional bond between people of all faiths. Perhaps even more pertinent is the bridge it provides between the races. Nothing is more corrosive to the social fabric than ethnic antagonism and its stimulus to deep-seated tribal loyalties. The fact that black churches have equal standing with all the others, and Martin Luther King is widely accepted as a national figure of transcendent moral authority, provides a strong signal of inclusion to African Americans.

A pertinent question about American Civil Religion is whether or not this meta-creed possesses the necessary cohesive power to bind an increasingly disparate nation to common standards of morality and a common purpose in warfare. The United States, as its ethnicity grows less British and European, has few sources of cohesion save language, and even its common language is under threat in some regions from Spanish.

Conservatives fear damage to the social fabric from the decay of religious values. In the United States, they see the once unifying culture of
Anglo-Protestantism as being under steady erosion from the pressures of
secularism, multiculturalism, and the divisive assertion of group rights
of various kinds over and beyond the individual rights promised in the
Constitution. An obvious way to strengthen cohesion would be through
religious education in the school years, the one major experience that
everyone has in common. But religion has been largely evicted from
American public schools, an event that would doubtless have dumb-
founded the framers of the Constitution. They directed Congress to make
no law respecting an establishment of religion but that was not because
they were secularists. It was because they didn't want the members of any
Christian sect taxed to support another sect.

In the eighteenth century, some 95 percent of the American population belonged to Protestant sects of one kind or another. Almost everyone
accepted that morality must be taught through religion, and that religion must be taught in schools. At that time, in the words of Noah Feldman, a legal scholar who has written about the history of church-state
issues, "The notion of teaching children morality by some means that
did not involve religion would hardly have entered the American mind.
Morality, it was understood, derived from religion, and for even the most
liberal of the Protestants who made up the northeastern elite in the 1820's
and '30s, that meant morality came from the Bible, especially the Gospels. Without religion there could be no foundation stone on which to
rest the basic values of honesty and rule following. None of the theorists
of the new common schools advocated keeping religion out of the classroom. No religion would have meant no morality, and no morality would
have meant that the schools could not achieve their society-shaping
function."[312]

The political solution arrived at under the founders and their immediate successors was called nonsectarianism. It consisted of teaching in
schools a generic form of Protestantism that was acceptable to all the

various sects and was based on reading the King James Version of the Bible. Nonsectarianism worked well until the tide of Catholic immigration starting in the 1820s.

The Catholics began to object that it was a Protestant idea to learn religion from the Bible, not from priests' interpretation, and that they were being taxed to support schools they could not use. The Protestant majority said, in effect, that that was tough luck. This failure of the two Christian denominations to agree left them vulnerable, a century later, to a movement Feldman calls legal secularism. The legal secularists did not explicitly seek to abolish religion, merely to build a wall of separation between church and state with the formal goal of protecting religious minorities. The chief minority in the legal developments of the 1950s was that of Jews who, like the Catholics, did not welcome paying for religious instruction they had no use for. "American Jews," Feldman writes, "gradually began to play an important part in the development of the strategies of legal secularism beginning in the postwar era."[313]

The Christian churches felt secure in the 1950s and did not oppose the legal secularists until too late. Legal secularism was not addressed to the electorate, which would doubtless have rejected it flat, just to the Supreme Court, an elite group culturally attuned to the secularists' arguments. "To embrace legal secularism was, for the Court, continuous with a set of liberal values characteristic of enlightened citizens and educated jurists," Feldman writes.[314] The outcome was that Christianity was evicted from the classroom.

Some 95 percent of Americans are Christians or belong to no religion. Minorities—including Jews, Buddhists, Muslims and Hindus, together make up less than 5 percent. To protect the rights of a 5 percent minority by denying religious education to 95 percent of the population was a solution that could seem satisfactory to few besides lawyers. As the continued tussles over religious education attest, particularly the assaults on teaching evolution, it is not a fully accepted or stable solution.

To anyone approaching the issue from the perspective of social cohesion, morality is one issue in which diversity and minority exceptions are distinct drawbacks. The educational years, it could be argued, are a unique and invaluable opportunity to inculcate a common frame of moral reference in an otherwise diverse and heterogeneous population.

Many liberals, however, see no need to strengthen religion as a source of national cohesion in the United States and regard the churches as wielding too much political power already. Conservatives fear that despite the United States' lively religious marketplace, religion in general is likely to yield eventually to the strong tides of secularism that have already undermined church-going in most European countries.

## Secularism and Sacred Texts

Two serious assaults on religious belief, or at least on the three text-based monotheisms, have been the rise of scientific knowledge, including especially the theory of evolution, and "higher criticism," the analysis of Bible texts spearheaded by nineteenth-century German scholars such as Julius Wellhausen.

Science has provided an increasingly comprehensive explanation for the material world, one which is now largely complete, in principle if not in detail, except for singular events such as the origin of the universe and the origin of life on earth. This knowledge, a soaring triumph of the rational mind, has from the seventeenth century onward eroded a major intellectual pillar of religious belief, that of religion's claim to explain the natural world.

A second challenge to religious belief emerged from the nineteenth-century practitioners of higher criticism who showed that the Bible, far from being the inerrant product of divine inspiration, was cobbled together by a number of different human hands whose varied stitching, once pointed out, was all too visible. In other words the Pentateuch, as one affronted cleric summarized the charge, was not Mosaic but mosaic.

Higher criticism was particularly painful for Protestant faiths.

Catholicism and Judaism had always emphasized their official interpretations of the sacred text rather than the text itself. But a major element of the Reformation was Luther's belief in the literal truth of the Bible, a tenet firmly endorsed by the Puritans.

Catholics and Jews, after the initial shocks had worn off, adapted to the challenges from higher criticism and science by interpreting parts of their sacred texts metaphorically. They were followed by liberal Protestants. But the conservative wing of the Protestant movement, instead of hedging its commitment to the literal truth position in light of all this new information, opted to double down its bet. Fundamentalists owe their name to a series of essays called *The Fundamentals: A Foundation of Truth*, which were published between 1910 and 1915 with the help of a large grant from Lyman Stewart, the head of the Union Oil Company of California. The five basic tenets of this position were the inerrancy of the scriptures; the virgin birth and the divine nature of Jesus; the doctrine of atonement; the resurrection; and the authenticity of Jesus' miracles.[315]

By the beginning of the twentieth century it seemed to many intellectuals that industrial societies like those of Europe and America would inevitably become more secular and that the role of religion would fade, perhaps to nothing. This prediction has turned out to be correct only in part.

Religiosity, as measured by church attendance and questions about the importance of religion, is consistently highest in agrarian countries (like Uganda and Peru), lower in developing industrial countries (like Mexico and Turkey) and lower still in advanced industrial countries (like France and New Zealand). This confirms the notion that religion tends to wane as countries modernize.

Further confirmation can be seen in the figures for religious participation in Europe, as measured by the proportion of people saying they attended church once or more times a week. Some 22 percent of the French population did so in 1975, a figure that had dwindled to 5 percent by 1998. Church attendance in Ireland fell from 93 percent to 65 percent over the same period, in Germany from 26 percent to 15 percent.[316]

Belief in God has also declined but not to nearly as low levels as church attendance. The proportion of the public saying they believed in God declined in Sweden from 80 percent in 1947 to 46 percent in 2001. In France the drop was from 66 percent to 56 percent over the same period. In the United States, ever the exception, 94 percent of the population said they believed in God in 1947 and exactly the same percentage did so in 2001.[317]

These fluctuations are easily explicable under the thesis presented here, that the capacity for religious behavior is inherent in human nature. The presence of the capacity does not mean it will always be fully exercised. People evidently feel less need to participate in religious activity when, as Norris and Inglehart propose, they grow up in Scandinavian-style states that are not threatened by war and that operate highly efficient welfare systems.

Conversely, a higher expression of religious behavior would be expected among populations that have endured severe stress, and in countries like the United States where there is a vigorous competition among churches for members.

Despite fluctuations, religious activity seems unlikely to disappear as long as the propensity for religious behavior is genetically embedded in the human neural circuitry. Moreover, even if only a small fraction of a population is highly religious, its values may still be shared by most other people and remain embedded in the national culture. "Although only about 5% of the Swedish public attends church weekly," write Norris and Inglehart, "the Swedish public as a whole manifests a distinctive Protestant value system that they hold in common with the citizens of other historically Protestant societies. . . . Today, these values are not transmitted primarily by the church, but by the educational system and the mass media." The result is a homogenization of values across different religions in a country, with the values of Dutch Catholics, say, being more similar to those of Dutch Protestants than to those of French or Spanish Catholics.[318]

The ancient function of religious behavior, to bind the in-group in defense against the out-group, seems likely to endure, even if fewer and fewer people attend church. And with the convergence of values between different branches of the same religion, the in-group/out-group polarization of society can occur on a scale that transcends the tribe or nation-state, that of a whole civilization.

## Religion and the Fault Lines Between Civilizations

The global politics of the twentieth century were long dominated by the rivalry between the Soviet Union and the West. With the collapse of this ideological struggle, new divisions have surfaced, notably a rekindling of the differences between Islam and the West, and a looming tension between China, a resurgent power, and its neighbors.

At first glance, these global fault lines have nothing to do with religion, as if this ancient coordinator of human societies had no role to play in a global economic order founded on rational pursuit of self-interest. But in fact religion, in some observers' view, has turned out to be more critical than either economics or ideology in shaping the highest level of political alignments.

In a 1993 essay in *Foreign Affairs,* Samuel Huntington predicted that the principal political divisions of the world would revert to being those that delimit civilizations. Since the Peace of Westphalia that separated church and state, Westerners have been used to thinking of nation states as the chief actors on the world stage. Tensions now occur across much larger groupings which are in effect those of civilizations, Huntington argued. A civilization consists of people who view themselves as belonging to a common culture. A civilization transcends two of the usual binding forces of nations, language and ethnicity. The binding force it does not transcend, and which is therefore most central to it, is that of religion.

"Religion is a central defining characteristic of civilizations," Hunting-
ton writes.[319] He sees the world as divided into seven principal civilizations—
Western (Europe and the United States), Confucian (China), Japanese,
Islamic, Hindu (India), Slavic-Orthodox (Russia) and Latin American.
These civilizations, he says, "are differentiated from each other by history,
language, culture, tradition and, most important, religion."[320]

These differences are of long standing and far more fundamental
than political differences. The fault line that divides Western Christianity
from Orthodox Christianity goes back to the great schism of 1054. Islam
and Western Christianity have been at war, on and off, for 1,300 years.
"The next world war, if there is one, will be a war between civilizations,"
Huntington writes.

He lists eight characteristics that define Western culture. These are
the legacy from the civilizations of Greece and Rome; Western Christianity in the form of its two main branches, Catholicism and Protestantism; European languages; the separation of church and state; the rule of
law; social pluralism; representative bodies; and a tradition of individual
rights and liberties.

Why is Slavic-Orthodox civilization so different? Because none of
these characteristics are familiar to it with the exception of the classical
legacy, and even that was bequeathed through the Byzantines with different overtones. The eight Western features are also alien to other civilizations, particularly that of Islam, which does not recognize any separation
between church and state.

Despite the profound differences between Western civilization and
the others, Americans often assume that their political values of democracy, pluralism and individual rights are universal and urge that they
be adopted everywhere. "What is universalism to the West is imperial-
ism to the rest," Huntington observes.[321] War between two or more of
the seven civilizations is far from inevitable, but the polarizing effect
of religion-based cultures causes many tensions to emerge as tensions
between civilizations.

The centrality of religion to these arrangements is no surprise, given the arguments developed in the preceding pages. Human societies have several kinds of linkage but religion is the only one that binds people on an emotional level, signaling who has common values and whose values are alien. Language and even ethnicity can be split—a person can be bilingual, or half French and half Dutch—but religion confers an indivisible identity; it's hard to be half Catholic and half Muslim.

Each society adapts its religion to its own needs, so it is no surprise that religion does not play the same leading role in every civilization. In China, unlike in Christendom or the Islamic world, a single ethnic group, the Han, constitutes a majority of the population and dominates all other ethnic groups. Ethnic cohesion among the Han is strong and it matters less if they share no particular religion or ideology. Indeed the Chinese government, officially atheist, has long regarded religions as potential sources of opposition and has not hesitated to bring them under control by whatever means necessary. The Falun Gong movement, a Buddhist-tinged mixture of morals and breathing exercises, has been severely persecuted by Beijing since the mid-1990s. Even the fading of communism in China has so far posed no obvious threat to stability, whereas the erosion of the same ideology in the Soviet Union led to that empire's disintegration into units shaped by the traditional cohesive forces of ethnicity, language and religion.

The cohesive powers of religion should be of particular interest to nations and civilizations in which other kinds of social bonds are being eroded, such as Europe and the United States. Europe is engaged in the bold experiment of integrating nations that have fought one another for centuries into a structure that will make serious internal wars much less likely. The shared heritage of Christianity would be a common bond. But the modern disdain for religion is evident in the new constitution of the European Union, which does not even mention Christianity, the historical creed of all member countries and an indelible part of their culture and history.

Religion continues to play a central role in the Islamic world, though not altogether happily. Islam began as a religion of empire, a seamless web of authority for a prophet-ruler, and for most of its history has been a highly successful religion. But in recent centuries most Islamic nations have failed to adapt to the more productive European model of competing centers of power within a state.

For the Islamic world, a civilization that until the Renaissance exceeded Europe in science, military strength, economic power and religious tolerance, decline has been steady and painful. "By all the standards that matter in the modern world—economic development and job creation, literacy and educational and scientific achievement, political freedom and respect for human rights—what was once a mighty civilization has indeed fallen low," writes the Islamic scholar Bernard Lewis.[322]

Many would blame Islam itself for some of this decline. The religion's grip on law and politics has been little modernized. Women are relegated to an inferior position in most Islamic countries.

Lewis, however, argues that Islam itself is not the problem, asking: "If Islam is an obstacle to freedom, to science, to economic development, how is it that Muslim society in the past was a pioneer in all three, and this when Muslims were much closer in time to the sources and inspiration of their faith than they are now?"

But if religion is the "central defining characteristic of civilizations," as Huntington asserts, Islam or the way it is interpreted seems likely to have something to do with Islamic decline. That is certainly the analysis of Islamic fundamentalists who believe the error has been to stray from the way the religion was practiced in the seventh century. Mustafa Kemal, the revolutionary founder of the Turkish republic, also believed Islam had played a central role, except that he saw the religion as the source of all backwardness and a central factor in the Ottoman empire's decline. From opposite extremes, Islamic fundamentalists and Kemal are agreed on the power of religion to shape society for good or ill.

In the progression from tribe to nation to civilization, religion has remained the most fundamental and distinctive of all social binding mechanisms. Rationality and security may moderate the expression of religious behavior. Warfare and uncertainty may fill the pews. Religion remains the essential means whereby people associate in solidarity with one another and in defense against their adversaries.

# 12

---

# THE FUTURE OF
# RELIGION

*Religion can never be abolished out of human nature. An
attempt to abolish religion would just lead to new religions
springing out of the old ones, by the culture of such men that
would use it for purposes of reputation.*

THOMAS HOBBES[123]

R eligion expresses a society's collective wisdom, past and present,
as to how its members should best behave in order to enhance
the society's survival. During the 50,000 years since modern
humans left the ancestral homeland in northeast Africa, religion has
guided people's actions at almost every turn. Among Australian Aborigines, month-long ceremonies absorbed almost every free moment. In
archaic states ruled by priest-kings, religion and government were inseparable. The church played a leading role in the politics of the later Roman
empire. It preserved Western civilization through the Dark Ages and was
in the forefront of European politics until the seventeenth century and
beyond.

Only in the last 350 years or so, the last 0.7 percent of modern human
existence, has the strength of religion started to falter, yielding to the

institutions of secular states and to the erosion of some of its premises by modern knowledge.

The dethronement of religion has been a necessary consequence of modernity. Religious leaders, being no better than other kinds, sometimes used their powers to persecute dissidents and stifle inquiry. Western nations could not function were not church and state separate. Theocratic regimes such as those of Iran seem seriously out of place in the modern world.

Less welcome than the church's loss of direct political power has been the ebbing of its moral authority. Even the most cynical of religion's critics have acknowledged its role in sustaining the moral fabric of society. "The various modes of worship, which prevailed in the Roman world," reported the historian Edward Gibbon, "were all considered by the people, as equally true; by the philosopher, as equally false; and by the magistrate, as equally useful."

Religious belief is waning in many countries, especially among the most educated classes. Many modern states are secular and, particularly in Europe, have confined the sacred to a separate sphere of seemingly limited relevance. The religious instinct, the inherited propensity for ritual and belief, is still wired into the human mind as much as ever before, but many people do not exercise it, whether because they choose not to or have lacked a religious upbringing. Many are driven by feelings of emptiness to search for transcendent meaning or spirituality in other ways and do not participate in organized religion, the form in which religious behavior exerts its cohesive powers. The low ebb that religion has reached in European countries may well presage its eventual decline in even the United States.

Is religious behavior in fact unnecessary in the modern secular state? Should we thank the gods for their long tutelage and bid them farewell? If history does not end in secularism, what is the future of religion?

The essential element of religious knowledge, from an evolutionary perspective, is not theology but the practical rules of moral, military and reproductive behavior, the distilled collective wisdom of leaders past and present as to the guiding principles most likely to ensure a society's survival. These rules, having been negotiated with the gods, may be embedded in a sacred ritual or narrative, sometimes explicitly, sometimes only becoming evident in the way a text or ceremony is interpreted. They are quite unlike the rules in statute books because they command not merely intellectual but also emotional commitment. In practicing the religion that embodies these rules, members of a community, or of a nation, signal their commitment to one another and to the common vision of how their society should operate.

This is the behavior, secured with a prayer or a pinch of incense, that has preserved the fabric of human societies through the centuries. It seems unlikely that suddenly it no longer has a useful role to play.

Religion may not seem so essential in times of security and prosperity, when the social fabric appears reasonably robust. The test comes in times of crisis, whether warfare or economic disaster. Social order, past a certain point of stress, can rapidly collapse.

Beyond its role in strengthening the social fabric, religion exerts a cultural influence so deep that it has in effect become a defining factor of the world's major civilizations. In even the most secular countries religion strongly influences the way people identify themselves. The quality or nature of a religion affects everyone through its shaping of their culture. And culture, though social scientists cannot measure it and economists largely ignore it, surely makes a difference. "One has only to ask," writes Samuel Huntington, "Would America be the America it is today if in the seventeenth and eighteenth centuries it had been settled not by British Protestants but by French, Spanish or Portuguese Catholics? The answer is no. It would not be America; it would be Quebec, Mexico or Brazil."[324]

If religion still has many valuable roles to play, how might religious leaders protect its foundations from erosion by the rising tides of secularism?

A central problem facing the three monotheisms has arisen from their claims to historicity. These helped recruit believers when the religions were starting to grow. But the price began to be paid when the textual analysts of the nineteenth century uncovered the composite nature of the sacred texts and when Darwin's theory undermined most of what religion had to say about the nature of life. Scholars like Wellhausen showed that the Old and New Testaments were the works of many human hands, and so seemed less likely to have been divinely inspired. Modern archaeology has provided substantial evidence that there was no exodus from Egypt and no conquest of the promised land: the Israelites had always lived in Canaan. The great patriarchs of Israel belonged to legend, not to history. Jesus was a historical figure, but an orthodox Jew who probably sought to reformulate Judaism, not to found a new religion; Christianity was developed by his followers from an artful blend of Judaism and the mystery cults that had penetrated the Roman world. As for Muhammad, there is a strange paucity of independent historical evidence about his life; some scholars doubt whether he lived in the Hijaz, where Islamic texts locate him, and a few wonder if he lived at all.

Does it matter that each of the three monotheisms asserts a historical basis not wholly in accordance with the textual and archaeological facts? In many ways it does not matter. Religion is about symbolic communication. The sacred texts of the three monotheisms include themes that symbolize the values and traditions of each religion. Their longevity is a testament to their emotional truth and their enduring value for the civilizations constructed around them.

But in other ways the assertions of historicity present a problem because they make it much harder for each of the monotheisms to adapt to changing times and needs. Once the sacred texts of a religion have been finalized, a religion must live within the framework set by its canon. The fixed texts of Christianity and Islam have made both religions hard to update, and this in turn has led to clashes with modernity. In the long run, it would seem that both religions need to adapt to new knowledge or be undermined by it.

Religion is often taken as fixed and unalterable, responsive only to its mysterious internal laws. But could it perhaps be changed, reshaped in a manner that enhanced its cohesive properties and diminished its clashes with modernity and rationality? If religions are the product of the society they reflect, as argued above, why should they not be reworked so that as many people as possible can exercise their innate religious instincts to their own and society's benefit? Judaism in particular has been quite successful in retaining the allegiance of secularists who do not believe in any deity but observe their faith because it is part of their culture and has preserved them as a people.

Can there be religion without gods? Buddhism formally has no gods, but has accreted many in practice. The ethical culture movement seeks to build a religion around ethics alone, but has few adherents. The New England transcendentalists of the nineteenth century sought to construct a religion on a mixture of Kant's philosophy and socialism. Scientists from time to time propose that awe of the natural world and of the marvels of science would be a fitting focus for a new, god-free religion. Such ideas go nowhere because they are far from capturing all the facets of religious behavior, and in particular its appeal to deep-seated emotions. No religion is likely to succeed unless it evokes all or most of the genetically prescribed features of religious behavior.

But is belief in a supernatural power—the stumbling block for many people in today's highly educated societies—an essential feature of religion? For those raised in any of the three monotheisms, which are centered on a single deity, a godless religion sounds self-contradictory. Yet consider how deftly modern societies have developed a secular version of religion's ancient role in training and motivating warriors. The deity is no longer essential to making men go into battle.

Another reason for inferring that gods may not always be essential to an effective church can be drawn from Durkheim's analysis of religion as embodying a society's moral conception of itself. If the gods play an essentially symbolic role in this conception, perhaps their roles could be successfully delegated to other elements in a religion, as has been accomplished in secular military training.

East Asian religions such as Taoism, Confucianism and Buddhism are without gods, at least at their philosophical core, even though all have adherents who also worship gods. The Falun Gong movement of China is a novel religion centered on ethics and exercise, with the supernatural playing no prominent role. The exercises are presented as health giving but, since they are performed in unison, clearly have the potential to induce feelings of togetherness. Falun Gong is familiar to Chinese because it draws on Buddhist traditions, but also has adherents in many other cultures, presumably because of its emphasis on universal ethical principles, the attraction of its exercises and the lack of specific theology.

A Western religion without gods could perhaps be made compatible with scientific knowledge about the human condition. But how, then, would such a religion assure people that their lives had a significance beyond material existence and that there was some larger purpose that transcended the cycle of birth, reproduction and death?

At first glance, science has nothing to offer in this regard. Evolution is driven by the three forces of mutation, drift and selection, of which the first two are random and the third is blind and purposeless. Yet there is another force at work within human evolution that has not yet been given its due, perhaps because its fingerprints are only just now becoming visible.

That force is human choice. People choose, to some large extent, the nature of the societies and economies in which they live. Over the course of generations, as people adapt genetically to their social environment, cultural changes operate like a force of natural selection, favoring certain behaviors and the genes and neural circuitry that underlie them. Culture thus feeds back into and shapes the human genome. The best documented case so far concerns a fine nutritional detail, the emergence of lactose tolerance among the cattle herding culture of north-central Europe 5,000 years ago. Here a cultural practice—keeping cattle and drinking raw milk—has led to changes in the human genome, giving northern Europeans the unusual genetic ability to digest milk in adulthood.[325] Many other instances of genetic changes in response to culture will doubtless come to light, including some to do with human nature.

.

The role of human choice in shaping human evolution is far from understood, in part because it has been found only recently that culture can feed back into the genome. But human preferences about the nature of society could have played a significant evolutionary role, accounting for at least some part of the vast difference between people and chimpanzees, their closest living cousins.

Indeed, looking back at the broad sweep of human evolution over the last 50,000 years, it is easy enough to recognize the ways in which societies today are vastly preferable—kinder, more prosperous, less warlike, less profligate of the environment and far more knowledgeable—to those of earlier times. This, however much historians may hesitate to use the word, looks a lot like progress.

Such substantial and fairly steady progress cannot have been directed by evolution, a blind and largely random process with not a flicker of interest in human welfare. Surely the only possible origin of progress is human choice. For generation after generation, people have passionately sought the better course for themselves and their families and their community and, despite many dead ends and reverses, they have in general attained it.

These collective choices about how a society should behave could well have left their imprint on the human genome, or rather, a multitude of imprints depending on each society's circumstance. If people choose to devote their interests to warfare, then warriors are likely to have more children, as is known to have happened among the Yanomamo, and both the genetics and the culture of violence will be perpetuated.[326] But in societies that see conciliation and commerce as the better choice, the creators of wealth will leave more progeny and the character of society will change accordingly.

Thus it is certainly possible to argue that a beneficial direction has been imposed on the course of human evolution over the last 50,000 years or more; that the course has been set by human choice, acting as a force within the evolutionary process; and that this favorable vector has had, as one of its components, the evolved propensity for religious behavior.

Might this not be described, from a theological point of view, as the hand of the deity in action? Perhaps religious leaders interested in evolutionary theory may see some way to make use of this possibility.

The discovery that society molds and modulates the human genome is one that Durkheim would surely have appreciated. Not only do religions embody society's moral authority, he would have said, but the gods may have shaped human societies in their own image. We are not just the product of a blind and random process but something more, a creature shaped for good or ill by the collective choices of all our ancestors for thousands of generations. Is there a metaphorical validity to ancestor worship after all? New religions can only emerge out of old ones, but perhaps the originator of a new sect might one day see how to draw inspiration from Durkheim's analysis of how religions function.

For thousands of years people have negotiated with supernatural powers with prayer and sacrifice, and the religions they thus brought into being have shaped the moral nature of each society, reflecting the collective knowledge and desires of their people. Cruel and rapacious religions, like that of the Aztecs, have in the end led their societies to disaster. The winners of the Darwinian struggle between societies have been, surprisingly, not the most brutal and bellicose faiths but those that chose a more sustainable balance between warfare and conciliation.

Religion is not entirely unique. There is another cultural creation that stirs the emotions, conveys wordless meaning, and exalts the mind to a different plane. This strange parallel to religion is music. Like the propensity for religious behavior, the appreciation of music is a universal human faculty. Like religion, music is primarily a social activity, though it can be pursued privately too. As with religion, music draws people together. And religion of course draws heavily on music, from which it may once have developed.

Those who head religions today have a task analogous to that of the producers of operas. Both stage public performances that involve music and the singing of a libretto. But the bishop has fewer freedoms than the opera director. No one minds if the plots of operas are ridiculous—their only purpose is to provide the context for emotions too deep for speech. But the librettos sung in church express sacred truths; the church must stick to the sacred text century after century, regardless of the changes in society and advances in knowledge.

Conservatism has its virtues. People like their religion to embody values and principles that do not shift or yield. But culture has changed vastly since the advent of the three monotheisms. Secularism is on the march because religions, within the framework of their sacred narratives, are losing their hold on people's belief. They endure more because people want to believe in something than through the plausibility of their historical assertions.

Is there not some way of transforming religion into versions better suited for a modern age? The three monotheisms were created to meet conditions in societies that existed many centuries ago. The fact that they have endured for so long does not mean they were meant to last forever, only that they have become like some favorite Mozart opera that people are happy to hear over and over again. But the world of music did not achieve final perfection in Mozart.

Religion can be seen, from one perspective, as a high form of creativity. Music appeals to the auditory part of the brain, poetry to the language faculty, dance to the centers of rhythm and movement, art to the visual cortex. Religion plays on all these faculties, and through them arouses the deepest emotions of which the mind is capable, inspiring people to look beyond their own self-interest to something they may value more, the health and survival of their society, culture or civilization.

As a product of human culture, the three monotheisms seem long ago to have reached the limits of their development, lagging behind the increasing complexity of human societies and the vast growth of organized knowledge. Many people no longer develop their innate propensity for religious behavior, leaving unfulfilled a substantial component of human nature. Is this their fault, or society's fault, or perhaps the fault of the unchanging religions on offer?

Religious behavior evolved for a single reason: to further the survival of human societies. Those who administer religions should not assume they cannot be altered. To the contrary, religions are Durkheimian structures, eminently adjustable to a society's needs. They are shaped in implicit negotiation with supernatural powers who then give instructions to promote society's interests. Much of course depends on the craft and inspiration of the negotiators. But first it is necessary to understand that negotiation is possible.

Maybe religion needs to undergo a second transformation, similar in scope to the transition from hunter gatherer religion to that of settled societies. In this new configuration, religion would retain all its old powers of binding people together for a common purpose, whether for morality or defense. It would touch all the senses and lift the mind. It would transcend self. And it would find a way to be equally true to emotion and to reason, to our need to belong to one another and to what has been learned of the human condition through rational inquiry.

# NOTES

1. Edward O. Wilson, *Consilience* (New York: Vintage, 1999), 281.
2. Karen Armstrong, *A History of God* (New York: Knopf, 1993), xix.
3. Roy Rappaport, *Ritual and Religion in the Making of Humanity* (Cambridge, UK: Cambridge University Press, 1999), 1.
4. Roy Rappaport, "The Sacred in Human Evolution," *Annual Review of Ecology and Systematics* 2 (1971): 23–44.
5. William James, *The Varieties of Religious Experience* (New York: Penguin Books, 1982 [first published 1902]), 31.
6. Émile Durkheim, *The Elementary Forms of Religious Life,* transl. Karen E. Fields (New York: Free Press, 1995), 227.
7. Ibid., 44.
8. John Henry Blunt, *The Annotated Book of Common Prayer* (London: Rivingtons, 1885), 455.
9. Bronislaw Malinowski, *Magic, Science and Religion* (Prospect Heights, Illinois: Waveland Press, 1992 [reissue of 1948 edition]), 54.
10. Letter to Peter Carr, 1787.
11. Edward O. Wilson, *Sociobiology* (Cambridge, Mass.: Harvard University Press, 2000 [first published 1975]), 562.
12. Edward O. Wilson, *Consilience* (New York: Vintage, 1999), 290.
13. Ibid., 272.
14. Ibid., 277.
15. Jonathan Haidt, "The Emotional Dog and Its Rational Tail: A Social Intuitionist Approach to Moral Judgment," *Psychological Review* 108 (2001): 814–834.
16. Jerome Kagan, "Morality and Its Development," in *Moral Psychology*, ed. Walter Sinnott-Armstrong, vol. 3 (Cambridge, Mass.: MIT Press, 2008), 299.
17. en.wikipedia.org/wiki/Phineas_Gage/.
18. Nicholas Wade, "An Evolutionary Theory of Right and Wrong," *New York Times*, October 31, 2006, F1.
19. Nancy Howell, *Demography of the Dobe !Kung* (London: Academic Press, 1979), 119.
20. Bronislaw Malinowski, *The Sexual Life of Savages in North-Western Melanesia* (London: Routledge, 1932), 219.
21. Marc Hauser, *Moral Minds* (New York: HarperCollins, 2006), 128.
22. Fiery Cushman, Liane Young, and Marc Hauser, "The Role of Conscious Reasoning and Intuition in Moral Judgments: Testing Three Principles of Harm," *Psychological Science* 17, no. 12 (2006): 1082–89.
23. Charles Darwin, *The Descent of Man,* 2nd ed. (New York: Appleton and Company, 1898), 105.

24. George Williams, quoted by Frans de Waal in *Primates and Philosophers* (Princeton, N.J.: Princeton University Press, 2006), 9.

25. George C. Williams, *Adaptation and Natural Selection* (Princeton, N.J.: Princeton University Press, 1966).

26. Lawrence H. Keeley, *War Before Civilization* (New York: Oxford University Press, 1996).

27. Frans de Waal, *Good-Natured* (Cambridge, Mass.: Harvard University Press, 1996), 18.

28. Richard D. Alexander, *The Biology of Moral Systems* (Hawthorne, NY: Aldine de Gruyter, 1987), 142. Alexander should probably have conceded that in many ant species too the principal threat is from other ant colonies.

29. de Waal, *Good Natured*, 61.

30. Sarah F. Brosnan and Frans B. M. de Waal, "Monkeys reject unequal pay," *Nature* 425 (2003): 297–299.

31. Jessica C. Flack and Frans B. M. de Waal, " 'Any Animal Whatever': Darwinian Building Blocks of Morality in Monkeys and Apes," in *Evolutionary Origins of Morality*, ed. Leonard D. Katz (Thorverton, UK: Imprint Academic, 2000), 69.

32. Donald E. Brown, *Human Universals* (New York: McGraw-Hill, 1991), 108.

33. Hauser, *Moral Minds*, 48.

34. Edward O. Wilson, *Consilience* (New York: Knopf, 1998), 286.

34A. I. M. Lewis, *Ecstatic Religion* (London: Routledge, 3d ed., 2003), 15.

35. Several observers have attempted to specify the universal elements of religious behavior, but tend to differ as to its components. This is perhaps to be expected. Because most genetically based human behaviors are flexible, not deterministic, it is probably unrealistic to require that a behavior be exhibited by every known society in order to be accepted as having a genetic basis. Avoidance of incest, for instance, is almost certainly under genetic influence, yet cases of incest occur nonetheless. If a behavior is ancient and reported from a preponderance of societies, that is sufficient to consider it likely to have a genetic basis. Religious behavior in general is clearly universal, and it should not be surprising if its various components are expressed to different degrees in various societies, leading observers to differ somewhat in their descriptions of what is found universally.

Here are lists of universal religious behaviors compiled by two anthropologists:

    Religious or supernatural beliefs
    Conflicts structured around in-group/out-group antagonisms
    Divination
    Rituals including rites of passage
    Dream interpretation
    Dance and music
    Taboos on certain utterances and foods.
    (Donald E. Brown, *Human Universals* [New York: McGraw-Hill, 1991], 139–40).

    Afterlife
    Beings with special powers
    Signs and portents
    Spirit possession
    Rituals
    The Sacred
    Deference
    Moral obligation
    Punishment and reward.
    (Harvey Whitehouse in *The Evolution of Religion*, ed. Joseph Bulbulia et al. [Santa Margarita, California: Collins Foundation Press, 2008], 32).

Following are some statements from various authorities about the universal aspects of religious behavior:

"The psychological foundation [of religion] is universal among human populations but very flexible. It consists of elements of the human mind which make it easy to learn the local religion and other local commitment devices and signals." (William Irons in Bulbulia, ed., *Evolution of Religion*, 55).

"Throughout the world the developmental period deemed most appropriate for 'learning religion' is adolescence. Adolescent rites of passage are found in 70% of the world's societies . . . all share a common structure, and all include music as a common element." (Candace S. Alcorta in ibid., 265).

"In all human cultures, people believe that the soul lives on after death, that ritual can change the physical world and divine the truth, and that illness and misfortune are caused and alleviated by a variety of invisible personlike entities." (Steven Pinker in *Where God and Science Meet*, ed. Patrick McNamara [Westport, Connecticut: Praeger, 2006], 1).

"The rituals that accompany all religions almost always include music and other sorts of voluntary rhythmic stimulations. . . . Prayers in all religions involve the same gestures of submission: outstretched arms with chest exposed and throat bared, genuflection, prostration and so on." (Scott Atran in ibid., vol. 1, 183).

"These three structural features of religion—belief in supernatural agents, music-based communal ritual, and the emotional significance of the sacred—are elements common to all religions." (Candace S. Alcorta in ibid., vol. 2, 63).

36. Henri Hubert and Marcel Mauss, *Sacrifice: Its Nature and Function* (Chicago: University of Chicago Press, 1964), 101.

37. E. E. Evans-Pritchard, *Nuer Religion* (New York: Oxford University Press, 1956), 283.

38. Edmund Leach, *Culture and Communication* (Cambridge, UK: Cambridge University Press, 1976), 92–93.

39. Steven C. Schachter, "Religion and the Brain: Evidence from Temporal Lobe Epilepsy," in Patrick McNamara, ed., *Where God and Science Meet*, vol. 2 (Santa Barbara, California: Praeger, 2006), 171–88.

40. Brian D'Onofrio et al., "Understanding Biological and Social Influences on Religious Affiliation, Attitudes, and Behaviors: A Behavior Genetic Perspective," *Journal of Personality* 67, no. 6 (1999): 953–84.

41. Laura B. Koenig et al., "Genetic and Environmental Influences on Religiousness: Findings for Retrospective and Current Religiousness Ratings," *Journal of Personality* 73, no. 4 (2005): 1219-1256.

42. Charles Darwin, *Autobiography* (New York: Norton, 1969), 93.

43. Roy Rappaport, *Pigs for the Ancestors* (Long Grove, Illinois: Waveland Press, 2000 [first published 1984]), 131.

44. Christopher Boehm, *Hierarchy in the Forest* (Cambridge, Mass.: Harvard University Press, 2001), 69.

45. Lawrence H. Keeley, *War Before Civilization* (New York: Oxford University Press, 1996), 25.

46. Ibid., 93.

47. Ibid., 174.

48. Thomas Hobbes, *Leviathan* (New York: Pearson Longman, 2008), 83.

49. Raymond C. Kelly, *Warless Societies and the Origin of War* (Ann Arbor: University of Michigan Press, 2000), 160.

50. Ibid., 159.

51. Steven A. LeBlanc, *Constant Battles* (New York: St. Martin's Press, 2003), 8.

52. Keeley, *War Before Civilization*, 158.

53. Boehm, *Hierarchy in the Forest*, 69.

54. Evans-Pritchard, *Nuer Religion*, 18.

55. These facts about ant wars, as well as the quotation from Forel, are taken from Bert Hölldobler and Edward O. Wilson, *The Ants* (Cambridge, Mass.: Harvard University Press, 1990), 392–418.

56. Kelly Bulkeley, *Dreaming in the World's Religions* (New York: New York University Press, 2008), 3.

57. Harvey Whitehouse, "Cognitive Evolution and Religion; Cognition and Religious Evolution," in *The Evolution of Religion*, ed. Joseph Bulbulia et al. (Santa Margarita, California: Collins Foundation Press, 2008), 31.

58. Jesse M. Bering and Dominic D. P. Johnson, "O Lord . . . You Perceive My Thoughts from Afar: Recursiveness and the Evolution of Supernatural Agency," *Journal of Cognition and Culture* 5.1–2 (2005): 118–42.

59. Psalm 139:1–2, 23–24.

60. Laurence R. Iannaccone, "Why Strict Churches Are Strong," *American Journal of Sociology* 99 (1994): 1180–1211.

61. Ibid., 1204.

62. William Irons, "Religion as a Hard-to-Fake Sign of Commitment," in *Evolution and the Capacity for Commitment*, ed. Randolph M. Nesse (New York: Russell Sage Foundation, 2001), 293.

63. Richard Sosis, "Religious Behaviors, Badges, and Bans: Signaling Theory and the Evolution of Religion," in McNamara, ed., *Where God and Science Meet*, vol. 1 (Westport, Connecticut: Praeger, 2006), 61–86.

64. Scott Atran, *In Gods We Trust* (New York: Oxford University Press, 2002), 267.

65. Pascal Boyer, "Religious Thought and Behaviour as By-products of Brain Function," *Trends in Cognitive Neuroscience* 7 (2003): 119–24.

66. Steven Pinker, "The Evolutionary Psychology of Religion," in McNamara, ed., *Where God and Science Meet*, vol. 1, 1–9.

67. Richard Dawkins, *The God Delusion* (Boston: Houghton Mifflin, 2006), 161–207.

68. Darwin, *Autobiography*, 135.

69. David Sloan Wilson and Edward O. Wilson, "Rethinking the Theoretical Foundation of Sociobiology," *Quarterly Review of Biology* 82 (2007): 327–48.

70. Dan Levin, "A Display of Disapproval That Turned Menacing," *New York Times*, December 16, 2007, 49.

71. Samuel Bowles, *Microeconomics: Behavior, Institutions and Evolution* (Princeton, N.J.: Princeton University Press, 2004), 467.

72. Samuel Bowles, "Group Competition, Reproductive Leveling, and the Evolution of Human Altruism," *Science* 314 (2006): 1569–72.

73. David Sloan Wilson, *Darwin's Cathedral* (Chicago: University of Chicago Press, 2002). The theory is presented in summary form in Table 2-2 on p. 51.

74. David Sloan Wilson, *Evolution for Everyone* (New York: Delacorte Press, 2007), 256.

75. Owen Chadwick, *A History of Christianity* (New York: Thomas Dunne Books, 1998), 219.

76. William H. McNeill, *Keeping Together in Time* (Cambridge, Mass.: Harvard University Press, 1995), 2.

77. A. R. Radcliffe-Brown, *The Andaman Islanders* (New York: The Free Press of Glencoe, 1964), 251–52.

78. Bruno Nettl, "An Ethnomusicologist Contemplates Universals in Musical Sound and Musical Culture," in *The Origins of Music*, ed. Nils L. Wallin et al. (Cambridge, Mass.: MIT Press, 2000), 466.

79. Amy Waldman, "Word for Word/Taboo Heaven," *New York Times*, December 2, 2001.

80. Charles Darwin, *The Descent of Man*, 2nd ed. (New York: Appleton, 1898), 582.

81. Barbara Ehrenreich, *Dancing in the Streets* (New York: Holt, 2007), 15.

82. Charles Darwin, *The Voyage of the Beagle* (New York: Collier, 1909), 475.

83. Darwin, *Descent of Man*, 585.

84. Steven Pinker, *How the Mind Works* (New York: Norton, 1997), 534.

85. Sandra Trehub, "The Developmental Origins of Musicality," *Nature Neuroscience* 6 (2003) 669–73.

86. Geoffrey Miller, "Evolution of Human Music Through Sexual Selection," in Wallin, et al., eds., *Origins of Music*, 331.

87. Ibid., 351.

88. W. Tecumseh Fitch, "The Biology and Evolution of Music: A Comparative Approach," *Cognition* 100 (2006): 173–215.

89. Rodney Needham, "Percussion and Transition," *Man* 2 (1967): 606–14, , reprinted in *Reader in Comparative Religion*, 4th ed., edited by William A. Lessa and Evon Z. Vogt (New York: HarperCollins, 1979), 311–17.

90. Lorna J. Marshall, *Nyae Nyae !Kung Beliefs and Rites*, Peabody Museum Monographs No. 8 (Cambridge, Mass.: Harvard University Press, 1999), 79.

91. Darwin, *Descent of Man*, 585.

92. The point is made in Fitch, "Biology and Evolution of Music," 198.

93. This suggestion has been advanced by the paleoanthropologist Richard Klein, who argues that some kind of "neurological change" gave behaviorally modern humans an adaptive advantage over the Neanderthals and others; see Richard G. Klein, *The Human Career*, 2nd ed. (Chicago: University of Chicago Press, 1999), 452.

94. Erika Bourguignon, "Possession and Trance," in *Encyclopedia of Medical Anthropology*, ed. Carol R. Ember and Melvin Ember (Philadelphia: Springer, 2004), 137–45.

95. Gilbert Rouget, *Music and Trance* (Chicago: University of Chicago Press, 1985), 14.

96. Ibid., 175.

97. Mickey Hart, *Drumming at the Edge of Magic* (New York: HarperCollins, 1990), 176.

98. E. E. Evans-Pritchard, *Witchcraft, Oracles and Magic Among the Azande* (Oxford: Oxford University Press, 1937), 162.

99. McNeill, *Keeping Together in Time*, 42.

100. William J. Broad, *The Oracle* (New York: Penguin Press, 2006), 173.

101. Rick Doblin, "Pahnke's 'Good Friday Experiment': A Long-Term Follow-Up and Methodological Critique," *Journal of Transpersonal Psychology* 23 (1) (1991): 1–28.

102. David E. Nichols and Benjamin R. Chemel, "The Neuropharmacology of Religious Experience: Hallucinogens and the Experience of the Divine," in *Where God and Science Meet,* vol. 3, ed. Patrick McNamara (Santa Barbara, California: Praeger, 2006), 1–33.

103. Bronislaw Malinowski, *Magic, Science and Religion* (Prospect Heights, Illinois: Waveland Press, 1992), 39.

104. Lars Fogelin, "The Archaeology of Religious Ritual," *Annual Review of Anthropology* 36 (2007): 55–71.

105. Nicholas Wade, *Before the Dawn* (New York: Penguin Press, 2006), 67–69.

106. Lorna J. Marshall, *Nyae Nyae !Kung Beliefs and Rites,* Peabody Museum Monographs No. 8 (Cambridge, Mass.: Harvard University Press, 1999), 63–90.

107. Megan Biesele, "Religion and Folklore," in *The Bushmen: San Hunters and Herders of Southern Africa,* ed. Phillip V. Tobias and Megan Biesele (Cape Town: Human and Rousseau, 1978); quoted in Yosef Garfinkel, *Dancing at the Dawn of Agriculture* (Austin: University of Texas Press, 2003), 69.

108. Wade, *Before the Dawn,* 87.

109. A. R. Radcliffe-Brown, *The Andaman Islanders* (New York: The Free Press of Glencoe, 1964), 250.

110. Ibid., 253.

111. Ibid., 328.

112. Georgi Hudjashov et al., "Revealing the Prehistoric Settlement of Australia by Y Chromosome and mtDNA Analysis," *Proceeding of the National Academy of Sciences* 104 (2007): 8726–30.

113. Baldwin Spencer and F. J. Gillen, *The Native Tribes of Central Australia* (New York: Dover, 1968 [originally published 1899]), 272.

114. Ibid., 271.

115. Ibid., 321.

116. Ibid., 381.

117. Ronald M. Berndt, "Traditional Morality as Expressed Through the Medium of an Australian Aboriginal Religion," in *Religion in Aboriginal Australia,* ed. Max Charlesworth et al. (Queensland, Australia: University of Queensland Press, 1984), 207.

118. Baldwin Spencer and F. J. Gillen, *The Northern Tribes of Central Australia* (first published 1904), reprinted in Charlesworth et al., eds., *Religion in Aboriginal Australia,* 277–78.

119. Robert N. Bellah, "Religious Evolution," *American Sociological Review* 29(3) (1964): 358–74, reprinted in *The Robert Bellah Reader,* ed. Robert N. Bellah and Steven M. Tipton (Durham, N.C.: Duke University Press, 2006), 33.

120. Robert Tonkinson, "Semen Versus Spirit-child in a Western Desert Culture," in Charlesworth et al., eds., *Religion in Aboriginal Australia,* 118.

121. W. E. H. Stanner, "The Dreaming," in *Australian Signpost,* ed. T. A. G. Hungerford and F. W. Cheshire (Melbourne: F. W. Cheshire, 1956); reprinted in the first edition only of *Reader in Comparative Religion,* ed. William A. Lessa and Evon Z. Vogt (Evanston, Illinois: Peterson, 1958), 515.

122. Spencer and Gillen, *The Native Tribes of Central Australia,* 93.

123. Ibid., 98.

124. E. E. Evans-Pritchard, *Theories of Primitive Religion* (Oxford: Oxford University Press, 1965), 108.

125. Ibid., 104.

126. E. E. Evans-Pritchard, *Nuer Religion* (New York: Oxford University Press, 1956), 313.

127. Daniel L. Pals, *Seven Theories of Religion* (New York: Oxford University Press, 1996), 200.

128. Evans-Pritchard, *Theories of Primitive Religion,* 73.

129. Talcott Parsons, in Max Weber, *The Sociology of Religion* (Boston: Beacon Press, 1963), xxxvii.

130. Franz Boas, *Anthropology and Modern Life* (Mineola, NY: Dover, 2004 [first published 1928]), 111.

131. Steven Pinker, *The Blank Slate* (New York: Viking, 2002), 23.

132. Carl Degler, *In Search of Human Nature* (New York: Oxford University Press, 1992), 84. The quotation is cited without source.

133. Christopher Boehm, *Hierarchy in the Forest* (Cambridge, Mass.: Harvard University Press, 2001), 42.

134. Yosef Garfinkel, *Dancing at the Dawn of Agriculture* (Austin: University of Texas Press, 2003), 100.

135. Roy Rappaport, "The Sacred in Human Evolution," *Annual Review of Ecology and Systematics* 2 (1971): 23–44.

136. Joyce Marcus and Kent. V. Flannery, "The coevolution of ritual and society: New 14-C dates from ancient Mexico," *Science* 101 (2004): 18257–61.

137. Kent V. Flannery and Joyce Marcus, "The Origin of War: New 14-C Dates from Ancient Mexico," *Science* 100 (2003): 11801–05.

138. Peter M. M. G. Akkermans and Glenn M. Schwartz, *The Archaeology of Syria* (Cambridge, UK: Cambridge University Press, 2003), 96.

139. Garfinkel, *Dancing at the Dawn of Agriculture,* 100.

140. I. M. Lewis, *Ecstatic Religion,* 3rd ed. (London: Routledge, 2003), 118.

141. E. R. Dodds, *The Greeks and the Irrational* (Berkeley: University of California Press, 1951), 270–82.

142. 1 Samuel 10:1–11.

143. 2 Samuel 6:12–20.

144. Wayne A. Meeks, *The First Urban Christians,* 2nd ed. (New Haven, Conn.: Yale University Press, 2003), 149.

145. Barbara Ehrenreich, *Dancing in the Streets* (New York: Holt, 2006), 76.

146. Paul Johnson, *A History of Christianity* (New York: Simon & Schuster, 1995), 105.

147. William H. McNeill, *Keeping Together in Time* (Cambridge, Mass.: Harvard University Press, 1995), 75–77.

148. Johnson, *History of Christianity,* 249–50.

149. Frank Lambert, *Religion in American Politics* (Princeton, N.J.: Princeton University Press, 2008), 172.

150. McNeill, *Keeping Together in Time,* 79.

151. Ibid., 94.

152. E. E. Evans-Pritchard, *Nuer Religion* (New York: Oxford University Press, 1956), 203.

153. David N. Keightley, "The Shang: China's First Historical Dynasty," in *The Cambridge History of Ancient China* (Cambridge: Cambridge University Press, 1999), 232–91.

154. Émile Durkheim, *The Elementary Forms of Religious Life,* Karen E. Fields tr. (New York: Free Press, 1995), 429.

155. Jonathan K. Pritchard et al., "Population Growth of Human Y Chromosomes: A Study of Y Chromosome Micro-Satellites," *Molecular Biology and Evolution* 16 (1999): 1791–98.

156. Roy A. Rappaport, *Ritual and Religion in the Making of Humanity* (Cambridge: Cambridge University Press, 1999), 337.

157. Quoted in ibid., 490–91.

158. Bronislaw Malinowski, *Magic, Science and Religion* (Prospect Heights, Illinois: Waveland Press, 1992), 39.

159. William G. Dever, *Did God Have a Wife?* (Grand Rapids, Michigan: Eerdmans, 2005), 267–69.

160. Ibid., 263.

161. Ibid., 295.

162. 2 Kings 22.

163. James L. Kugel, *How to Read the Bible* (New York: Simon & Schuster, 2007), 74–79.

164. Genesis 8:21.

165. Genesis 7:1–2.

166. Genesis 7:15–16.

167. Israel Finkelstein and Neil Asher Silberman, *The Bible Unearthed* (New York: Simon & Schuster, 2001), 37.

168. William G. Dever, *Who Were the Early Israelites and Where Did They Come From?* (Grand Rapids, Michigan: Eerdmans, 2003), 228.

169. Ibid., 235-6.

170. Ibid., 167.

171. Kugel, *How to Read the Bible*, 381–82.

172. Finkelstein and Silberman, *Bible Unearthed,* 249.

173. 2 Kings 22:20.

174. Paul Johnson, *A History of Christianity* (New York: Simon & Schuster, 1976), 43.

175. Ibid., 12.

176. Rodney Stark, *The Rise of Christianity* (Princeton, N.J.: Princeton University Press, 1996), 63.

177. Ibid., 7. The numbers generated by this simple calculation agree well with estimates derived independently by several historians.

178. Ibid., 160.

179. Sarah B. Pomeroy, *Goddesses, Whores, Wives and Slaves: Women in Classical Antiquity* (New York: Schocken, 1995), 49.

180. Stark, *Rise of Christianity*, 128.

181. Henry Chadwick, *The Early Church* (New York: Penguin Books, 1993), 127.

182. Ibid., 72.

183. Matthew 5:17.

184. E. P. Sanders, *The Historical Figure of Jesus* (New York: Penguin Press, 1993), 224.

185. Matthew 10:5–6.

186. Matthew 28:19.

187. Sanders, *Historical Figure of Jesus*, 192.

188. Barrie Wilson, *How Jesus Became Christian* (New York: St. Martin's Press, 2008), 167.

189. Galatians 1: 11-12.

190. Bart D. Ehrman, *The Lost Christianities* (New York: Oxford University Press, 2003), 23.

191. Peter Brown, *The World of Late Antiquity* (New York: Harcourt Brace Jovanovich, 1978), 143.

192. James Frazer, *The Golden Bough*, (abridged) (New York: Oxford University Press, 1994), 389.

193. Chadwick, *Early Church*, 24.

194. Frazer, *Golden Bough*, 346–52.

195. According to Leviticus 17, Yahweh himself told Moses that "the life of the flesh is in the blood" and that blood must on no account be eaten. "And whatsoever man there be of the house of Israel, or of the strangers that sojourn among you, that eateth any manner of blood; I will . . . cut him off from among his people."

196. The Apostolic Fathers: *Early Christian Writings* (New York: Penguin Books, 1987), 194.

197. Of the fourteen letters attributed to Paul in the New Testament, seven are generally agreed to be authentic. They are, in order of probable composition, with estimated dates: 1 Thessalonians (A.D. 46 or 49), 1 Corinthians (A.D. 49 or 52), 2 Corinthians (A.D. 50 or 53), Philippians, Philemon, Galatians, Romans (A.D. 51–52 or 54–55). The letters to the Philippians, Philemon and Galatians are of unknown date but seem to have been written between 2 Corinthians and Romans. Donald Harman Akenson, *Saint Saul* (New York: Oxford University Press, 2000), 145.

198. 1 Corinthians 11:23.

199. The phrase occurs in 1 Corinthians 11:20. It is sometimes translated "the Lord's supper," as for example by James D. G. Gunn in his *Christianity in the Making* (Vol. 2: *Beginning from Jerusalem*, Michigan: William B. Eerdmans Publishing Company, 2009, p. 645), but this is probably incorrect. Greek preserves the same distinction as does English between "a lordly supper"—*kuriakon deipnon*—and "the Lord's supper"—*deipnon tou Kuriou*; Paul uses the former. According to Hyam Maccoby in *The Mythmaker* (New York: Harper and Row, 1986, 116), "The same expression was used in the mystery religions for the sacred meals dedicated to the saviour-god. . . . The early Fathers of the Church became embarrassed by it, and they substituted for it the name 'Eucharist,' which had Jewish rather than pagan associations. Thus the Fathers sought to align the Christian ceremony with the non-mystical, non-magical *Kiddush* of the Jews, in which the wine and the bread were 'blessed' (or, more accurately, God was blessed for providing them)."

200. 1 Corinthians 15:5–8.

201. Eusebius, *Quaestiones ad Marinum*, available online in Greek and French at http://www2.unil.ch/cyber documents/pratique/acces/theologie/theses_theologie.html as pdf attached to thesis by Claudio Zamagni.

202. The practice began following a decree of the Roman emperor Elagabalus before his death in A.D. 222. The earliest known record of Jesus' birthday being celebrated on December 25 dates to 243. See Wikipedia entry on Sol Invictus.

203. Chadwick, *Early Church*, 25, footnote.

204. Patricia Crone, *Meccan Trade and the Rise of Islam* (Princeton, N.J.: Princeton University Press, 1987), 204.

205. Jonathan P. Berkey, *The Formation of Islam* (Cambridge: Cambridge University Press, 2003), 40.

206. Hugh Kennedy, *The Great Arab Conquests* (Philadelphia: Perseus Books, 2007), 83.

207. Yehuda D. Nevo and Judith Koren, *Crossroads to Islam* (Amherst, NY: Prometheus Books, 2003), 234.

208. David B. Cook, "Islam: Age of Conquest," in *Encyclopedia of Religion and War*, ed. Gabriel Palmer-Fernandez (London: Routledge, 2004), 203.

209. Patricia Crone and Michael Cook, *Hagarism: The Making of the Islamic World* (Cambridge: Cambridge University Press, 1977), 23.

210. Patricia Crone, "What Do We Actually Know about Mohammed?" www.opendemocracy.net/faith-europe_islam/mohammed_3866.jsp/, August 30, 2006.

211. G. R. Hawting, "John Wansbrough, Islam, and Monotheism," in *The Quest for the Historical Muhammad*, ed. Ibn Warraq (Amherst, NY: Prometheus Books, 2000), 522.

212. Al-Bukhari, quoted in Bernard Lewis, *Islam*, vol. 2 (New York: Oxford University Press, 1987), 2.

213. John Wansbrough, "Res Ipsa Loquitur: History and Mimesis," lecture reprinted in *The Sectarian Milieu* (Amherst, NY: Prometheus Books, 2006), 162.

214. John Wansbrough, *Quranic Studies* (Amherst, NY: Prometheus Books, 2004 [first published 1977]), 179.

215. Estelle Whelan, "Forgotten Witness: Evidence for the Early Codification of the Qur'an," *Journal of the American Oriental Society* 118 (1998): 1–14.

216. Nevo and Koren, *Crossroads to Islam*, 248.

217. Nevo and Koren, *Crossroads to Islam*, 279.

218. Crone, *Meccan Trade and the Rise of Islam*, 203–30; quoted in Ibn Warraq, "Studies on Muhammad and the Rise of Islam," in *The Quest for the Historical Muhammad*, ed. Ibn Warraq (Amherst, NY: Prometheus Books, 2000), 29.

219. Ibid.

220. Nevo and Koren, *Crossroads to Islam*, 230.

221. Whelan, "Forgotten Witness."

222. Volker Popp, "The Early History of Islam, Following Inscriptional and Numismatic Testimony," in *The Hidden Origins of Islam*, ed. Karl-Heinz Ohlig and Gerd-R. Puin (Amherst, NY: Prometheus Press, 2009), 35–36, 62.

223. Christoph Luxenberg, "A New Interpretation of the Arabic Inscription in Jerusalem's Dome of the Rock," in Ohlig and Puin, eds., *The Hidden Origins of Islam*, 131–32.

224. Karl-Heinz Ohlig, "Why 'Shadowy Beginnings' of Islam?", in ibid., 10.

225. Philip Jenkins, *The Lost History of Christianity*, (New York: HarperCollins, 2008), 193.

226. Luxenberg, "New Interpretation," 143.

227. Ibid.

228. Napoleon A. Chagnon, *Yanomamo*, 5th ed. (Florence, Kentucky: Wadsworth, 1997), 76.

229. Max Weber, *The Sociology of Religion* (Boston: Beacon Press, 1963), 1.

230. This account of the Kula exchange is based on Bronislaw Malinowski, *Argonauts of the Western Pacific* (Long Grove, Illinois: Waveland Press, 1984 [first published 1922]).

231. Ibid., 83.

232. Details of this picturesque male fantasy would doubtless tire most readers, so are relegated to this footnote: Malinowski writes (223), " . . . Kaytalugi is a land of women only, in which no man can survive. The women who live there are beautiful, big and strong, and they walk about naked, and with the bodily hair unshaven (which is contrary to the Trobriand custom). They are extremely dangerous to any man through the unbounded violence of their passion. The natives never tire of describing graphically how such women would satisfy their sensuous lust, if they got hold of some luckless, shipwrecked man. No one could survive, even for a short time, the amorous yet brutal attacks of these women. The natives compare this treatment to that customary at the *yousa*, the orgiastic mishandling of any man, caught at certain stages of female communal labour in Boyowa. [Malinowski here refers to the report that men who disturbed women ritually weeding their gardens in the south of the main Trobriand island were liable to be raped and otherwise abused by the women.] Not even the boys born on this island of Kaytalugi can survive a tender age. It must be remembered that the natives see no need for male co-operation in continuing the race. Thus the women propagate the race, although every male needs must come to an untimely end before he can become a man."

233. Marcel Mauss, *The Gift* (London: Routledge, 1990), 37.

234. Mary Douglas, Foreword to ibid., ix.

235. Roy A. Rappaport, "The Sacred in Human Evolution," *Annual Review of Ecology and Systematics* 2 (1971): 23–44.

236. Robert Bellah, "The R Word," *Tricycle: The Buddhist Review*, Spring 2008.

237. Oliver Goodenough and Monika Gruter Cheney, in *Moral Markets*, ed. Paul J. Zak (Princeton, N.J.: Princeton University Press, 2008), xxiii.

238. E. E. Evans-Pritchard, *Nuer Religion* (New York: Oxford University Press, 1956), 192.

239. Ibid., 17–18.

240. www.http://avalon.law.yale.edu/18th_century/washing.asp.

241. Will Herberg, *Protestant-Catholic-Jew* (Chicago: University of Chicago Press, 1983), 84.

242. Stephen E. Ambrose, *Eisenhower*, vol. 2 (New York: Simon & Schuster, 1984), 38.

243. Francis Fukuyama, *Trust* (New York: Free Press, 1995), 7.

244. Ibid., 319.

245. Max Weber, *The Protestant Ethic and the Spirit of Capitalism* (Mineola, NY: Dover, 2003), 172.

246. Renee Rose Shield, *Diamond Stories* (Ithaca, N.Y.: Cornell University Press, 2002), 1.

247. www.sec.gov/investor/pubs/affinity.htm.

248. Robin Pogrebin, "For Jews, Madoff's Scandal Brings Feelings of Betrayal and Shame," *New York Times*, December 24, 2008, 1.

249. Richard Sosis, "Does Religion Promote Trust? The Role of Signaling, Reputation and Punishment," *Interdisciplinary Journal of Research on Religion* 1 (2005): article 7.

250. Deuteronomy 23:20; Luke 6:35; Koran, Surah 2:275.

251. Marc Hauser, *Moral Minds* (New York: HarperCollins, 2006), 421.

252. Richard Dawkins, *The God Delusion* (Boston: Houghton Mifflin, 2006), 227.

253. Deuteronomy 13:8–10.

254. Sam Harris, *The End of Faith* (New York: Norton, 2006), 15–18.

255. Christopher Hitchens, *god Is Not Great* (New York: Hachette, 2007), 106.

256. http://come-and-hear.com/kethuboth/kethuboth_61.html/.

257. Vernon Reynolds and Ralph Tanner, *The Social Ecology of Religion* (Oxford: Oxford University Press, 1995), 69.

258. Ibid., 38–39.

259. The Pew Forum on Religion & Public Life, *U.S. Religious Landscape Survey 2008*, 68. Available online at http://religions.pewforum.org/.

260. Samuel Huntington, *The Clash of Civilizations and the Remaking of the World Order* (New York: Simon & Schuster, 1996), 265.

261. Rodney Stark, *The Rise of Christianity* (New York: HarperCollins, 1996), 128.

262. Paul Johnson, *A History of Christianity* (New York: Simon & Schuster, 1976), 141.

263. Gregory Clark, *A Farewell to Alms* (Princeton, N.J.: Princeton University Press, 2007), 99–102.

264. Erik Eckholm, "Boys Cast Out by Polygamists Find New Help," *New York Times*, September 7, 2007, A1.

265. J. B. Peires, *The Dead Will Arise* (Bloomington: Indiana University Press, 1989), 99.

266. Ibid., 145.

267. Ibid., 158.

268. Revelation 11:3: "And I will give power unto my two witnesses, and they shall prophesy a thousand two hundred and threescore days, clothed in sackcloth."

269. en.wikipedia.org/wiki/"Heaven'sGate"/.

270. Lisa J. Lucero, "The Politics of Ritual," *Current Anthropology* 44 (2003), 523–58.

271. J. Stephen Lansing, *Priests and Programmers* (Princeton, N.J.: Princeton University Press, 2007 [1st edition 1991]), 75.

272. Roy Rappaport, *Pigs for the Ancestors* (Long Grove, Illinois: Waveland Press, 2000 [first published 1984]), 126.

273. Ibid., 3–4.

274. Thomas Babington Macaulay, *Lays of Ancient Rome* (London: Longmans, Green, 1884), 25.

275. Deuteronomy 20:1 and16–17.

276. Hugh Kennedy, *The Great Arab Conquests* (Philadelphia: Da Capo Press, 2007), 50.

277. Bernard Lewis, *What Went Wrong? The Clash Between Islam and Modernity in the Middle East* (New York: Harper-Collins, 2002), 100.

278. Samuel P. Huntington, *The Clash of Civilizations and the Remaking of the World Order* (New York: Simon & Schuster, 1996), 114.

279. Noah Feldman, *The Fall and Rise of the Islamic State,* (Princeton: Princeton University Press, 2008), 79.

280. Ibid., 136.

281. Samuel P. Huntington, "The Clash of Civilizations?" *Foreign Affairs,* Summer 1993.

282. Geoffrey W. Conrad and Arthur A. Demarest, *Religion and Empire* (Cambridge : Cambridge University Press, 1984), 38.

283. Quoted in ibid., 28–29.

284. Ibid., 47.

285. Ibid., 69.

286. Richard Sosis, Howard C. Kress, and James S. Boster, "Scars for War: Evaluating Alternative Sig-
    naling Explanations for Cross-cultural Variance in Ritual Costs," *Evolution and Human Behavior* 28
    (2007): 234–47.

287. Quoted in William H. McNeill, *Keeping Together in Time* (Cambridge, Mass.: Harvard University Press,
    1995), 104.

288. Dominic Johnson, "Gods of War—The Adaptive Logic of Religious Conflict," in *The Evolution of Religion*,
    ed. Joseph Bulbulia et al. (Santa Margarita, California: Collins Foundation Press, 2008), 111–17.

289. Johnson, "Gods of War," 112.

290. McNeill, *Keeping Together in Time*, 127.

291. Sam Harris, *The End of Faith* (New York: Norton, 2004), 26.

292. McNeill, *Keeping Together in Time*, 105.

293. Paul Johnson, *A History of Christianity* (New York: Simon and Schuster, 1976), 249–50.

294. Greg Austin, Todd Kranock and Thom Oommen, "God and War: An Audit & an Explanation," Depart-
    ment of Peace Studies, University of Bradford, unpublished. http://news.bbc.co.uk/1/shared/spl/hi/
    world/04/war_audit_pdf/pdf/war_audit.pdf/.

295. Kevin Phillips, *The Cousins' War* (Philadelphia: Basic Books, 1999), xii–xiii.

296. Alexis de Tocqueville, *Democracy in America*, Vol. 1 (New York: Vintage Books, 1945), 314.

297. *Economist*, December 23, 1999.

298. Phillips, *Cousins' War*, 21.

299. Frank Lambert, *Religion in American Politics* (Princeton, N.J.: Princeton University Press, 2008), 17.

300. Roger Finke and Rodney Stark, *The Churching of America 1776–2005* (New Brunswick, NJ: Rutgers
    University Press, 2005), 175.

301. Quoted in ibid., 124.

302. The Pew Forum on Religion & Public Life, *U.S. Religious Landscape Survey 2008*, 6. Obtainable from
    http://religions.pewforum.org/religions/.

303. Finke and Stark, *Churching of America*, 246.

304. Ibid., 23.

305. Pippa Norris and Ronald Inglehart, *Sacred and Secular* (Cambridge: Cambridge University Press, 2004), 100.

306. Pew Forum on Religion & Public Life, 22.

307. Ibid., 5.

308. Robert N. Bellah, "Civil Religion in America," reprinted in *The Robert Bellah Reader*, ed. Robert N. Bellah
    and Steven M. Tipton (Durham, N.C.: Duke University Press, 2006), 229.

309. Robert Booth Fowler, Allen D. Hertzke, Laura R. Olson, and Kevin R. Den Dulk, *Religion and Politics in
    America*, 3rd ed. (Boulder, Colorado: Westview Press, 2004), 301.

310. Samuel P. Huntington, *Who Are We?: The Challenges to America's National Identity* (New York: Simon &
    Schuster, 2004), 68–69.

311. George McKenna, *The Puritan Origins of American Patriotism* (New Haven, Conn.: Yale University Press,
    2007), xiii.

312. Noah Feldman, *Divided by God* (New York: Farrar, Straus and Giroux, 2005), 59–60.

313. Ibid., 170.

314. Ibid., 183.

315. Lambert, *Religion in American Politics*, 107.

316. Figures taken from Norris and Inglehart, *Sacred and Secular*, 72.

317. Figures taken from ibid., 90.

318. Ibid., 17.

319. Samuel P. Huntington, *The Clash of Civilizations and the Remaking of the World Order* (New York: Simon &
    Schuster, 1996), 47.

320. Samuel P. Huntington, "The Clash of Civilizations?" *Foreign Affairs*, Summer 1993, 22–49.

321. Samuel P. Huntington, *Clash of Civilizations*, 184.

322. Bernard Lewis, *What Went Wrong?* (New York: HarperCollins, 2002), 152.

323. Thomas Hobbes, *Leviathan* (New York: Pearson, 2008), 77.

324. Samuel Huntington, *Who Are We?: The Challenges to America's National Identity* (New York: Simon &
    Schuster, 2004), 59.

325. Todd Bersaglieri et al., "Genetic Signatures of Strong Recent Positive Selection at the Lactase Gene," *American Journal of Human Genetics* (2004) 74:111-1120.

326. The Yanomamo, a tribal people who live in villages in the border forests of Brazil and Venezuela, engage in frequent warfare with their neighbors. Some 30 percent of adult men die violently. Those who have killed other men—called *unokais*, after the purification ceremony they must go through—have more wives and three times more children than do non-*unokais*. Napoleon A. Chagnon, "Life Histories, Blood Revenge, and Warfare in a Tribal Population," *Science* 239 (1988): 985–92.

# ACKNOWLEDGMENTS

This book grew out of an earlier one, *Before the Dawn,* which examined the last 50,000 years of human evolution in the light of new explorations of the human genome. In writing that book it became clear to me that religious behavior had played a greater evolutionary role in shaping human societies than could be described at the time. *The Faith Instinct* is an attempt to remedy that neglect.

I thank Peter Matson of Sterling Lord Literistic for shaping the idea of the book and Vanessa Mobley, its first editor at Penguin Press, for her unfailing encouragement and advice. I am much indebted to Laura Stickney, its second editor, for her fine judgment and many deft suggestions and improvements.

I am most grateful to the Templeton Foundation, both for a generous grant and for the advice of its expert reviewers, who scrutinized the project at its outline and first-draft stages. The reviewers were anonymous so I cannot thank them by name, with the exception of Christopher Boehm of the University of Southern California, who kindly let his name be known to me. Further conversation with him allowed me to close several significant conceptual gaps in the argument.

I have benefited greatly from the advice of friends who read early drafts of the book and saved me from many errors, obscurities and infelicities. These include Caleb Crowell, Nicholas W. Fisher, David H. Levey, Jeremy J. Stone, Richard L. Tapper, and my wife Mary V. Wade. I thank them for their considerable help in improving the book. I am also indebted to Jonathan Haidt of the University of Virginia for reviewing the chapter on morality.

Erica Harris, of Boston University, and Prometheus Press were kind enough to make important books available to me in advance of publication.

My religious education I owe to Henry VI, who founded a school for poor scholars in 1440. He built at Eton one of England's most beautiful chapels, in which I attended services every day and twice on Sunday during my school years.

# INDEX